Follow Me!

JEAN

BAER

Follow

Me!

THE MACMILLAN COMPANY, NEW YORK ▶

For my father

Contents

Follow Me!

Introduction

Unless you travel with a man, go by yourself. In my own case, I went abroad for the first time because I was alone and miserable and because the only alternative was staying home.

I'll never forget that May morning thirteen years ago when my section chief at the U.S. Information Agency summoned me to the inner sanctum. Sitting back in his swivel chair, soberly elegant in neat tweed suit and narrow black tie, he said sympathetically, "Sorry, Jean, but this is government, and we're over our budget. Since you're on temporary payroll, we'll have to lay you off for the next six weeks."

My world collapsed. Since my mother had died the year before, my job had been the only pleasant part of my day. All that was left—the love of my life having run off with a bleached blonde—was the dreary task of keeping house for my father and younger brother and sister.

The boss eyed me. "Why don't you go abroad?" he offered diffidently. "You're the only writer here who has never traveled overseas."

Actually, I *had* dreamed of escaping to some European Eden, where there would be handsome strangers and never any dishes to wash or bathrooms to scrub, but even though I had the inclination and $1,500 in the bank, no one wanted to go with me, and my heart plummeted at the terrifying thought of going abroad on my own.

That night I missed the last fast commuter train and burned the roast. But the high point of the evening was when the mother of my recently engaged best friend called to demand that I give a shower for her daughter. "Maybe it will bring you luck," she chirped. With that, my cup of acid ran over. I would go to Europe. In fact, I would go next week. Moreover, I would go alone.

It was the happiest month of my life.

Since then I have made sixteen overseas trips that have taken me from the Amazon in South America to Samarkand in Central Asia, plus eight journeys to various Caribbean islands, and I have learned this guiding precept for women travelers: *unless you travel with a man, go by yourself.* For she travels fastest, most happily, and most productively who travels alone.

I made my travel debut alone because the urge to escape from Mount Vernon outweighed my fears and phobias. Others are not so adventurous. For them, the perils and problems surmount the pleasures.

Recently, I overheard two gray-haired women chatting on a bus.

"What are your summer plans?" asked Mrs. A.

"Back to Maine," answered Mrs. B. "But I'm so sick of it."

"What would you like to do?"

"Oh, I've always wanted to go to Europe. John and I had always planned to. But now I'm afraid to go alone."

This was a widow in her sixties, but the same attitude exists in twenty-year-old secretaries, teachers with two-month vacations, career girls who have three-weeks-with-pay holidays, elderly spinsters with cash but no courage. They all may have coped with death and taxes, matrimony and mothers-in-law, earning a living and getting out the local vote, running an organization and chairing the women's club, but faced with traveling out of the country alone, they throw in the beach towel and head for Cape Cod.

If you're a typical American female from twenty to seventy, single, divorced, or widowed, with a secret desire to yodel on a Swiss mountaintop, steam in the mixed company of a Japanese bath, and cross-examine the Sphinx, you may feel these insecurities about going alone:

No one will talk to me. Unless you are a lady hermit, a novelist with a long-past deadline, or the proud plagiarizer of Greta Garbo's famous line, this is impossible. Be prepared to meet and influence people within one hour of quitting your homeland—and be prepared to meet them in the Excelsior bar, halfway up an Alp, or in the middle of the Egyptian desert. Everyone is going somewhere, and everyone likes to talk about it. Unless you scare people off with a "go-away" tilt of the nose and an "I-want-to-be-alone" attitude, you'll have plenty of company.

How can I meet people? How do you meet people at home? You'll encounter them in the same way abroad, plus all the special ways that have been designed just for you, the woman traveler. You can make connections by playing bridge or gin on the boat, soaking in a Finnish sauna, watching people in a hotel lobby, getting lost in a strange city, taking tours, or looking so confused that someone comes to your rescue.

Everyone will be in twosomes but me. Many of the people you meet traveling will be married. There's no getting away from that fact. But they may even envy your freedom. And if you're smart, you'll chart your trip so that you stay away from places that reek of that honeymoon atmosphere.

It's so expensive—and I have only a three-week vacation. Weigh the cost of the trip against its worth to you. A gay whirl through London and Paris can cost no more than a sojourn in Yosemite—and feeding Continental men a line is much more fascinating than feeding grizzly bears lump sugar. Economize a bit one year on American clothes; the next year you can

afford to buy yours in Rome. Save for three years and you can
have outfits made to order in Hong Kong. If you're lucky
enough to belong to a club that likes to travel, you may join
a charter flight with a round-trip fare by jet between New
York and Lisbon at $150—less than the fare from New York to
Los Angeles and back.

Will I have to eat alone? If the worst comes to the worst,
is the pleasure of your own company so bad? At least it's
familiar. But you shouldn't have to resort to this too often.
Men have been known to pick up the tabs for lonely ladies.
And even if you can't find a man to do this, there are lots of
other women who would be glad to join you at a restaurant.
If you can't find one lone woman, approach two. They are
probably so sick of each other's company that they will welcome you as though you were royalty.

Who will take care of me if I get sick? Doctors exist in
foreign countries, too. Travel equipped with your favorite
remedies, stay away from tap water and unpeeled fruit, and
you probably won't need medical attention. If you do, call the
hotel manager or the American consulate.

In any case, getting sick in a foreign country has its benefits
—or can have. My friend Soni was in Ocho Rios, Jamaica,
when she was felled by acute appendicitis. There was no seat
on the New York–bound plane. Frantic, she somehow got to
the Myrtle Bank Hotel in Kingston. The friendly manager gave
her a bed at the hotel until arrangements could be made at the
hospital for an emergency operation.

The next day she was deluged with flowers and gifts—from
fellow patients, townspeople, visiting Americans, and all the
guests of the hotel. A week later, still shaky, she boarded the
plane home. Her Jamaican doctor knew a planter who was
traveling on the same flight and asked him to look out for Soni.
He did—and the romance lasted for two years.

Suppose I get lost? If you do, sit back and enjoy it. After
all, a girl can lose her way in Philadelphia, Boston, or San

Francisco. It's much more exciting to be lost among the ruins of Delos, the Indians of Huancayo, or the bazaars of Istanbul.

How will I manage without knowing the language? You do know one language—English—and it's spoken all over the world. In countries such as Holland, Norway, Finland, Sweden, and Denmark, it is required of every high-school student. In tourist centers such as Tokyo, Manila, Rome, and Paris, hotel-men, storekeepers, restaurateurs are used to tourists and their "How much?" "Where to?" and "Why?" queries. Other places use your Handy Phrase Book.

How can I cope with porters and conductors? If you can manage your own financial affairs, you should be able to tip a waiter, find your own luggage, and buy a ticket to Versailles. If you feel you can't do such things, yet still want to see the world, try a conducted tour. Remember that helplessness in a woman can be irresistible. My stepmother credits half the fun of her many trips abroad to the fact that she has never been able to read a map or fasten her seat belt.

What will I do at night? You can enjoy your evenings, even if you spend them alone. After all, you spend time alone in your own living room. In large cities, there are always movies, theater, concerts, and you don't have to understand the language to enjoy them. In smaller towns, a gathering in your hotel will be like a large house party; you will automatically be part of a group with your fellow tourists. Evenings don't have to loom as a major problem. If you've walked four miles through ruins, climbed countless castle steps, and absorbed a multitude of impressions during the day, you may actually be glad to go to bed early.

To be a success abroad on your own, you need:

Interest in other people, other lands;

Initiative to make some first moves yourself;

Intelligence to pick places to go and things to do where you will stand out as a person and not just another single woman;

Inclination to leave your everyday self back in Albany, New

York, or Appleton, Wisconsin, and be the woman you've always wanted to be;

Internationalism that will make you respect the customs of other countries and not resent them or laugh at them because they are different from yours.

With these attitudes, you can travel alone and love it. And you'll be completely mistress of the situation if you follow these three basic rules:

Leave your best friend back home.

Stop worrying about being alone and concentrate on being a woman. Femininity is your chief asset abroad.

Go. It's much better to have been than never to have dared to try. However you travel, whether by cargo boat or clipper, car or train, don't waste time agonizing over what may happen. Go and find out for yourself.

CHAPTER 2

Travel Debut

"Let's see, you've got fifteen hundred dollars and a four-week vacation," summed up the travel agent, a blasé, worldly-wise woman with the nondescript name of Alice Peterson.

I nodded blankly. I was so ignorant that my tongue had quit cold in the presence of this formidable figure.

"Well, we'll give you the standard tour for first-trippers— London, Paris, Brussels, Lucerne, and a side trip to the Alps; Italy and down to Naples to see Vesuvius, Pompeii, Capri, and the Blue Grotto. If it works out, we'll schedule a few days on the Rhine. That ought to use up your time and money nicely." In just five minutes, without my uttering more than a single sentence, Miss Peterson had planned my trip for me.

Something in me woke up. It was my money. I had earned it by saving $15 a week for two years. I didn't want to sail along the Rhine. I've always been frightened by grottoes, I loathe mountains en masse, and have no interest in Belgian lace.

The independent in me spoke up. "I want to go to Greece."

"Oh, that's miles out of the way. It will cost $100 more. Besides, no one but Englishmen and archaeologists goes there."

I've always had an affinity for Greece. In college, Greek drama was the one course where I rated an A. My senior term

paper had been written on Euripides' *Medea;* if I could be
authoritative on any subject in the world, it was Greek theater.
Just recently a new-found friend had introduced me to Katina
Paxinou and Alexis Minotis, stars of the Greek National
Theater. They had said, "Look us up if you ever get to Athens."

"I won't eat lunch and I'll make up the money that way,
but it's the one place I want to go."

The travel agent snorted her disapproval, but I was firm.
Out went the Rhine, Switzerland, Belgium, and the Blue
Grotto. In went Athens.

By sheer accident and stubbornness, I had discovered the
guiding precept of travel success:

RULE 1: **Go where you really want to go—never where the
travel agent says you should.**

It took exactly one week from the moment my boss broke
the news that I was a strain on the USIA budget until I got on
the plane for Europe. During those seven days, my stomach
muscles got more and more rigid. People kept asking, "Why
are you going alone? Why don't you wait and go with a
friend?" I couldn't tell them the truth—that I was going because I felt I was a failure, that a lifetime in Westchester
County, with a four-year interval at Cornell University and a
terrifying expedition on muleback down the Grand Canyon,
was somehow inadequate. On the few occasions I had been
away from home, it had been with a friend, a roommate, or a
relative. I had never really severed the cord between myself
and Mount Vernon. Now I was going to be on my own. I was
scared.

I made one last effort to find company for the trip. "Please
come," I begged Carol, my second-best friend.

"Sorry, but the answer is still 'no,' " was her response. "I don't
want to see monuments. I'm going to a resort to meet men."

For seven days I was frantic with last-minute preparations—
passport, wardrobe, travel agent, and answering cracks like,

"*You* travel *alone?* Why, it takes you a month to get ready for a week out of town. How can you prepare in a week for a month abroad?" I was too busy to be afraid of what lay ahead. But suddenly, when the day came to leave, my stomach knotted into a cold, hard lump.

My father drove me to what was then Idlewild Airport and cheerfully waved me through the gate.

"I hope nothing goes wrong," I said. My knees quaked.

"I hope not, honey," said he, not too sympathetically. As I went slowly up the ramp, I heard a fatherly shout: "Jean, did you take a warm coat?" Somehow, at that moment, I crossed the bridge from childhood to adulthood. If I could still be asked a question like that, it was time to cut the silver cord.

Ever since I had made the fateful decision to go on my solitary expedition, I had been building castles in the air about the flight. I saw myself sitting next to an Italian count who would tender invitations to a whirl of gala dinners and dances in Rome. Or perhaps in the cocktail lounge of the double-decker plane, I would meet an English duchess. Enchanted by the simplicity of this unsophisticate from Mount Vernon, New York, she would insist I spend the next weekend at her country estate, "Manderly." There, maids would draw my bath and serve kidneys and kippers from a breakfast table of solid silver.

This was before the days of economy flights, and the trip started out in deluxe fashion. The stewardess handed out makeup cases and orchids to the women passengers. Pinning the corsage on my new (and still unpaid for) traveling suit and walking to my seat, I felt very *soignée* and woman of the world. Unfortunately, no handsome man was sitting next to me, but surely one would arrive as the evening wore on.

On came the *apéritifs*, and I—whose alcoholic intake usually consisted of a weak predinner highball—was suddenly sipping my second Scotch. A split of champagne accompanied the pheasant; a pony of brandy followed the crêpes Suzette. I drank everything. It cost nothing, and I wanted to get the most out of my trip. The next thing I knew, the stewardess was shaking me.

"Wake up," she exclaimed in her precise British accent. "This is London." We had landed, and I hadn't even felt a vibration. I had been deep in an alcoholic doze. As I think back on it, I probably drank so much to avoid thinking about what the next four weeks, alone, held in store for me.

When I bounced out of the plane at London Airport on a rainy Sunday morning, there was London all curled up like a sleepy kitten. All around me were people and things that were almost identical with the people and things I had known all my life, but everything was different. The porters were carrying baggage the same way they did at Idlewild, but this wasn't Idlewild. The men hurrying past me at the airport were almost like the men at home, but they carried umbrellas and wore bowlers. As the taxi sped along the wrong side of the street, there was all the noise and all the quiet of a big city on a Sunday morning. It wasn't so different from Fifth Avenue and Times Square, but it wasn't Fifth Avenue or Times Square. It was London. I was three thousand miles from home. I wanted to cry.

My mother's remedy for the blues had always been a good hot bath. Suddenly I wanted to lie in a large tub for an hour and soak. Pilgrimages to Piccadilly and Peter Pan's statue could wait. I wanted to clean off the grime of the trip, crawl into a good bed with a soft mattress, and call room service for a hot cup of tea with lemon.

Since every penny was a problem, the travel agent had suggested an inexpensive hotel. "I know a quiet little place near Euston Station," she had said. "It's small but spotless and very cheap."

The cab driver took me to the hotel, where I was greeted with a cheery Cockney, "So sorry, ducks. We've no room for you."

It was too much. "But I've a confirmed reservation," I stammered.

"Now, don't you worry," said the clerk. "We've got you a
lovely bed and breakfast in a boardinghouse round the corner."

That seemed odd, but off I trudged to the address, which
turned out to be a narrow yellow row house with a sign outside that read "Lodgers." Inside, the manageress, a lusty, gusty
type who might have been a chorus girl thirty years ago, welcomed me with, "I'll take you right to your room."

There was no lift, and we plodded up three flights of stairs.
The manageress was over sixty, so the only polite thing to do
was to hoist my two bags myself. The room was no bigger than
my bathroom at home. In fact, the whole room resembled my
bathroom: in one corner was a battered zinc sink that looked
as if William the Conqueror and all his men had fought the
war of 1066 in it, and behind a pink cretonne curtain, a toilet
seat. The carpet was strewn with faded cabbage roses. As a
matter of fact, the whole house smelled of cabbage, a vege-
table I detest. But worst of all, the most important thing was
missing. There was no bed.

Timidly I inquired, "Where do I sleep?"

"Oh," said the woman, "that wooden chair unfolds into a
lovely bed at night. You'll sleep fine, lovey."

This didn't present a very restful prospect. Moreover, the
neighborhood struck me as something out of Dickens; I half-
expected Fagin or Uriah Heep to come walking around the
corner at any moment. I told myself, I am experiencing Life—
but I didn't like it very much.

Suddenly I knew what was wrong with me. I needed someone to talk to, someone who would make me forget my sudden
loneliness and the notion that London was a foreign wilder-
ness.

"May I use your phone?" I asked.

"Go right ahead. It's tuppence a call." She gave me some
British coppers and led me to the telephone in the hall. Only

the phone wasn't like the simple affair I knew in the United States where you drop in a dime and dial the number. This strange apparatus was full of slots and plungers and metal placards covered with instructions in English, which seemed to me a foreign language because I was so overawed. I put the big pennies in, waited for the operator's voice, pushed the plunger just the way the directions said—and the pennies came back. It took a good half hour until I acquired the technique and managed a connection with my only London contact, a friend of my mother's.

The call made me feel I had never left home.

"Where are you staying?" demanded Mrs. Thompson.

I told her.

"Where?" And a long pause. "That's not a proper place. You can't stay there. Now, it's just two o'clock. You go out and walk to Westminster Abbey and back, and we'll come by for you at teatime. By then we'll have you registered at a decent hotel."

Making an attempt at independence, I hedged. "But I can't afford it."

"Nonsense," was the motherly response. "I wouldn't let a child of mine stay in that neighborhood. I can't let you."

Two hours later to the minute, an aristocratic Daimler drove up in front of the row house. In it was Mrs. Jones, lately from Mount Vernon; only now she was English and her name was Mrs. Thompson. She wore a flowered hat, a print dress, and sensible shoes, and she looked ready to take off for clotted cream at the vicar's. With true British efficiency, she had found me a room at the Howard for only $3 a day more than the boarding house rate.

"Hop in, my dear," she commanded. "We'll take you to the Howard, and you go right upstairs and have a strong cup of tea. Tea is the best thing in the world for you, you know. Then we'll come back and take you to supper at our house. It's Sunday, you know, so everything will be cold."

I moved into the Howard, on a quiet side street off the Strand. There were clean linen, a hot bath, a soft bed, and room service. And when that tea wagon, pushed by a frail, white-haired British waiter, rolled solidly into my room, I thought to myself, Luxury! It's wonderful! For the first time, I felt the thrill of being abroad.

RULE 2: **Don't save money at your own expense.** *Economy is fine in its place—but its place should not be on your vacation.*

For three days I was probably the most industrious sightseer to visit England. I hit every high spot in the guidebook. I rushed to Harrods to see the china collection, watched the Changing of the Guard at Buckingham Palace, rode out to Hampton Court and walked the same paths where Henry VIII had walked with his many wives. One morning I visited the Tower of London, talked with the Beefeaters—and suddenly realized I wasn't a bit interested. To me, one tower is like another, whether it is located on Riverside Drive or in Australia.

It was far more meaningful to go to the theater. The play was a real tearjerker called *Down by the Sea*, and I queued up at the end of the line to buy a ticket. When the man ahead of me reached the window, there was just one seat left for the performance. Hearing my American accent, the man refused to take it. "You go. I can see it another time," he said.

During intermission, my left-hand neighbor, a Cambridge don, started talking to me. He ordered tea, and when I offered to pay my share, he said, "Oh, no, you are a stranger in our country." And at the second intermission, the man on my right bought me a drink, and I made the lovely discovery that London theaters have bars.

RULE 3: **Do the things you enjoy doing—never mind whether you miss a few sight-seeing "musts."**

London had been dignified, historical, and fascinating with
its royal pomp, but in some peculiar way, because the language was the same, it had not seemed really foreign. When
May 17 dawned and I was on my way to Athens, I felt, now
I'm really going abroad. As I got on the plane, I kept pinching
myself. "This can't really be me. . . . I can't really be going
to Greece, when just five days ago I was typing stories in New
York. In just a few hours, I'll be seeing the Acropolis and the
Parthenon, standing where Plato stood, drinking *retsina*. . . ."

My seat companion eyed me curiously. In my excitement,
I had been uttering these thoughts quite audibly.

"First trip?" asked the tweedy stranger pleasantly.

That was all I needed. Between the eggs *à la russe* and the
cold ham and chicken, I found myself telling him all about my
troubles, my excitement about Greece, and the fact that today
was my birthday and I would be six thousand miles from
home.

Then it was his turn. He was a Scot (not a bit dour) who
was going down to spend his "holiday" in Athens, where he
would visit his sister, married to a Greek.

During the eight-hour flight, we became quite well acquainted. So much so that I felt completely deserted when I
saw him kissing his relatives at Hellenikon Airport and realized that there was no one even to wish me a happy birthday,
let alone give me a present.

After going through customs, I prepared to go off by myself
to the Grand Bretagne Hotel, when my traveling companion
reappeared, smiling. "We're giving you a party," he said.

"Me?"

"Yes, the Greeks are the most hospitable people in the
world. My brother-in-law says he can't let you come to Athens
without giving you a birthday party. We'll pick you up in an
hour at the hotel."

So my first evening in Athens, instead of being spent in
solitary confinement, was celebrated in a Greek *taverna*, where

a group of new-found friends joined in singing "Happy Birthday to You," complete with Greek accents, Scottish burrs, Levantine music, and toasts in *ouzo*.

RULE 4: Always talk to strangers.

Nowadays, everyone has a word for Greece, but thirteen years ago only a few tourists ventured that far off the grand-tour path. I was determined to see *Medea* performed by Katina Paxinou and Alexis Minotis at the Greek amphitheater at Delphi. It wouldn't be all Greek to me. I knew every word of the play; I had lived with it for a whole year while I did my senior thesis at Cornell. To see this play done in the original Greek in the original theater was a dream that could now come true.

But when I started scouting the "hows" of getting to Delphi, the only way seemed to be by hiring a car and chauffeur. For me, on a continuing battle of the budget, that was out. Eating all the bread-and-cheese lunches in the world wouldn't make up for that extravagance.

A visit to the tourist office produced more hope. "Two girls from my department are driving up for the play tomorrow," said the director. "But in a very old car. If you contribute $10 toward the cost, you can be the third passenger."

The price was right, and the next day, off I went in a blaze of dust with my non-English-speaking companions in a Ford, vintage 1928.

From the beginning, there was trouble. Every few miles, the car halted, the driver disappeared into the barren mountains searching for water, and my two traveling companions talked compatibly in Greek of life, love, and the pursuit of drachmas. I had never been silent for so long.

Finally, some eighty-five kilometers from Athens (about fifty American miles), the car stopped dead. The girls and driver waved me to wait and disappeared. At first I didn't mind being alone. I thought about *Medea* and about my approaching

trip through Italy. I even mentally decorated a few brown-
stones back in New York. After forty minutes. I grew impatient,
but I was still calm.

At the end of an hour, I was bored, beaten, and beleaguered.
I had always had a fatal attraction for mosquitoes. Now they
had the opportunity of a lifetime. Dust clung to my dress,
shoes, face, hands. At first I was just uncomfortable, then
frantic, finally furious. From anger my feelings changed to
hopelessness and despair. Why hadn't I listened to the New
York travel agent? What was I doing in the far-off hills of
Greece? More important, how would I get back to civilization?
Visions of horrors yet to come leaped through my head. I
imagined spending the night on the deserted mountainside
without food or water. Night? Probably nights. Furthermore,
my passport was in my good purse back in the Athens hotel,
so if I fainted from thirst and hunger and some stranger did
find me, he wouldn't even know my name. I could picture a
grave for the unknown girl on the Greek hilltop.

The hours rolled on relentlessly. When a donkey ambled
up and tried to make small talk, I was beside myself. I remembered mountain climbers who had spent weeks in lonely
ravines. But those were the ones who had been saved. Meanwhile the sun beat feverishly down on my bare head, the
donkey brayed, and the hills seemed to echo with my heart-
sickness. "Why did I ever come abroad alone?" I cried as the
tears poured down my dirty face. "I wish I were home."

Suddenly everyone reappeared. Miraculously, after two
twists of the wrist, the car started again. A short while later
we drew up to the hotel at Delphi. A friendly Englishwoman
took one look at me and said, "Wash your face. You'll feel
better." Mr. Minotis appeared and offered me a lift back to
Athens the next day in a Cadillac. The lonely, silent hours on
the deserted mountaintop began to fade, and only the adventure was left.

Soon I found myself writing my first postcard home. "Dear

all," I penned. "Everything wonderful. So thrilling to be on foreign soil. Just spent three hours with a donkey. Having wonderful time and glad you aren't here."

Every traveler has a moment such as I had on that mountain; you wonder, "What am I doing here? . . . Why did I come alone?" Those terrible hours in the Greek hills when I felt deserted by the whole world have always lived in my memory as my worst traveling experience. Having lived through that and emerged whole, I could venture anything—and have.

RULE 5: Expect to be lonely on at least a few occasions. But don't let this ruin your trip. You can be miserable at home, too.

The trip had been wonderful so far, but as the time for my Roman holiday neared, I knew it was only logical that something would go wrong. But that Greek experience had helped. Keep a stiff upper lip, I cautioned myself as the airport bus careened down the Appian Way.

So in Rome I did as tourists do. I took tours—two a day—and they were wonderful. The buses were new and neat, and a pretty girl served orange-juice cocktails. I stood below the balcony from which Mussolini used to harangue his Black Shirts and felt I was reliving history. The stiff Swiss Guards at the Vatican made small talk with me. I stole a two-thousand-year-old stone from the Forum, threw a penny and made a wish at the Fountain of Trevi. On these solo expeditions, I met other lone voyagers—a journalist from Berlin, a teacher from Marseilles, a ceramist from Denmark, a handsome bachelor from Chicago, and a publisher from New York. I saw more of Rome than I've seen in six subsequent visits. And at night my feet hurt so, I would have been glad to have had a solitary dinner, sip my Chianti, watch the passersby, and digest my impressions—but I didn't have to. The bachelor from Chicago turned out to be staying at the same hotel.

RULE 6: **It helps to have friends or introductions abroad, but you can have a good time without them. Whatever you do, don't despise fellow Americans. Some of them may turn out to be friends.**

At luncheon one day at my hotel, I experimented with Roman artichokes, the lovely breaded kind that take hours to make. They were so good I ordered a second portion. The waiter, a handsome youth with an aristocratic Roman nose, smiled approvingly. I wasn't sure whether it was a compliment to my appearance or appetite, but it was nice to be smiled at by such a good-looking man. So I smiled back. After the meal, I went up to my room before taking the next tour. Suddenly there was a knock on the door, and there stood the waiter with a gift—a plate piled with artichokes.

At that point, I had had artichokes up to my collar, but I tried to thank him. He didn't seem to understand, so I added a few gestures. Those he misunderstood. The artichokes suddenly went sailing to the bureau top as he clasped me in a fervent, moustached embrace. He paid no attention to my protests until I threatened, "I'll report you!"

He saw I meant it and swept me a courtly bow. "Signorina," he said, "I thought you wanted me. You smiled at me."

RULE 7: **Use a little judgment when you flirt.**

Venice was the last stop on my Italian itinerary. I couldn't wait to see the famous Piazza San Marco with its pigeons, the glassblowers, and the Lido, but it was no fun. The two days there were the unhappiest of my life abroad. The pigeons didn't seem any different from the ones in Central Park. The glassblowers were just one more way of commercializing sight-seeing. The gondolas made me want to cry, and Jones Beach seemed better than the Lido.

For it was June, the time for honeymooners in Venice, and everyone seemed to be in love but me. This was before

Katharine Hepburn starred in *Summertime*, but that's just how I felt—an unloved American spinster without even a Rossano Brazzi to chase after me. I was so depressed by the constant sight of couples that in a fit of frenzy, I washed out all my underwear. Then I dashed off to catch the launch that would take me to the Riviera train, leaving all my pants and bras decorating the hotel room.

RULE 8: **If you're alone and feel alone, leave. The world is full of pleasant places. Never stay somewhere that doesn't give you peace of mind.**

Every traveler has one place in which he feels completely at home. For me it was, and is, Paris. The very minute I arrived in the City of Light and saw for myself the arrogant independence of the taxi drivers, the sensible frugality of the average Frenchman, the snobbishness of the intellectual set, the heated political discussions over an interminable cup of coffee in cafés, the strong egos of the middle-class shopkeepers, I thought, This is for me. This is what I dreamed Europe would be like.

Yet Paris was the very place everyone had warned me against:

"Too expensive," advocates of Scandinavia had announced.

"It was *the* place during the twenties, but now all the creative people go to Rome," said the fans of Italy.

Others proclaimed, "The French are so inhospitable. They think they're doing you an enormous favor if they buy you a piece of cake. Some Americans live there for years without being invited to a French home for dinner."

Maybe I was lucky, for Paris was the place where I had people to meet. I had met a Frenchwoman journalist at a party just before Christmas. She didn't seem to know many people in Manhattan, so I invited her to our Yuletide family dinner. She accepted. The dinner was a typical American ham-to-nuts meal, and I was afraid this sophisticated woman was just a little bored by a group of relatives devouring food without wine.

Yet, the minute I arrived in Paris, the phone started ringing. "Marcelle wrote me about you. Will you have dinner with me tomorrow?" asked a man who sounded everything Frenchmen are supposed to be.

"Nothing is too much for the young lady who took care of my sister," announced Mrs. George Arents, adding in true sisterly fashion, "Tell me frankly, do you think she'll marry again?"

With the help of the hotel telephone operator, I called every name in my little black book, and at least six different persons tendered invitations—to dinners *en famille*, to Sunday-morning antique hunting at the Flea Market, to a Balenciaga fashion show, to Left Bank cabarets and fancy Right Bank bistros.

One woman provided more than hospitality. "Is Mount Vernon near Yonkers?" she asked.

"It's the next town," I said.

"When you get home, I want you to call up Perry Lansing and say hello for me," said Mimi. "He visited us last month; such a nice man—and single!"

RULE 9: Go with a list of names to look up if you can, and, if possible, let them know ahead of time just when you are arriving. Most people are more than willing to be nice to a stranger.

A telegram from the office arrived the day before I was scheduled to leave for home. "Can't hire you back yet. Stay another week," it read. But how could I? My extravagances in Paris had left me with just $40.

Quick calculation made me realize that if I changed to another airline, I could travel free to Holland and use the next week to see another country. So the next day I started.

At the end of two days, I knew Amsterdam was too expensive. I had spent $10 on a hotel room, $7 on food, $3 on tours, so I would have to move on. I took the train and tram to Scheveningen, where, since it was still off-season, I could enjoy sun and surf for $2 a day.

I figured everything to the last guilder. Breakfast was free. Lunch was a twenty-cent sandwich on the beach. My room was $2, and I had $14 and small change left.

The final night abroad, I decided to splurge and went to the Bali Restaurant for dinner.

"What will you have, madame?" asked the waiter.

Too shy to ask for advice and unable to read the menu, I said, "The specialty." Platters of steak, chicken, and ham were going by my shoulder, so whatever the dish was, I thought it would be fine.

A small army of waiters brought on all sorts of sauce dishes full of strange foods—spiced shrimps, tiny dried fish, fried bananas, curried eggs, rice, grated coconut, chutneys, chicken livers on skewers. . . . Seasoned, sophisticated veteran of four countries that I had now become, I immediately recognized that this was the Dutch version of the French *hors d'œuvres variés*. Not having the nerve to ask for an explanation, I ate sparingly so as to leave room for the main course—unaware that I had already had it. The next course was a bill for $5.

Without knowing it, I had eaten—or barely tasted—the famous Indonesian *rijstafel*. I left the restaurant still ravenously hungry. I tried to ignore the pangs, but finally had to go out again for another dinner, which used up two more of my fast disappearing dollars.

RULE 10: Don't be afraid to ask questions. People want to befriend the stranger within their gates. They are not out to cheat you or do anything but make you feel at home.

On the windswept beach in front of the Kurhaus Hotel at Scheveningen, I had an experience which brought home to me the wide, wide world of travel. A girl of my own age, simi-

larly dressed in a brief bathing suit, approached. We chatted
—clothes, dates in America and Europe, fads. Anne lived in
Rotterdam and was my own age. Yet to me she seemed like
Anne of the thousand days, for Anne had seen Rotterdam
almost razed to the ground, her father arrested by the Gestapo
during World War II. She had lived through the rigors of the
German occupation. All during the early forties, when I had
been a schoolgirl relatively untouched by the war, she had
been living under The Terror. Yet there we were, contempo-
raries but centuries apart in experience, discussing the new
fashions and whether or not bikinis were becoming.

RULE 11: The most important thing about travel is not the
places or things but the people.

The time for the homeward flight came all too quickly. It
was ridiculous, but poverty was making me miserable. By now
I had one fifty-cent piece left, which I had found in the inner
lining of my coat, and I finished with an IOU to the airline
for ten pounds of overweight. Outward-bound, I had dozed
all the way across the Atlantic in a drunken stupor; all the way
home, I was in a dither lest my father fail to meet me at the
airport. I just didn't have the $1.25 bus fare to Manhattan or
the seventy-five-cent fare to Mount Vernon.

However, as I left the plane bearing the five-pound Dutch
cheese that had made me so unpopular with my fellow passengers, there were my father and brother Bob. Bob looked
just the same, but my father seemed older and frailer. They
kissed me warmly, saying, "Did you have a good time?" and,
"You look wonderful," along with, "Why didn't you write
more?" as they led me toward the car.

"So glad your flight came in on time," said Bob. "You're
just in time to cook us a good lunch."

Instead of annoying me, the remark struck me as funny. I
could see that nothing had changed at home.

"Oh, your friend Carol said to tell you she didn't meet a

single decent man at the resort," informed my father. "She wants to go abroad with you next year."

"Oh, she does, does she?" I retorted, with all the superiority of someone who has gone, seen, and conquered. "That's what she thinks. It's much more fun to travel alone."

CHAPTER 3

Two's a Crowd

I didn't realize how much the combination of instinct and ignorance had helped make my first trip abroad a delightful experience. It was on my second expedition, when I let others' heads prevail over my own heart, that I went wrong. This second time, I did not travel alone. Barbara went along.

My first trip had been accomplished with a minimum of preparation and fuss. The second was different. I discovered that when you decide to go abroad and six months elapse between the decision and the departure date, you might as well be going to your own graduation exercises all over again. You work yourself into a frenzy—and everybody wants to get into the act.

Said one travel expert, "You've tried it by yourself; this time go with a friend."

A well-meaning relative cautioned, "Go by boat, where you'll meet some people."

My boss, who had welcomed me back with a raise now that I had crossed the Atlantic Ocean, suggested, "Go back to some of the same places. You'll enjoy them more now that you've seen the standard sights."

Over and over, acquaintances reiterated the tired refrain,

"You've shown that you can stand on your own two feet; now go with someone."

I made a reservation for the June 4 sailing of the *Ile de France*. The plan was simple: six days on the boat, two weeks in Paris, Lisbon, and Madrid, and then home by plane. When Barbara, a perky brunette who worked as a sales promotion assistant for a radio network, decided she wanted to go on the same crossing and spend a week in Paris, it seemed fortuitous. We made a practical pact. We would be together but not together. We would share a ship cabin, stay at different hotels in Paris, and seek each other's company only when nothing better came along.

Sailing day I deposited my luggage in the pint-size cabin and rushed to the dining room. "This is my first trip by boat," I confided to the chief steward, "and I'd like to sit at a table with someone young, interesting, and who speaks French." I didn't actually say the word "male," but the steward, with all his experience, should surely understand.

He nodded.

I pressed the point. "Many of my friends have traveled on your ship, and they all tell me the most important thing is to be at the right table. If I could sit with someone attractive, sophisticated, someone of my sort . . ."

He looked up from the master plan with travel-weary eyes. "Table 22. Second sitting."

He couldn't get rid of me that easily. "Look. I work in the communications field. I'd like to be with someone who could be a friend."

"I'll do my best, mademoiselle."

All day I was breathless with anticipation. During the afternoon, I caught sight of Barbara batting her false eyelashes at whatever eligible male sauntered past, but since I was busy doing likewise, I didn't pay much attention. Once, in the privacy of our tiny cabin, we checked results.

"What sitting did you get?" I asked.

"Second."

"Me, too."

Nighttime came. All the guidebook instructions had cautioned, "Don't dress the first night out," so I put on my top casual costume—the casual red dress from Bergdorf's sport shop, the waist cincher from Bergdorf's Lingerie, the gold chain from Bergdorf's Costume Jewelry, the red-satin pumps from Miss Bergdorf's Shoes, and went in to dinner. I was a little disappointed to find myself at a table for two, but then natural optimism perked me up. Why shouldn't I have the male partner all to myself for three meals and eighteen courses—all day, every day?

The dining room filled. I sat alone facing a bleak array of empty wineglasses.

Concerned, the waiter inquired, "Are you expecting someone?"

"Well, yes," I replied uncertainly. I was getting jittery.

The minutes dragged. The seat opposite me remained vacant. Finally, just as I signaled the waiter to bring on the *purée mongole*, I saw someone coming toward the table. Someone charming, sophisticated, attractive, and dressed in casual blue from Bloomingdale's, black belt from Bloomingdale's Main Floor Accessories, black slippers from Bloomingdale's Better Shoes, and real gold earrings filched from mama. It was Barbara.

No matter how we tried, Barbara and I couldn't escape our mutual annoyance—or each other. On the boat train, I tried to organize details. "I'll tend to the luggage; you get seats for the second sitting at dinner," I instructed with all the wisdom of someone who knew the ropes. But when the waiter banged his bell for *deuxième service*, I learned that Barbara hadn't bothered to do her share. There were no places left, so we went without dinner. She didn't care; she already weighed ten pounds too much and felt virtuous resisting French fare, but I was starved.

When we arrived at the Gare St. Lazare, I started to feel really excited. I had made a reservation at the Hotel Cambon, and Barbara's cousin, who worked in the Paris office of a merchandising corporation, was taking care of her reservation for her. From now on, I thought, it would be easy. I could check in with Barbara for the next few days, perhaps meet her for tea or lunch, but I would be able to go my own way.

You can imagine my surprise when Larry, the merchandising executive, and his slick-looking ex-Baltimore-resident wife, who, after six months in Paris, looked like an *Elle* model, greeted us at the station. "Where are you staying?" questioned Larry.

I told him.

"How funny," he chortled. "That's right across the Rue Cambon from the hotel where we've put Barbara."

I didn't think it was funny at all, particularly when my phone rang at one o'clock in the morning and it was Barbara asking cheerfully, "May I come over?" I began to feel as if Paris and Mount Vernon shared a common problem—Barbara. She finally went home at three o'clock, and I went out on my balcony to look at Paris by moonlight. Silhouetted against the sky, on the corresponding balcony across the street, was a familiar plump figure in a familiar pink peignoir. My last view of Paris on this first night in Paris was Barbara.

For six days she drove me crazy. When I lunched with my French friend Mimi, she wanted to come along. Since her French was even worse than mine, it made everything very awkward. When I was at loose ends and she had a date, she turned on me with sweet reasonableness, "Now, Jean, we did agree to go our separate ways." She suggested that we go to a really good restaurant, and we went to Lucas Carton for dinner. But Barbara was so overawed by the prices that she ordered only a dish of asparagus. I was so embarrassed by her stinginess that I ate for two, and my bill came to $16.

She wasn't all bad. A little embarrassed by the fact that I

had more connections than she did, she inveigled Larry and
his wife into taking me to the races at Longchamp. I didn't
have the nerve to refuse. But the truth is that I'm bored by
horses and would have had a much better time taking myself
to a matinee.

On Barbara's last night in Paris, we agreed to celebrate by
attending the Opéra. "You get the tickets, Jean," she commanded. I did. But at the last minute, Barbara preferred to
brood in front of the Seine, so I attended *Faust* alone.

Late at night, she called to apologize. "I'll pay you back for
the ticket later," she promised. "But since you're going to
Spain and I'm not, would you buy me a bottle of sherry? I'll
trade you for a bottle of Grand Marnier when we get back
home."

Good sport to the bitter end, I agreed. I would have given
away my favorite garnet bracelet to get Barbara out of my
life. I had already forfeited two weeks of my vacation.

Once Barbara had taken off for Rome, things began to happen to me just the way they had on the first trip. I sobbed my
heart out at *Œdipe Roi* at the Comédie Française and was so
moved by the way the king tore his eyes out that I went back-
stage to congratulate the actor who played Oedipus. He was
so flattered by this attention from an American girl that he
bought me a drink.

In Lisbon, I stopped for a lemonade one evening at a sidewalk café. I did notice that I was the only woman on the
terrace, but I was a little astounded when a policeman started
muttering something in Portuguese that obviously meant,
"Please depart." I went with what dignity I could muster and
didn't realize until hours later that he had taken me for a
streetwalker.

In Madrid, I was invited for dinner at the home of a Spanish couple. "Come at ten o'clock" they ordered. Politely, I
arrived exactly on time. No one else showed up until eleven.
and I had to wait forty-five minutes until even the patrician

host and hostess descended the stone stairs. My advance research had not included the fact that it is customary to arrive an hour late for dinner in Spain. But my dinner partner turned out to be a bullfighter, who invited me to a *feria* and eventually honored me with a rare trophy—the tail of the bull he had killed, presented to him for his artistry. I knew this was supposed to be a great tribute to my feminine charms, but the tail still smelled alive, and I had no intention of stuffing it and framing it, as custom decrees in Spain. When the chambermaid wasn't looking, I left it in the hotel wastebasket. But I did buy Barbara the bottle of sherry.

On the plane ride home, I reviewed this second trip. The split vacation had taught me a travel lesson. The least satisfactory way to travel is with another woman. The best way must be to go with the man you love. But failing that, the second most rewarding is to venture on your own.

Whatever the object of your overseas trip may be—to sightsee, shop, or study ancient Greek at the foot of the Acropolis —leave your best friend, or any other female, behind to plan her own itinerary. You have much more chance of seeing the world and letting the world see you when you go globetrotting on your own.

Perhaps you are fortunate enough to have one female pal, whether fellow worker, ex-roommate, or next-door neighbor, whose company you can stand for X hours a day and still be friends. If so, you are the exception to my rule, and togetherness may work for you. But for most women, traveling as a female twosome has just one advantage: you are sure of someone to pass the salt at mealtimes. Against this limited social security, weigh the freedom of thought and action that you have traveling alone. A female partner is fine for tennis but not for travel.

In case your fears about traveling alone are clouding your normally clear thinking, let's tote up the practical and psychological advantages of going it alone:

You Make Your Own Timetable—or None. Go alone and you can sleep till noon, skip Venus de Milo's armless beauty for a Left Bank atelier, pick up men, change your plans in midstream, and not talk when you are spoken to. Go with a friend, even one with a sugarcoated disposition, and life becomes one long period of adjustment. For example, at the age of fifty, my grandmother traveled around the world with her best friend of many years' standing. They returned home and never spoke to each other for the rest of their lives. "She doesn't wear well," was Grandma's explanation.

You Leave Home Behind. You may think that traveling thousands of miles can separate you from your existence on Main Street, U.S.A., but you can't enjoy Notre Dame or the Pitti Palace if Joannie continually carps, "We haven't sent a card to Mary Jones yet," or, "I forgot to send my fur coat to the cleaners." Without the drag of an equally scared traveling companion who knows you as a timid-rabbit type, you are free. At least there isn't going to be any criticism if you sport a low neckline and eyelashes out to there. A stranger will be delighted to accept the New You—for the simple reason that he never saw the Old You.

You Can't Help Meeting People. With a constant cohort, you can travel around the world and hardly talk to anyone else but tour conductors, porters, concierges, and ticket takers. Alone, the monotony of your own company virtually forces you to make overtures to other travelers. And desperation can lead to delightful consequences.

You Don't Have to Change Personality. If you are accustomed to living alone, it is difficult to adjust to another woman on vacation. It's tough enough to live with someone you love. To experiment in international living with some comparative stranger whom you know merely from coffee breaks, occasional lunches, and a few congenial evenings can be a bore or even a disaster.

You Don't Scare Away Men. Adult wolves do not travel in

a pack. They blaze solitary trails, and the surest way to scare off the male animal is to appear with a friend. There is nothing like one dame, but two spell trouble. If your friend is ugly, the lone man will avoid both of you because he doesn't want to be stuck with her. If she's pretty, he makes his choice—and you take your chances. The grown-up male over thirty is usually adult enough to travel alone—and he likes his women equally adult.

Even if you finally realize that the heaviest baggage a woman can carry on a trip abroad is a girl friend, there are a few other companion possibilities you may want to consider—and, I hope, reject:

([*An Aunt Susie who offers to foot the bills.* If, along with her offer of bed and board, she also promises to take a nap every afternoon and carries plenty of sleeping pills for evenings, you might try. Otherwise don't—that is, if your Aunt Susie is anything like mine. Life as an unpaid companion is not beautiful if you have all the duties of a wife and none of the privileges. It is much better to save $10 a week for the next year, rob your Christmas Club account, and go on your own for three weeks.

([*A gigolo who wants a free ride.* If you're bound for Riviera society, where a penniless count still has status, you may want to consider engaging a professional escort who is ornamental and has social contacts. But why pay his passage? Gigolos can always be found at deluxe Continental hotels such as the Excelsior in Rome and the George V in Paris, but they also abound at the Negresco in Nice, the Carlton in Cannes, and any other place frequented by rich widows with poodles. If you must take one along for the ride, make sure you hold on to the tickets. Gigolos have a way of disappearing in search of fairer game and turning *your* tickets in for *their* cash.

([*A platonic friend who wants the security of your sex minus sex.* Many a man, fearing loneliness, has suggested, "Since we're both going abroad, why don't we travel together?" That's his problem, not yours. Meet frightened Tom, Dick, or Harry if you must en route, but pick the cities where you don't know a soul and can use an escort for nightclubs and theaters. You definitely do not need him on a ship, at a resort, or any-place where you have letters of introduction.

Besides, these platonic friendships have a way of turning out unexpectedly. I was once going on a tour to Latin America. By chance a new acquaintance was leaving for the same place, same day, same flight. He called and suggested, "Jean, instead of leaving on Monday afternoon, why don't we go on Friday to Tobago and spend the weekend there? It won't cost much more, and we'll have two days in the sun."

I deliberated. Certainly there was no romantic interest on either part, but you never can tell what men will do away from home. Did it look right? Was Richard interested in Tobago or in me? Finally, I decided that Richard was unim-portant and that lying on the beach would be pleasant. Off we went. I had a harbinger of things to come when Mama brought him to the airport and eyed me with great suspicion. When on the plane he borrowed $15, I knew that romance was out.

The hotel looked very glamorous as we checked in. Men in dinner jackets stood on the veranda, Martinis in hand. Women wearing bouffant tropical prints looked at me and took a second look when they saw my companion but no wedding ring on my left hand. I was a little amused, but when I saw the romantic pink-and-white flower beds that guarded the low-slung, white, beach-front hotel, I thought, What a won-derful place for a honeymoon, and wished I were there with almost anyone but Richard. The hotel clerk looked at us strangely as we signed our separate names and requested separate bedrooms. The soul of cooperation, he immediately offered adjoining bedrooms—and winked.

As we walked down the garden path in the moonlight, the spicy scent of bougainvillea became stronger and the sea crashed and sighed into the sand with magic rhythm. "Your room," said the clerk obsequiously bowing me into a charming chamber. "Your room, sir," I heard him say to Richard as he led him next door.

The next thing I heard was a click. Richard had locked me out. Although I had faith in his honorable intentions, he apparently was not sure of mine.

What about your own case? Are you anxious to go abroad but afraid you aren't the "type to do it successfully alone"?

The first thing to realize in traveling alone is that you start with one major advantage. You are not just any woman. You are an American woman, and you have three valuable assets:

Looks. American women are generally conceded to be the best-looking women in the world. Indonesian women have beautiful bodies, but they are old at thirty. Italian women rate for their bosoms, but they get fat. Frenchwomen have chic, charm, and a captivating walk, but they win few beauty contests. Arabs age. But Americans stay younger and look better longer than the women of any other country.

Cash. You have your own money and the right to spend it as you please. You've earned it yourself, and it belongs to you. You don't have to get a husband's or father's permission to open a bank account, as is the case in some countries.

Independence. Other travelers have set the stage for you. The world expects American women to be adventurous and dare to do things other women would not do.

Whether you can travel successfully alone has nothing to do with age, appearance, or the knack of making small talk. It is simply a question of attitude and action. You must go with an open mind, enjoy your own company, and maneuver well in your own behalf. But don't expect the trip to change your basic personality. You take yourself with you wherever you go.

At the conclusion of my second trip abroad, I came home

feeling that I was the very quintessence of the worldly traveler. As I entered the house, the phone was ringing. It was Barbara, and the dialogue went something like this:

I asked, "How was your trip?"

"Just wonderful. The minute I left you, things began to happen."

"For me, too. A top star at the Comédie Française bought me a drink."

"How exciting. A friend of my Aunt Jane's in Milan *gave* me a set of tablecloths and napkins. They would cost $200 at Bloomingdale's."

No one had given me anything. I tried for shock value. "Can you imagine—a Lisbon policeman thought I was a prostitute."

She wasn't going to be outdone. "I met an Italian count who wanted to marry me."

Nobody had asked for my hand. I countered. "Did you gain weight?"

There was a minute of silence. I had definitely said the wrong thing. "A little, but it was worth it," said Barbara airily.

I remembered the liquor. "Barbara, I did get you the sherry. I'll bring it over tomorrow and exchange it for the Grand Marnier."

Barbara had evidently learned that her liqueur was worth much more than my sherry. "Oh, never mind, I'll keep the Grand Marnier."

It was too much. She had forced herself into my company, ruined my boat trip and most of my stay in Paris, and now she was repudiating the bargain she had offered in return for the favor I had done.

A long pause. "Barbara, you are terrible," said I.

"And so are you," said she. "I wish I'd never gone with you."

Two telephones slammed simultaneously. It was the end of a beautiful friendship. And I realized anew that one woman traveling alone spells adventure; a pair is clearly a case of two's a crowd.

CHAPTER 4

Decisions, Decisions

You don't need beauty, brains, background, or the ability to speak a foreign language to have a successful trip abroad. You do need to recognize your type and pick the type of travel that suits you.

Before you look at a single glamorous travel folder, sit down and take a long, soul-searching look at yourself. Analyze your capabilities, interests, needs, yearnings—and earnings. When you know *who* you are and *why* you want to go adventuring, then and only then are you ready to take up the all-important decisions of the "when," "how," and "why" of your trip abroad.

If you're a woman who loves the luxury of room service, bath salts, and ringing imperiously for the *femme de chambre,* the last thing you should do is suddenly develop a taste for Somerset Maugham islands or the desire to call on Albert Schweitzer. You'll end up having a hate affair with a mosquito and wishing you were back in the Duncan Phyfe comfort of your own living room.

If you are a twenty-two-year-old secretary with a limited budget and a completely withdrawn bank account, splurging on a first-class boat passage and stays at the swank hotels of Europe will rarely result in a fun trip or a rich husband. You are far more apt to have an uncomfortable holiday and spend the next two years dining on baked beans.

The woman traveling alone, without benefit of husband, escort, or feminine companion as a shock absorber, is bound at times to be lonely, desperate, bored, and restless, and such feelings create problems. But she will go a long way toward solving these problems if she casts her travel to type.

Do any of these familiar travel types fit your personality? Are you *The Neophyte,* anxious to see and do everything, in case you never go again, but unsure of your own judgment? *The Adventuress,* who travels for the sake of adventuring and dreams of having a bearded, helmeted stranger emerge from the African jungle and say, "Miss Livingston, I presume?" *The Sophisticate,* who wishes you could have seen Budapest in '29 and who finds everything today old hat and expensive? *The Joiner,* extroverted, sure of yourself as Madam Chairman, but unsure of your ability to manage abroad, who wants somebody else to worry about hotels and baggage? *The Career Girl,* buyer, stylist, copywriter, executive secretary, a refugee from a year under pressure, who longs for three weeks to collapse on some beach, petted and fussed over by a series of handsome bachelors? *The Budgeteer,* who has saved for years, skipping lunches, eschewing taxis, and wearing last year's dress to parties, more interested in guidebook monuments than in *haute couture? The Widow,* well-off, abroad alone for the first time, frightened, in search of new places without memories? *The Lady Executive,* who has already seen the Continent on an expense account and wants a relaxing vacation with people in the same salary bracket?

Your answer will determine whether you are a tourist type or a go-it-aloner, a woman who likes capital cities or who wants to hide in the hinterlands, a lady who craves luxury or a budgeteer by necessity or choice.

Now, ask yourself *exactly why you want to travel abroad.* Do you want to find out whether European men live up to their reputation? Do you genuinely want to stroll through churches, or do you prefer to eat your way around the world? Your reason for going may be just old-fashioned curiosity, jealousy, or just that you think travel is a status symbol. Whatever your motivation, you must know this from the start, or you will come home disappointed because you haven't seen what you really wanted to see.

Once you understand the "why," you are ready to come to the basic decisions of your expedition. And this is when you should start to rejoice that you will be alone. You can be as self-centered, self-willed, and selfish as you want. You don't have to make one single judgment on the basis of anything other than your own preference.

HOW LONG

This depends on you and your time schedule. Many travel authorities agree that six weeks is the perfect time length and that after that you tend to reach a certain saturation point. On the other hand, you may be like my friend who went to Paris for a ten-day visit and decided to stay there forever. But what about the working woman who doesn't have six weeks—and may never have? Remember that two-letter word: "go." You can see a great deal in the space of three weeks or even seventeen days. It does seem a shame to spend all that money on transportation and stay such a short time, but it's even more of a shame to procrastinate and never go at all. Only one of my overseas expeditions has been for more than a month.

If you smile prettily, most bosses will allow you a few extra days on your own time or will let you take your overtime pay in days instead of dollars. You might schedule your trip around Thanksgiving, Labor Day, or Memorial Day, which provides you with extra time. Remember, it may cost you a bit more to go to Spain and Portugal for three weeks than it would to spend your customary two weeks at a holiday resort at home, but it will be worth much more to you. The fact that you have only a short time at your disposal should never interfere with taking the trip.

WHEN

If possible, the woman traveling alone should avoid travel to Europe during the peak months of July and August because she is apt to find herself in the position of the girl who came calling and found the family out. The very people to whom she has so carefully wangled letters of introduction have probably fled to hiding places in the hills to escape the heat and the hordes of tourists.

There will be no room at the inn, for the hotelkeeper will be reluctant to fill his hostelry with a lone female in a double room when he can get two for the price of one.

The man to whom you may have a letter of introduction may be in town but not to you. It's one thing to take Jane Jones out to dinner on Tuesday night, but it gets expensive when you have to escort Tibby Thompson from Detroit on Wednesday, Sally Simpson from Cleveland on Thursday, and Eugenie Edwards from Syracuse on Friday. After all, the same person who provided you with the foreign gentleman's name probably has turned it over to others, and the turnover can be terrific. Also, Europe is crowded in summer—so crowded that you don't even have enough room to change your mind. Just waiting in the line at the airline counter to reroute yourself uses up a precious afternoon.

The best travel months in Europe are from March through June, or September through December. Then you are assured of moderately good weather, off-season prices on ships and planes, and can avoid the swarms of tourists that overflow

▶

hotels, restaurants, galleries, trains, and buses. You don't even need reservations in most cases.

However, if you can go abroad only during July and August, console yourself. Some excursions are available only at these times. There are events, such as the Sound and Light festivals, that require bulk patronage and really warm weather. Transportation is most adequate then. You never have to be lonely, even if you are minus letters of introduction, for there will be scads of compatriots at every American Express mail counter. Formerly, all Parisians fled the City of Light in August; now the smart ones stay home, for that's the only month of the year they can find a parking place easily.

Good judgment will not recommend the Italian lakes in February or Cornwall in the dead of winter, but it is better to go at a bad time of year than not to go at all. I went to Samarkand in the middle of August, when the sun beat down at 110 degrees. I was hot, but I saw Samarkand. Remember, too, that below the equator, seasons reverse; when it is summer in the United States, it is winter in South America, the southern half of Africa, and Australia.

HOW

You can travel via three major systems: tour, planned independent, or do-it-yourself.

1. *The Guided Tour.* Guided tours provide a way for twenty or more people to travel together, with the help of a conductor, for a lump sum and follow a general itinerary. I feel that the prepackaged variety is only for the girl who hasn't the guts to go any other way. You live a rigid existence, see too much, learn too little, follow too strict a schedule, and miss the elements that are really important—such as people. However, special-interest tours are different and can be both pleasant and productive. The cost runs high, but so do the results.

2. *The Foreign Independent Tour.* This is what travel
agents call FIT and what I call "For Idiot Tourists." Here, the
agent maps out an itinerary that includes everything the
traveler wants—or the agent thinks she should have. She pays
for everything in advance—transportation, hotel accommodations, sight-seeing tours. Often, arrangements are made for
you to be met on arrival at each stop (at a cost of $5 per
"hello"). Everything is scheduled, including visits to museums
and "free time" to get your hair done. You're apt to end up in
Venice and have all your time taken up by visits to glassworks,
when *you* want to flirt with a man and go gondola riding.
The FIT costs plenty and has the same rigidity as a guided tour.
You pay more because you fork over American dollars here
instead of getting the benefit of foreign exchange.

3. *Potluck.* This is the best way for the woman with the
courage, curiosity, and instinct for self-preservation. Plan what
you want to do, and then tell the travel agent what you want.
Buy your tickets here, make the basic hotel reservations (but
pay a deposit for one night only), and arrange for everything
else when you get there.

TRANSPORTATION

A transatlantic crossing is wonderful if you like to attend
movies daily, play gin, or if shuffleboard is your idea of good
sport. But don't kid yourself in the romance department. Those
stories about all the tall, dark, handsome Lotharios from
east, north, south, and west are strictly tall tales. Most of the
men on board ship are married or too young, so if you don't
bring your own man, you're out of luck. However, for those
who like to smell sea air, sip bouillon in midmorning, and
watch other ships that pass in the night, an ocean voyage can
be relaxing.

If you are very young or pinching pennies hard, go tourist. Otherwise, beg, borrow, hock your gold earrings, sell a savings bond if you must, but go first class. Don't make the mistake of choosing cabin class because you've heard "all the fun is there." That's just rationalization from those who can't or won't pay for the best. Cabin class is comfortable, filled with pleasant couples, and complete with moderately gracious living, but most of the interesting, famous, and fascinating people go first class. Certainly all the lone men on company expense accounts do.

I've tried cabin class on the British, French, and Italian lines, and usually I've fled to first the second day at sea.

For example, my most recent transatlantic crossing was on the *France*, the year of its debut. "First class will be so stuffy," advised my knowing friends. "Tourist is definitely the thing on a new boat." I listened, and I booked return passage from Le Havre.

Things went wrong before the voyage even began. The eve of my departure, I returned late to the Hotel Bristol in Paris, only to hear that the crew of the *France* had gone on strike and all passengers would be marooned for at least two days. Since I had exactly $50 left, half of which had to be saved for shipboard tips, I was in a quandary.

"Are you stuck too?" inquired a pleasant, plump-faced, elderly woman with a cheerful Midwestern twang.

"I am," I confessed sadly. "And I've run out of money."

The lady turned out to be a pleasant Mrs. Settel from Chicago, and her husband turned out to be even pleasanter; he cashed a $50 postdated check for me.

We waved at each other frequently in the Bristol lobby, usually as they were emerging from the dining room and I was furtively coming back from my quick snack in a side street. When we finally left for the boat train in separate cabs, they cordially called, "We'll be in Cabin 608A. Where will you be?"

I didn't want to tell them that a series of doors marked "First Class—Do Not Enter" would separate us. "I'll be around," I promised, with firm intentions of breaking through that class barrier.

When I finally boarded the ship, I found my cabin already filled to overflowing with a fat bourgeois mama and a mousy daughter from the French provinces. Both were bound for New York to make their fortune as dressmakers. Their day began at 7:15 A.M., when the stewardess brought them breakfast (no brioches). I couldn't sleep through the clatter of their dishes and the clucking of their French. I found it equally impossible to sleep at night. Mama was awake until all hours, cutting the pages of her French paperbacks, and daughter snored on the offbeat.

My dining companions were even worse. I asked to be put at a table with "interesting people," and drew five beardless young Frenchmen with hairline moustaches. Profession: hairdressers. A little talk about the respective merits of hair sprays went a long way, and I requested a switch in tables. Next I drew a dull young widow from Rochester who had spent her whole European holiday looking for other people from Rochester who might know men back home. Since I knew no one in Rochester, she deserted me. Her replacement was a Boston bore who wore print ascots that clashed with his striped suit and didn't like conversation with his meals. For two days I talked to hardly anyone except the Polish cook who sat next to me on deck, and exchanging recipes in French was hard going. I was getting hungrier all the time, since tourist-class menus offered little choice and much monotony.

On the late afternoon of the second day at sea, I sat down for a long heart-to-heart talk with myself. "Jean," I argued, "you have spent $900 on a four-week vacation. It is all being ruined by this dismal trip home. Forget economy and get to first class."

Ten minutes later I was in the office of the first-class purser. Fifteen minutes later I had handed over a check for the extra cost, and one-half hour later I had a bed and cabin of my very own. As I was sorting out my belongings and getting ready to eat my way through a nine-course dinner, a note was pushed under the door inviting me to the purser's cocktail party that night. The first people I saw there were the Settels. "My dear, where in the world have you been? We've looked everywhere for you."

"It took me a little time to get located," was my response, "but here I am at last."

You may want to combine air and ship travel. If you do, cross by boat and fly back. Experts often advise doing the opposite because you can bring back packages of copper, brass, and breakables without excess-weight charges. But that's being practical in the wrong area. It's better to shell out for a few excess-baggage charges on the return trip by air and to enjoy the exhilaration of a *bon voyage* party when your ship sails, the opportunity to meet new people on board ship whom you might possibly see abroad, and experience the "what's-ahead?" atmosphere that pervades shipboard. Going home by ship is like the last day at camp. You feel rested, but all anyone talks about is what's happening at home.

Take a chance on seasickness and travel by ship in winter, fall, or spring, but avoid crossing during the summer season, when the vessel will be full of anxious mothers, noisy children, and spinster teachers on their annual holiday.

The ads for cruises make them sound tempting. The ship is your home, so you have no hotel expense. The purser organizes onshore expeditions for you. And among all those fellow voyagers, there must be someone you will like, you probably reason to yourself. But statistics tell a sad story. According to a spokesman for American Express, men on cruises are the minority group. The average cruise totals five hundred passengers. This breaks down into two hundred couples, seventy-five single women, and twenty-five single men. Of course, maybe you'll be one of the lucky ones who will nab one of the twenty-five, but, remember, at least half of them will be too young or too old. The story becomes worse in summer. On summer cruises, of the five hundred passengers, you have one hundred teen-agers, aged fourteen to eighteen, whose grand-mothers are taking them abroad to improve their minds.

If cruise abroad you must, bear in mind that there are Major and Minor cruises. The Minors are under four weeks and generally offer more unattached people for company. The Majors take from one to three months and go to the Orient, South Seas, Africa, or around the world. These are for retired people or the very rich.

This doesn't mean that you must rule out all cruises. Elimi-nate those that originate in New York or other American points, but you can have a gala time on offbeat cruises. The excitement of traveling with foreigners to foreign places is far superior to keeping company with couples who want to play bridge. Also, on these foreign cruises, you will never be asked to participate in a "make-the-best-hat" contest by a social director.

For example, you can take the *Transylvania* out of Con-stansa, Romania. This one calls at Black Sea ports, and your fellow passengers will be Russians, Bulgarians, and Roma-nians. From Bergen, Norway, you can cruise to the North Cape for two weeks of the Midnight Sun via coastal steamer. Or go to New Zealand and sail on the Union Steamship Cargo boat out of Auckland for a two-week tour of offbeat South Sea islands. At Marseilles, France, you can pick up one of the French liners that go to Dakar and other African ports. One word of warning: manners and ideas of hygiene vary with latitude, diminishing as you go south from Scandinavia.

I give a firm veto to travel by tramp steamer unless you have all the time in the world and are not particular about the company you keep. You may think you'll meet fascinating novelists and famous actors who shun publicity, but chances are you won't. Usually there are just twelve people on a cargo ship, and when you're stuck, you're really stuck. Furthermore, tramps are frequently tied up in some smelly port, loading a cargo of copra, hemp, or guano—which can make life difficult if you're due back on the job.

Unless you are an ocean fanatic, travel by plane is by far the swiftest, most satisfying, and cheapest. Your chances of meeting a worthwhile man are minuscule, but you will have more of your precious time to spend abroad. Incidentally, save your dollars and travel tourist. The few air travelers who go first class are usually widows with vast amounts of AT&T stock and snobs who want to impress other snobs. Many cagey men traveling on expense-account money turn in their first-class tickets and pocket the difference.

One plane tip to the wise: while transatlantic jets offer few social opportunities, planes to remote parts of the world offer excellent chances to meet other wayfarers. After all, if there are three English-speaking foreigners on a plane bound for Tashkent, they can't very well avoid talking to each other.

If you've a choice between five days on board ship and five days abroad, elect the latter. You can catch up on your sleep after you get home.

WHERE TO GO

Whether you are a buyer, housewife, typist, writer, or dilettante with dollars, I repeat: *go where you want to go.* One woman's champagne is another woman's poison. Travel agents can make the necessary reservations, but the rest of the trip should be your idea. Never take the trip that has worked for someone else unless it fits your tastes, too.

Tote up your own assets. In addition to asking what the

country can do for you, analyze what you can offer. Maybe
your talent can open certain doors for you. If you teach Spanish, to take only one example, the teachers' association of
Spain would be glad to welcome you and exchange ideas, and
one day with a Spanish teacher of your own age can teach
you more about her country than a whole week of tours.

In planning your itinerary, keep in mind that there are two
types of trips. If this is your first visit abroad and you have a
limited amount of time, you may want to pack in lots of
people, places, things. Or you may want to see just one
or two countries thoroughly. With the new charter flights and
reduced airline prices, it becomes less expensive each year to
venture abroad, and other chances may come your way. You
don't have to accomplish everything on one trip:

1. *Plan with a Purpose.* A grand tour of famous places can
be stimulating, but a trip with a purpose will be even more
memorable. Are you an amateur horticulturist? Why not go
to Holland during the tulip season? Is fashion your forte?
Schedule your trip for right after the Paris, Florence, and
Madrid openings. The music lover can go to Salzburg for
Mozart, to Helsinki for Sibelius, to Bayreuth for Wagner, to
Bergen for Grieg, and to Duszniki in Poland for Chopin. For
the religious, there are the Passion plays in the Austrian Tyrol,
the Lutheran World Foundation in Helsinki, the pilgrimages
to Fátima in Portugal and Lourdes in France.

Camera addicts can shoot exotic scenes of the Devil Dancers
of Oruro in Bolivia, the Whirling Dervishes of Konya in Turkey, the gilded elephants at Mysore, India, during the Dasara
festival in the fall.

Travelers who wish to obtain a copy of the current Calendar
of Overseas Events should write to Pan American Airways, P.O.
Box 431, Boston, Massachusetts, 02102.

I can't emphasize enough how much an interest other than
sight-seeing will add to your life abroad. I am a theater buff.
Wherever I go, I make a beeline for the box office, whether

the performance takes place in French (of which I understand about half), Spanish (I understand little of the language, but Spanish actors have most expressive bodies), or Russian (where nothing is clear except that women love machinery more than they do men).

Several years ago, I was in Berlin at the height of an international crisis. All Americans were warned to stay clear of East Berlin, but there happened to be a special performance of Brecht's *The Three-Penny Opera* that Friday, before all the Communist brass at the Theater am Schiffbauerdamm in East Berlin. I wanted to go.

The manager of the hotel thought I was crazy. "No, madame, we'll make no arrangements for you," he stated firmly.

The American Embassy curtly said, "We take no responsibility," and the Berlin Tourist Office refused my request for help. All these negatives just made me more positive about going.

At a cost of $10 for full day and evening use, I hired a car and chauffeur and swept through the Brandenburg Gate in deluxe fashion to the theater. There, the English-speaking chauffeur translated as I begged the box-office attendant for a ticket.

"Impossible," she told me. "We've been sold out for weeks. All the top Party leaders are coming."

Difficulty whetted my appetite. "I leave tomorrow. I won't get another chance."

A second look at my determined face and she recognized the true theater addict. "Come back at six," she said.

At six on the dot, I was back. I was certainly getting my money's worth out of that car.

"The director has agreed to let you sit in his box." My sympathetic box-office friend beamed with a sort of Lotte Lenya expression. And sit there I did, the only foreigner in the audience, composed of top Karl Marx Allee dignitaries.

Later I went to see *Three-Penny Opera* in New York.

"Wonderful, isn't it?" asked the man who took me.

"Oh, yes," I concurred. "But I wish you could have seen it in the original version in East Berlin!"

2. *Use Your Connections.* If someone you know has relatives in Verona, Italy, and proffers an introduction, head for Verona. If your college chum married a Foreign Service officer who now is heading the consulate in Tours, spend some time at a nearby château and postpone the weekend at Deauville. Remember, the farther away you get from major capitals, the more of a welcome you will receive.

3. *Allow Free Time to Think.* You may feel you have to telescope a lifetime of thwarted traveling into a four-week period, but your life will be much more fun if you allow time for leisure and relaxation. At home, you have one or two days off each week. Have them on your trip. On one thirty-day trip to four countries, I scheduled two days at a different beach resort at the conclusion of each stop in a big city. Torremolinos was quick-change artistry from Madrid, and those heated bath towels in Nice a wonderful antidote to the furor of life in Paris.

If you are going to an exotic spot like Angkor Wat in Cambodia, Hong Kong, Moscow, or Beirut, plan your next stop to be a restful chance to re-examine and classify your kaleidoscope of impressions. London is always a soothing end to a trip because there are no language complications.

4. *Go to Your Heart's Desire.* Don't let anyone sell you the idea that London, Paris, and Rome are "musts" for the first trip. They may not be right for you. Go to Rio at carnival time if you've dreamed all your life of wearing a mask and dancing along Copacabana Beach.

Things will happen to you if you like what you're doing. My friend Ruth had always dreamed of going to the Middle East, and that's where she went on her maiden adventure overseas.

Asked what impressed her most, she blithely dismissed the

Pyramids, the Sphinx, and the desert. "It was the night the car got stuck," she confessed. "Four of us hired a car and drove out to see the Egyptian countryside. The roads were muddy, the car got stuck, and we became terrified. And then, of all things, the local sheikh came to our rescue. He organized his men into a rescue crew, and they swept out a room in a tent for us, brought water, and cooked lamb for dinner. The next morning, these same men pushed the car out of the mud, and they cried—and so did we—when we said good-bye. It wasn't elaborate, but they gave us the best they had—their hospitality."

5. *Be Prepared for Quick Departure.* The place may be lovely, but the single woman always should travel armed with an alternate destination. If you go to an out-of-the-way place like Dubrovnik, Yugoslavia, you must know how to beat a quick exit—just in case. I always travel with a batch of airline schedules so that I don't even have to waste a moment at the local airline office. It is important to know in advance that the only direct flight from Dubrovnik to Paris is on Wednesday—in case you are the only woman alone in a hotel full of loving couples.

6. *Jettison the "Single" Psychology.* Never ask the travel agent, "Where do single people go?" Instead, query, "Where does my type of person go?" And go where you want to go with the attitude that if you don't meet a single soul, you will still enjoy the trip. You must do what's right for *you.* Don't go just to say, "I've been in Japan," or wherever.

7. *Be an Extraordinary Tourist.* Plan one extra enterprise that will take you away from the grand-tour stops, even for a weekend. One young woman retraced the footsteps of Thomas Jefferson in Italy. Another followed the route of Eleanor of Aquitaine through France. My friend Lillian, a still-stagestruck graduate of Carnegie Tech Drama School, decided to look up the place where the Brontës (Charlotte, Anne, Emily, and brother Branwell) had lived in Haworth,

Yorkshire, just because she had starred in a college production of *Moor Born,* the drama about the girls and their troubles.

As another example of how to be an extraordinary tourist, let's take Alice Sheldon. She was making her first trip abroad and decided she'd like to spend a week with an archaeological expedition. She had no idea of where to get the necessary information, so she wrote her college for names of U.S.-financed diggings currently in progress. From the list she acquired, she wrote to ten universities, stating that she would like to work for a week of her vacation and that she would pay her own transportation, room, and board. From the ten letters, she got back an acceptance from the University of Pennsylvania, which had an expedition in Gordium, Turkey: "You can come for a week."

So Alice went off to Gordium and spent seven days recording what the diggers dug. "Everything was so technical that I felt pretty useless," she said, but from this unique holiday, Alice went on to archaeological studies at Columbia University evenings.

8. *Make Your Life Easy.* If the language problem worries you, you might consider choosing a place for your first trip where the native tongue is English or where, at least, English is spoken as an important language. London, Amsterdam, Dublin, Helsinki, Oslo, Copenhagen, Stockholm immediately will give a woman the feel of a foreign city, but also will make her feel at home.

9. *Keep Your Itinerary Flexible.* Adaptability is a great asset for the lone woman traveler. Travel with too rigid a schedule and you may miss out on the best travel has to offer. I learned this on my second trip abroad. I was in Paris, bound for a week on the Riviera and thence to Portugal. It just happened that I had a date with an official from French National Railroads.

"Can you go to a beach at home during the summer?" he asked.

"Sure," said I.

"Skip the Riviera," he counseled. "You're not rich enough to stay at the top places, and at the second-rate ones you'll just meet English people on limited budgets. Why not spend a week traveling to Portugal by train, with stopovers in France? It will cost you less [always an important factor to the French], and you'll see more."

Pierre planned the whole trip for me, taught me that *consigne* means a baggage checkroom, and supplied me with a few introductions en route. I left Paris at eight in the morning, lunched in Lyons, and spent the night in Avignon. From there, I went off to Nîmes, Carcassonne, and Biarritz and picked up the train to Portugal at Hendaye. On the train, I met a Lisbon newspaper publisher and his wife, who insisted I be their guest in Lisbon. It was one of my cheapest and most satisfactory trips.

10. *Be Practical.* Classification of places according to the age of the traveler is controversial. A sixty-year-old sport may have a wonderful time in Lisbon, while a twenty-year-old sex symbol may fizzle at St-Tropez. But, for what it's worth, I'd like to offer a list of where to go at what ages:

FOR WOMEN OF ALL AGES: Paris (the perfect city for everyone), London (like wine, it improves with age), Athens, Vienna, Moscow (you can always make friends standing in line at Intourist), Tokyo, Berlin, and Munich.

FOR OVER SIXTY's, I recommend three weeks at the health baths of Wiesbaden or Baden-Baden. It's nip and tuck whether or not you'll make many friends, but you'll feel clean when you leave.

GOOD FOR OVER FORTY's: Jerusalem, Cairo, Johannesburg. Ischia, companion island to Capri in the Bay of Naples, is recommended to addicts of mud baths. Other good bets for the middle brackets are Corfu (the Greek isle beloved of Ulysses and Kaiser Wilhelm II), Majorca (crowded with retired Indian Army British colonels), and Monte Carlo (where the gaming tables offer opportunities, but most gamblers have café society wives).

THE THIRTY-TO-FORTY BRACKET will find good pickings at Deauville in August and Biarritz in September.

UNDER THIRTY'S can find fun and frolic at Málaga, Spain; St-Tropez, France; and Capri, Italy.

VERY DIFFICULT FOR WOMEN OF ANY AGE WITHOUT INTRO-DUCTIONS: Lima, Buenos Aires, Quito, Istanbul (drop quietly in the Bosporus if you are alone here), Lisbon (a small, closed city where wives stay at home and men prowl by night; better stay at nearby Estoril, where you can win at the casino if nowhere else), and Madrid (hard going without an escort; people don't dine until 10 P.M., and you'll have plenty of time on your hands).

SHOULD YOU USE A TRAVEL AGENT?

Choosing a travel agent is like picking a doctor. You want one who is warm and knowledgeable and who understands you. While any travel agent can arrange for visas and health certificates, baggage insurance, steamship tickets, and sight-seeing, he can't always know what will be a rewarding trip for the woman alone.

How do you find the paragon to help you plan a perfect trip? In much the same way you locate the perfect dress. You inspect, reject, then select. Visit several agents. Sound them out to find whether they are "your kind of person." You wouldn't keep going to a doctor who sets your teeth on edge with his attitude toward life. The same holds with travel agents.

Remember, too, the travel agent has his own insecurities. Since he doesn't know you, he may be afraid to suggest the spot that may be perfect for you.

On one occasion, a woman travel-bureau head sent me to an expensive, fashionable hotel in Antigua instead of to the little offbeat one I had heard about. I took one horrified look at the formal layout and the potbellied men with cigars and promptly switched hotels. When I got home, furious over the loss of my deposit, I rushed to the agent's office.

"Why did you send me to that gilded mausoleum, when all the interesting people go to the other hotel?" I complained.

"I was afraid," she answered truthfully. "I had just met you, and the second one is faded, shabby, and full of characters. I thought if you didn't like it, you might come home and tell everyone I had sent you to a dirty place."

Travel agents also try to force their "little-work" ideas upon you—tried-and-true standbys that make up the stock tour. Don't buy unless you like the merchandise.

In a large city, you have a choice of travel agents and are free to shop around until you find the one you want. In smaller towns, it may be more difficult, but always pick an agent with affiliations abroad; that is where you really may need help.

If you do not track down an agent who is truly a kindred soul, handle your own arrangements. The kindred-soul travel agents, the ones who really understand women, are typified by Walter Plaut, a former president of the American Society of Travel Agents and a New Yorker.

Mr. Plaut genuinely wants his clients to have a good time. "They think I pry, because I ask so many questions," he confesses. "When people come into my office, I give them a quiz. 'What profession? What hobbies? Did you ever work?' I ask them if they would like introductions. If so, I send them to art dealers, curators, bird watchers—even members of Planned Parenthood."

Mr. Plaut goes far beyond the call of duty. He once had two clients, a businessman and a spinster schoolteacher, sailing on the same boat. He introduced them, and six months later they were married. He also has produced several other matches through his annual New Year's Eve party. But—"I'm still single," he admits. "After all, a bachelor can always tell better what's good for a woman."

CHAPTER 5

The Organization Woman

"You could do some work for the office on your trip."

The suggestion came from my boss, the same public servant who had launched me as a world traveler, as we discussed my next European expedition over nut-topped sundaes at Schrafft's.

"Work?" I exclaimed. "This is vacation. I want to have fun."

Jim looked at me with the air of a senior Senator talking to a fledgling Congressman. "This will be much different from writing copy all day. I'll give you eight days of assignments in the four cities you'll be visiting anyway. You can meet the information officers, find out what we are doing wrong from this end, and write me a report on how we can improve our servicing of propaganda material. You'll receive $15 a day for expenses for the eight days you work."

I hesitated. "I'm not sure it's worth it."

He showed he was of the stuff bosses are made of. "It's a good deal. Take it or leave it."

I took it. In Paris, the information officer briefed me on copy needs for two hours and then escorted me to an Embassy cocktail party, where I acquired dinner dates for the next three nights. In Lisbon, the cultural attaché fed me Portuguese cod for lunch, apologized for not being able to entertain me in the evening, and to make up for this lack, provided me with a car and chauffeur for the next two days. In Tangier, the press attaché's Moroccan secretary helped me exchange my American dollars at top black-market rates, divulged the name of her dressmaker, treated me to green mint tea at a dark Arab café, and introduced me to a real live count, complete with monocle, moustache, and honest Hungarian accent.

By the time I arrived in Madrid, I was enjoying my work mission, with all its corollary benefits. Once my interview with the information section chief ended, I asked, "Could I possibly see a fashion show at Rodríguez?"

"No trouble at all," responded Mr. Jones and immediately made an appointment.

When I arrived, I found only one other person in the audience, a world-famous, 250-pound novelist who peoples her books with romantic characters with such names as Paul D'Arcy D'Artagnan and Solange D'Epry. It was a sad showing: I had no cash, she had no figure; and the chief *vendeuse* nearly collapsed on a pile of velvet when Miss Size 50 remarked, "I'll buy that little gray silk with the low V neck and the black lace with the hip flounce. My dressmaker in Philadelphia can copy them in my size. Of course, I'll have her take off the flounce and fill in the neck with tulle."

When I arrived home, heavier from the free meals and richer from all my freeloading, I handed a carefully typed report to my boss. He shoved it into a desk drawer.

"Aren't you going to read it?" I asked.

"One day," he said. "But I really wanted you to learn that sometimes you can have a better time traveling by doing a little work."

How right he was. In the years since, I have danced the samba with a Chilean newspaperman in Rio, nearly been arrested for talking too freely with local teen-agers in East Berlin, and ladled out hot coffee at an Austrian border point to refugees fleeing a Hungarian revolution—all because a boss was nice enough to show me that travel abroad can be much more interesting if you transport a little of your own workaday world to the workaday world overseas.

Work has proved my passport to people. Others may find their link through clubs, personal connections, hobbies, official greeting programs of foreign governments, or an interest in international folk music. The important thing is to mobilize your forces before you leave the U.S.A.

If you are a veteran traveler, you may skip the rest of this chapter. The next few pages are not for the sophisticate who is greeted by name at the desks of all the great hotels of the world, who has crossed the Atlantic and the Pacific, the Andes and the Alps a dozen times, and who travels with a letter of credit rather than letters of introduction.

This chapter is for the woman traveling alone who wants to know how to meet people—and how to talk to people—because travel not only is broadening but is much more fun if you can enjoy the company of others and know how to make them enjoy yours.

Any woman, regardless of age, appearance, occupation, or economic status, can meet people abroad if she embarks on an intensive homework program before she leaves her own front door. The way she studies can mean the difference between an A for accomplishment and an F for fiasco.

A MORE KNOWING "YOU"

Enlist the help of your local librarian, acquire a stack of books, and study. That way you'll know some of the offbeat things to do as well as the fact that you want to see the Taj Mahal or the Mannekin Pis. Far more important, the very fact that you have taken the time and trouble to learn something about their nation will make its good impression on the people of the country. Do not limit yourself to travel books. Read history, documentaries, even fiction. Bastille Day will come much more alive for you if you have reread Dickens' *A Tale of Two Cities* and "listened" again to Madame Defarge clicking those knitting needles in what is now the Place de la Concorde.

I stayed at the antique Hotel Beaujolais in Paris just because it was part of the Palais Royal, where Richelieu died, where Louis XIV lived as a child, and where Colette wrote novels about Chéri and lived with her cat collection. And each day, I would spy on Maurice Goudeket, Colette's husband, who, in my eyes, had done the unspeakable by remarrying. In Leningrad, fresh from my research, I asked to see the palace where Count Yussupov had lived and where he and his cohorts had gathered to murder Rasputin. My guide promptly obliged —with a look of astonishment that an American knew who Yussupov was—and informed me that the Count was still alive, lived in Paris, and came home almost every year to visit his former mansion, now a workers' club.

You must also know something about your own country. Many foreigners have the idea that the United States is composed of chewing-gum and comic-book addicts and mass-produced goods, that everyone has a new car every year, cocktails before dinner each night, and owns fifty mechanical gadgets. They know little about our laws on child labor, our five-day workweek, and our national preoccupation with public health and hygiene—and sometimes they don't care. One day my guide, at my request, took me to a small beach near Moscow. She went off to swim and left me supine on the ground. Suddenly I became aware of a face bending over me.

"Are you an American?" asked a young man, obviously a member of the *stilyagi*, the Russian beatnik set.

"Yes, I am," I replied.

"How much money do you earn a week?" was his next question.

I pretended I didn't understand. Unabashed, he went on, "How does your electoral college work?" . . . "What is the principle of American trade unions?" . . . "What percentage of boys and girls go on to college?" To my chagrin, I couldn't answer one query, and he was not interested in the data I offered about abstract art, Broadway plays, or specialized college courses.

So be prepared to answer questions about American politics, civil rights, and the price of a cotton dress.

THE STRATEGIC "YOU"

After you have accomplished your reading and research, you are ready to attack the all-important problem of developing friends abroad. If some kindly soul offers, "I've got four wonderful friends in Paris. I'll write them today and tell them to expect your call," your life is coming up roses. Otherwise you must employ all the energy, contacts, and tricks at your command to secure names and letters of introduction abroad. For there is no doubt about it, get them you must if you are to do more than take bus tours in a large foreign capital.

Organize your own "meet-the-people" program. Give it the same amount of study that you would if you were taking College Boards and needed to win a scholarship. You can still go to college without the scholarship, but the struggle to make ends meet will be difficult. The same applies to the woman traveling alone; she can go abroad without connections, but the going will be hard.

At this point, you despair, "I don't have a single connection." Of course you do. Everyone does if she looks into the past, utilizes the present, and plans for the future. You might try some of these stratagems:

1. *Talk About Your Trip.* Mention it in the office, at club meetings, cocktail parties, to friends, on dates. Don't overlook your sorority sister in Peoria, your neighbor down the street, your relatives whom you haven't seen in years, and even the

corner grocer. You never know who will say, "Oh, you're going
to Portugal. Why don't you look up Antonio Calvara?"

Keep talking and you'll find that even people you don't
know can be of service. Recently a friend of mine was detailing to a companion in the apartment-house elevator her approaching trip to the Orient. The next Saturday morning, her
doorbell rang, and Mrs. Evans from 6C said, "May I come in?
I couldn't help hearing you in the elevator. My daughter-in-
law's brother is with the State Department in Tokyo, and he's
a bachelor. I wonder if you'd like to look him up." My friend
did. Not only was he good for a tour of night spots on the
Ginza, but he sent her on to friends in Hong Kong.

2. *Call Friends of Friends for Advice.* This can be productive, but never ask them directly for names to look up, even
if this is what you have in mind. Instead, say, "I'm bound for
Bangkok, and I know you know the city well. Could I possibly come over to see you and get some pointers?" Flattery
may get you names and addresses.

3. *Check Your Alumnae Listings.* These provide names of
fellow graduates who now make their homes abroad. Nancy
Smith, who was such a scatterbrain at State University, may
be married to the press attaché in Athens and may now be an
authority on everything from the Acropolis to icons.

4. *Act Boldly.* One friend of mine was bound for India. She
noticed a picture in an American newspaper of a young
American rabbi who headed a Bombay temple. Intrigued by
the idea of an American and his wife ministering to a con-
gregation of Indian Jews, she wrote a letter to the publication.
The editor forwarded her missive to the rabbi, who sent an
immediate response. They corresponded. By the time Lucille
arrived in Bombay, they were old friends. She had even
brought a present for the baby.

Therefore, don't hesitate to write to the English newspaperman whose articles you have noticed in the *Manchester
Guardian*, the Hawaiian sportscaster whom you've heard on

shortwave, the Japanese designer whose technique you've admired at the local museum. I had always been an admirer of the late Truman Bailey, the silver craftsman who lived in Peru. Before going to Lima, I wrote to him. In Lima, he gave me pisco sours and *anticuchos* and an hour of his time.

5. *Consult Your Airline.* For the woman tourist, the airline that transports her abroad can turn out to be a good friend. Many of the international carriers offer services that go far beyond those covered by the sale of a ticket. Air France arranges invitations for first-class passengers to view the couturier collections. Women flying to Europe via SAS can obtain information on travel wardrobes from Sally Ann Simpson, a pseudonym used by the women's representative in the Scandinavian airline's American sales offices.

In my opinion, the best of the international carriers' free guidance programs is that offered by Pan American Airways. Its New Horizons Club for lady travelers costs just $3 for a lifetime membership, for which you receive a copy of the *New Horizons World Guide,* a beach bag, and periodic booklets and bulletins about travel news and services, and it is open to women living anywhere in the world. Upon arrival in a foreign city, a member who visits the Pan Am ticket office will receive a "Welcome Envelope" containing maps and tour guides to the city, lists of local stores that give discounts or gifts to members, and a list of restaurants that welcome women without escorts.

The club features a Traveling Companion Referral Service, which introduces, via mail, members who have similar travel plans and who seek company. You might write to Miss Mary Connolly, at Pan American Airways, Pan Am Building, New York, New York, 10017, and say: "Dear Miss Connolly: Do you know anyone going to Europe in October?" Miss Connolly may write back: "Here is a list of members. For your information, Doris Jones of New Rochelle is going at the same time and will be in many of the cities you list on your itinerary." Another New Horizons Club program provides members with the names of others in foreign countries with whom they can correspond—and meet when they travel abroad.

6. *Use Your Clubs.* Organize a "meet-the-local-people" plan through the organizations in your life—whether professional, cultural, or just plain goodwill. Many American clubs have sister groups across the seas. Investigate every club of which you are a member to see just what international facilities might be available to you. If your group doesn't offer anything, be forehanded and join one that does. Some of the various leading organizations that have active international programs are: International Federation of Business and Professional Women, General Federation of Women's Clubs, American Association for the United Nations, Young Women's Christian Association, National Council of Jewish Women, United Church Women, International Soroptimists, Federation of University Women, International Alliance of Women, Associated Countrywomen of the World.

The best way to utilize your club membership for contacts abroad is to write a letter to the national president, detailing the length of your stay abroad, arrival dates, languages spoken, personal background, and purpose of trip. Accompany your letter with a note from your local club president telling how much work you have done for the organization. If the national president feels that you merit attention, you'll get it. Another device is to write directly to the president of the woman's club abroad and ask whether it would be convenient for you to meet club members.

From Mrs. Douglas Johnston, chairman of the Council of International Clubs Division of the General Federation of Women's Clubs, comes this succinct advice: "If it's convenient, national headquarters and local chapters overseas will cooperate. But don't expect free meals. Don't expect red-carpet treatment. Surprise the foreign members by making a gesture of hospitality—*you* invite *them* to tea! Remember that in all probability they will ask you to speak. Be briefed on your club; they'll want to hear what the mother organization is like. The more off the beaten track you go, the more of a welcome you'll receive."

Namesake Towns Association is a special group that runs programs between cities in the United States and their counterparts abroad. Three hundred American towns are members. For instance, Middlesex, New Jersey, is paired with Middlesex, England; Toledo, Ohio, with Toledo, Spain; New York City with Tokyo; and Rockingham, South Carolina, with Rockingham, Australia. If your city is a member, you may write to Mrs. Barbara Spencer, Namesake Towns Association, 45 East Sixty-fifth Street, New York, New York, 10017, and explain, "I'm Janet Jones, and I live in (such and such a city). I am visiting _____ and would like to go to (namesake city) and spend two days there. I am interested in gardening and old churches and will arrive on November 20 at 10:30 A.M. by Pan Am." Mrs. Spencer will write to the city official and make all sorts of arrangements. If you are interested in this kind of person-to-person program and your hometown is not a member of this club, write to Mrs. Spencer anyway. Your civic interest may be enough so that she will want to do something for you —and perhaps you can do something for her by bringing your own city into the association.

7. *Utilize the Free Services of the Foreign Government Tourist Offices in the United States.* Almost all tourist offices can provide prospective visitors with a list of organizations and groups willing and eager to arrange meetings between individual Americans and local people or to arrange for visits to industrial plants, schools, craft workrooms, hospitals, courtrooms, hobby clubs, farms, professional groups, distilleries, or whatever interests you. Several national tourist offices have organized programs such as "Meet the Danes," "Get in Touch with the Dutch," "Find the Finns," "Meet the Irish," "Know the Norwegians," "Sweden at Home," and "Meet the Israelis."

These programs have fringe benefits. My friends the Berkes met a charming couple in Copenhagen through "Meet the Danes." The next year, when I descended on Copenhagen, the Berkes introduced me to the couple. "What would you like to see in Copenhagen?" the Sorensons asked politely.

I had been briefed by Scandinavian experts. "The night spots where the sailors go," I said.

The dignified Sorensons looked surprised for a moment and then smiled. "Good," they chorused. "We have never been there. You are giving us a chance to know our own city." It made me resolve to climb the Statue of Liberty the minute I got home.

8. *Never Refuse a Letter of Introduction.* Welcome it, no matter how slight the connection between you and the writer, even if you have five other letters to people in the same city and expect to be there only two days. You may be surprised at the hospitality shown you by the distant cousin once removed of a distant friend.

There is a definite technique in presenting letters of introduction. It is one thing to be given a name, to call up and say, "This is Mary Jones," and be greeted with a curt, "Who?" If you are preceded by a letter, detailing all your endearing and enduring charms, you will receive a warm welcome instead of, "Didn't quite get the name."

Ask your friends to write their friends and let them know the exact day of your arrival. You might also write a note yourself to the effect that "Anita Berke has told me so much about you, and I look forward to meeting you. My hotel will be the Grand, and I'll be checking in at five o'clock in the afternoon." If you are fortunate enough to be given the name of an eligible bachelor, be doubly sure to write him ahead of time. He's as apt to be pursued by local girls as by visiting ladies. Furthermore, write your note on your best letter paper. He might as well be impressed. After all, that "might-as-well-marry-a-rich-girl-as-a-poor-one" theory originated overseas.

Delivery of a letter of introduction can have surprising twists. My friend Marcelle suggested that I get in touch with her best friend in Paris, a Mme. Suzanne Martin. She gave me a little note that read, "This will introduce Jean Baer, one of my good friends."

Suzanne had no telephone, so the minute I checked into the French hotel, I sent a *pneumatique* (a letter which, for a little extra postage, travels by pneumatic tube and arrives anywhere in Paris within two hours) that said in my schoolgirl French: *"Je suis un ami* [sic] *de Marcelle Henry et j'espère de vous voir pendant ma visite à Paris."* I signed the letter, *"Sincèrement, Jean Baer,"* but forgot to enclose my letter of introduction.

Shortly afterward, I found a letter in my box. Mme. Martin would come to my hotel at five o'clock with her husband. When I went down to meet them, she and her husband gave me a startled look and exclaimed in unison, *"Une petite demoiselle!"* Because my first name is masculine in French and I had unwittingly failed to add a final "e" to *un* and *ami,* this bourgeois housewife had thought me to be a wolf in American clothing and had brought M. Martin with her for protection.

YOU—ON THE JOB

All play and no work can sometimes make for a relaxing, educational, but dull trip. For the working woman traveling alone, it is much better to combine pleasure with a little foreign business—and businessmen.

You may not have such a worldly-wise boss as I did. You may think your nonglamour-type work permits no opportunity for on-the-job action in a foreign country. You are wrong. You can put your job to work no matter what kind of work you do. Some effective techniques:

❡ Convince the company that giving you a free trip abroad will be to its benefit. A friend, designer for a pattern company, now takes a three-week trip on firm time and money every summer because she convinced the president that the ideas she gets for new-style dresses help him make a profit.

❡ If your company has a foreign branch, try to work in the office there for a week. You'll benefit by simultaneously being kept on salary and meeting the same kind of people you work with at home—and like—abroad.

❡ Check your personnel office to discover whether there is a foreign representative for your company abroad. Secure a letter of introduction, and make sure to meet him or her. The meeting may result only in a discussion of business problems, but it should be good for an invitation to dinner and a personal tour of the city.

❡ Meet your counterpart. If you are a teacher, you can always write the foreign school of your choice and ask to meet the English teacher. A nurse can write to a hospital or medical school and say, "I'd like to meet your chief nurse." Whatever you do, someone overseas does it, too.

❡ Volunteer to perform an office chore overseas on your own time. Getting ready for my third trip abroad, I felt that I was the experienced traveler. In fact, I felt more sophisticated in every life area. My father had remarried; instead of running a suburban household, I had my own apartment, one that had once belonged to nineteenth-century show girl Lillian Russell, at Thirtieth Street and Fifth Avenue in New York. From an underpaid government worker, I had moved to the post of publicity director for a major women's magazine. To celebrate my new status, I decided that on this trip I would go only to Paris and would live as if I were rich for three weeks. I would buy my fall clothes, breakfast on *croissants* and *café au lait*, drench myself in French bath oil and perfume, and, in general, live a sybaritic existence for twenty-one days. Because I would have free time in Paris, when the possibility of a joint promotion with a French magazine arose, I volunteered to talk with the editor in Paris.

This time my lady-editor boss was the one who hesitated. "I don't like to interfere with your vacation."

"It's perfectly all right," I assured her. By now I knew what unexpected delights could result from foreign work assignments.

In Paris, the French lady editor invited me to lunch. Expecting a chic, elegant, high-fashion type, I was quite surprised when she appeared wearing a little blue skirt, a white cotton shirt, and a rather shabby wool cardigan. Knowing how reluctant the French are to entertain strangers in their homes, I was even more amazed when, over the fruit compote in a bistro off the Champs-Elysées, she asked, "Will you come to a party at our home tomorrow night?"

"Why, that would be very nice," I said, imagining the pleasant family dinner I would have with the lady editor, her husband, three teen-age sons, and a few French friends.

"Don't dress," she cautioned. "It will be simple."

The next evening I carefully donned a no-sleeved basic-black wool with a cardigan jacket. If by any chance she had invited a partner for me, I would remove the jacket. I hailed a cab, and my first surprise came when we turned off Avenue Foch, the Gold Coast of Paris, onto a quiet side street where you literally couldn't see the houses for the trees.

When we finally found the discreetly hidden number, I left the cab, pressed the bell, and waited for what seemed like an interminable time until a tiny, birdlike woman with two front teeth missing appeared from a modest five-room house. "Your name," she asked.

I told her.

"Ah, yes, Mme. Janine expects you."

When I started to enter a French version of ancient Main Street middle-class housing, the concierge shook her head. "Oh, no, mademoiselle, that way." She pointed toward a broad path leading to a tall eighteenth-century mansion that might have been the home of Madame de Pompadour. I began to have slight "what-am-I-doing-here?" feelings and doubts about that little dinner *en famille*. At the door a butler waited. He said something, but by then I was so rattled I couldn't understand a single word. Eventually, by pantomime, I realized that he wanted to get his clutches on my three-year-old black silk coat. He held it rather gingerly, and I had the feeling that he was used to better material.

Up the parquet stairs, carpeted in a red plush fabric, we walked together almost as if we were going up the aisle to the strains of the *Lohengrin* wedding march. "Mlle. Jean Baer," he announced, just as if I were a member of royalty, and I walked slowly into a room filled with gentlemen with that look of inherited money, ladies dressed divinely—but simply—by Dior, and such decorative accessories as ancestral portraits, draperies in $50-a-yard gold damask, and a solid gold piano. My first reaction was sheer instinct. I removed the gold bow (synthetic) from the shoulder of my dress; every other woman's jewelry looked real.

The people couldn't have been nicer. The lady editor's husband drew me out about life in New York, and as we talked I dimly remembered seeing his surname on a street, a square, and a building in the heart of Paris.

"Are you really traveling all alone?" asked a white-haired dowager; her tone evinced envy, not disapproval.

"Do girls in the United States really go out with men who just call up and say, 'I'm a friend of a friend?'" queried one sophisticated male, whose piercing look promised things to come if I'd allow him.

By the time we went in to dinner, I felt considerably more secure. "I didn't quite catch your name," said I in halting French to the blond, moustached gentleman on my left. "Rothschild," said he in perfect English.

That unnerved me so that for the first time in years, I

watched my hostess to see what fork she used. By the time we had drunk fifty-year-old brandy and entered the two-hundred-year-old ballroom (the first I had ever seen in a private house), I had recovered my aplomb. After all, it is nice to be among the rich—even if only for a night. And there is a certain Cinderella cachet in being the only poor girl in the room.

¶ Create your own work assignments that will pay off in contacts abroad, attention at home after the trip. You might write a three-part series for a local newspaper on "The Women of Rome" or "The Cuisine of Portugal." Almost any hometown paper will accept an article from a native daughter if it is free. A tape recorder is sometimes worth its weight. You can record the singing in a Greek tavern or the blues in a Paris nightclub. You are bound to meet people this way, and when you get home, the program director of the local radio station might well be interested in using the tapes and interviewing you. Before you leave home, you can make arrangements to address the local women's club or church sisterhood on "Continental Women and How They Live" or to show the pictures you take abroad at a series of club meetings.

¶ Get in touch with the department of the foreign government in the United States that will be most interested in you. Foreign-government tourist offices, most of which are based in New York City, are always interested in cooperating with newspaperwomen, radio commentators, television producers, photographers, and lecturers. The cultural attaché in Washington, D.C., handles teachers, professors, artists, sculptors, musicians, and actors. The commercial attaché will be glad to be of service to buyers, top secretaries, advertising executives, and any other type of businesswoman. The consulate aids mayoresses and mayors' wives, heads of the health services, and people engaged in any form of municipal service.

A few letters allow you to see things that the average person does not and have the fun of meeting people who earn their living just the way you do. But under no circumstances

bother the press attaché in Washington; his job is to handle
real political and economic problems. Do line up all appointments ahead of time from the U.S.A.; just calling up upon
arrival will get you about as far as the secretary, and she probably doesn't understand a word of English. And keep in mind
that certain occupations have much more status abroad than
here. My guide in Tbilisi, Georgia, informed me coolly, "We
see far too many journalists. We prefer teachers."

MEETING PEOPLE ON THE SPOT

If all your advance work has produced nothing but aggra-
vation and you have not made a single social or professional
connection when you depart from the U.S.A., you still have
the very best asset of all—yourself.

But only on one condition—that the "you" you take abroad
is a receptive, outgoing, approachable one; for that "give-
nothing, take-all" variety that announces, "I'm here—what are
you going to do about me?" is doomed to large doses of her
own company.

Before you leave, you must realize that everything you do—
whether you buy cheese in Holland, stroll through the Roman
catacombs, or just sit still on a park bench in Paris—can lead
to *people*. Whether the people you meet turn into companions
or remain just faces in a foreign crowd is up to you. Here are
some "woo-and-win" techniques that you should be prepared
to try:

❨ Do take attention-getting props. Tote a camera, and even if
you don't scare up kindred souls, you'll still have something
to show for it when you get home. As an icebreaker, the
sketchbook is superior to a poodle—but, remember, there are
two places where a sketchbook traveler is not welcome: one
is a military installation; the other, a Paris fashion house. A

movie camera, a colorful walking stick, or a Quechuan dictionary might also prove useful.

❡ Do be informative. A little black book full of names of people, places, things can prove an excellent person-to-person device. Rattle off a unique fact or two about the little antique shop in Bruges or the best place to get a dress made in Hong Kong and you will certainly impress your fellow tourists.

❡ Do take gifts—nothing elaborate or expensive, but practical and representative of America. Personally, I travel with a batch of stockings, size 9½ (this size not only fits most women but also fits me, in case there are leftovers), inexpensive costume earrings, paperback books, dime-store toys, and kitchen gadgets. These make a very good entry fee, and I don't have to feel like the woman who has come to dinner empty-handed.

Sometimes bearing gifts to others can lead to a new experience. Mr. Karinska, a family friend, asked me to deliver a watch to his niece in Leningrad. "I have not seen my sister in thirty years," he said. "This is a high-school graduation gift for her daughter. I think you will enjoy meeting the family. My brother-in-law is a successful doctor, and they live in a lovely flat on the Nevsky Prospect."

In Leningrad, I walked down the famous avenue, where characters strolled in all of Tolstoi's books, until I came to the home of the Volkonsky family. It was a large apartment house, and as I entered I saw that the complex extended in back for a full block and that the rear buildings were decayed and shabby. The front was for show.

Mr. Karinska had written the apartment number in Cyrillic script for me, and I, not knowing which of the maze of buildings to enter, kept showing the slip of paper to passersby. No one would listen to me. I kept trying to explain, but no one even tried to understand.

"*Amerikanski?*" asked one woman.

I nodded hopefully.

She shrugged and walked away.

In the center of the complex was a grassy park where a group of wrinkled, white-haired old ladies sat gossiping. Obviously I was the target of their remarks, for they kept casting glances in my direction to check on my progress. I didn't know what to do and began to think that that watch was going to go straight back to the United States. Suddenly, one old lady started screaming at the others, and it didn't take a knowledge of Russian to understand that she was berating them for their rudeness.

On squat legs, with firm steps, she walked up to me, looked at the paper, and led me to a dilapidated ocher-colored building on the rear right. Inside, hand in hand, we walked up four flights of stairs to an apartment door on which ten different names were lettered next to ten different bells. She pressed the one marked "Volkonsky" and fled.

Mrs. Volkonsky expected me. "Miss Baer?" she asked, taking one look at my American attire and indicating by pantomime that her brother had written and told her all about the watch. She showed me down a long, narrow hall, from which doors led off to apartments, into her family's quarters. It turned out to be one room, shared by Mama, Papa, soon-to-be girl graduate, and ten-year-old son. The room, about the size of a master bedroom in a housing project, was decorated with one samovar, a torn Bokhara rug, family photographs, inexpensive studio couches, and partitioned by clotheslines hung with blankets. At a table, obviously the same one used for meals, was daughter Anna doing her mathematics assignment. I delivered the watch; Mrs. Volkonsky served cake and tea in a glass. We communicated by sign language. But by delivering the present, I had experienced something rare for an American. I had been inside a real Russian home.

When I returned to America, Mr. Karinska called up to thank me. "My family telephoned all the way from Russia to say you had brought the watch. Tell me, is their apartment on the Nevsky Prospect as beautiful as I imagine?"

I didn't have the heart to tell the truth. "Lovely," said I.

⟨ Don't tie up with two couples or more or you'll feel like the outsider looking in. You can be a third wheel at times—but never a fifth or seventh.

⟨ Do put yourself out to be friendly. Europeans, South Americans, Arabs, and Asians are not lying in wait to rape you, steal your luggage, convert you to Buddhism, or force you into a harem. Leave your suspicions at home.

⟨ Do things. Staying in your hotel room and feeling sorry for yourself will result only in "having-wonderful-time-*but*" postcards home. Read the English-language newspapers for news of local events. Drop in at the university and see what is doing in the way of lectures. Go to local concerts. Talk to your neighbors. Shop. Take a nightclub tour; this is one way to see night spots without having to worry about an escort and to meet other souls in search of diversion—but don't expect men. Contact the local American Club (they exist from Santiago to Singapore) and take advantage of what is doing. Sight-seeing provides all sorts of social possibilities; even if you don't meet anyone at a palace or a waxworks, you can establish a tête-à-tête at the co-ed entrances to the johns.

⟨ Do attract attention to yourself in the nicest way possible. On a sight-seeing bus, offer candy to your fellow passengers. Be the one who organizes a special expedition for fellow hotel guests. Invite people you've met and liked for cocktails.

⟨ Don't get stuck with bores. If you don't like to be alone, there is always the danger that you will overlook shortcomings of strangers in order to keep company with someone—and this company may be much worse than your own.

⟨ Do look up every name you have acquired—no matter how much your feet hurt or how afraid you are of a rebuff.

⟨ Don't do anything you can get a man to do for you. One of the best things about foreign travel is that you never know whom you will meet. Home contacts can work unexpectedly in your behalf.

On one occasion, I was sitting over my *citron pressé* at the Café de la Paix when an attractive man, whose dark-brown hair, navy-blue suit, and white button-down shirt gave him (except for a marked French accent) the general air of a Madison Avenue executive, greeted me with, "Hello, Miss Baer."

He certainly looked familiar, seemed to know me well, but no matter how I tried, I couldn't place him. "Sit down," I suggested, staring into his eyes so that he wouldn't realize I didn't know him from Adam, Alan, or Alfred. It was to no avail; the face was familiar but not the origin. After we had exchanged mutual impressions of Paris and he had paid for my drink, he departed for the Opéra.

Two weeks later I arrived home. At lunchtime the next day, my first place of call was the hairdressing salon of a Fifth Avenue beauty shop. It certainly felt good to wash the grime out of my dark brown locks, and I sat, clean and relaxed, waiting for the hairdresser to start snipping.

"Did you enjoy the rest of your trip, Miss Baer?" asked a familiar accented voice.

I looked up. There was the Madison Avenue executive from the Café de la Paix—who was really the French hairdresser who had done my hair for the last four months.

CHAPTER 6

Men

MEN

How to Think About Them

If you are the typical female traveler, you long to tour Rome after dark, marvel at the Taj Mahal by moonlight, and sip champagne on Montmartre in the small hours of a Paris dawn. Naturally you yearn to do these things with a man.

Naturally. There is nothing unnatural about the wish, but wishing won't make it come true. Escorts abroad don't materialize just by rubbing Aladdin's lamp any more than they do at home. Finding them requires a combination of psychological attitude and practical attack.

Ask yourself these questions:

❮ Are you making the trip to find a husband?

❮ Is meeting men on the trip as important to you as sightseeing?

❮ Do you want to meet foreign men, or do you prefer Americans whom you may have a chance of seeing again in the U.S.A.?

Answer these queries honestly before you consider venturing forth into the international free-for-all.

First of all, if you think that hunting a husband abroad is

75

like shooting sitting ducks, forget it. You have a much better chance with the man next door. And you know how much chance you have with him.

Every woman on a trip dreams of meeting Prince Charming. Grace Kelly met and married a real prince, but she had advantages that you probably don't have. For the average woman, acquiring that gold ring for the third finger of the left hand takes concentration and time. And the here-today-gone-tomorrow schedule of a month's vacation militates against a permanent relationship. There isn't much point in meeting a divine man in the morning if you are taking the express for Florence in the late afternoon.

The emphasis on husband-hunting can color your whole vacation dark blue. Of course try to trap the male animal on foreign soil, but don't let failure ruin the rest of your trip. Simply aim for a Mr. Evening Date and not Mr. Right.

If your major objective is meeting men, pay no attention to those know-nothing travelers who advise, "If it's going to happen, it's going to happen. Don't try to meet a man while traveling, and then you will." You can push your luck too far.

If you want dates and diversions as well as excursions through museums, waxworks, and catacombs, keep your aim in mind when planning the trip. When a motherly soul offers, "I know a nice lawyer in Paris," and you've been mentally tossing a coin between Paris and Rome, deliberate no more. Head for Paris.

If another friend claims, "There's a perfectly charming off-beat island near Naples which no one knows about. I met a terrific guy there," stay away. He was probably the only eligible who ever hit that particular beach.

Before you even pick your destination, you might remember these salient points:

⟨[Transatlantic ships are full of happily married men, married men traveling alone on an expense account, and under-twenty's from Yale. *Caveat venatrix!*

❬ With a letter of introduction in any Latin country, you can have the keys to the city. Without one, as far as meeting men is concerned, you're reduced to pickups. The *senores* and *senhores* will jump at the chance to get to know you, but you must be prepared to reap the consequences.

❬ Meeting men of the right sort is easiest in England, Denmark, Norway, Sweden, Finland, and Holland because most of them speak English. They have to if they want to leave home.

❬ A guided tour will be full of fellow Americans. Pick the right one and you will probably find not only a few unattached men, but some assorted couples with eligible friends at home.

❬ The farther away you get from the United States, the easier it is to meet men.

Do not daydream your whole trip away. Instead of dreaming about an Adonis who happens to live in your hometown, romancing about romance aboard ship with an eligible widower, creating castles in Spain, *do the things that best reflect your own interests, personality, and ideology.* There are many wonderful people in the world. Best of all, they come in two sexes.

Don't give up the thought of meeting men because you are frankly fifty plus. If you are attractive, you are attractive to many types—the young Oedipus, the widower looking for a woman with money, the man of your same age seeking friendship and a possible love affair, the elderly rake who expects you to rejuvenate him, and just plain Bill Jones who is also traveling alone. One of the few women I know who actually landed a husband as a result of a trip abroad is well over sixty. Alice was crossing the North Sea from England to Hamburg, when her seatmate, a gray-haired, distinguished German who looked as if he might have dueled at Heidelberg, spoke to her. The dialogue went something like this:

HE (eyeing her wedding ring): You must be married.

SHE (faking it): Oh, this is my mother's ring.

HE (probing): Are you alone?

SHE (bluntly): Yes.

HE (frankly): Why are you not married?

SHE (coyly): I never wanted to marry.

HE (seriously): If you were married, what kind of man would you pick?

SHE (artfully): A man like you.

He invited the widow from Chicago to dinner in Hamburg. She went. Two weeks later they were married. And they lived happily ever after, after she took him back to Chicago!

Remember that love may make the world go round, but going around the world doesn't guarantee love. I spent years dreaming about marrying a Frenchman and living in Paris. My friend Marcelle provided the Frenchman. He proposed— both in person and through an official offer from his mother. And I said no.

MEN

Picking Your Destination

Let's get down to specifics. You have given up the idea of finding a husband en route, but you do want a series of pleasant flirtations. Use foresight, not hindsight.

Along with brushing up on your tennis, practicing a few helpful foreign phrases like, "Are all the men of your country so handsome?" and making sure you have a low-necked, close-fitting black dress, remember the following:

Don't flit about too much. Even if you're not taking off for Florence first thing in the morning, perhaps *he* is. So for one man-meeting destination, choose the sort of place where people seem to settle for a while. You don't want anything too far off the beaten path, of course; otherwise he cannot beat a path to your perch at the bar. But there are lots of

places that strike a happy medium between a remote wilder-
ness and the top tourist haunts, where feminine competition
is keen and buses, trains, boats, and planes bring in enemy
reinforcements every minute of the day.

Pick a good place, and stay for at least a week. If you're
young with a good figure, there is nothing like a beach resort
in summer or a ski spot in winter. Meeting people is the
primary aim in these places. You're there to make new friends,
and so is everyone else. If you're not so young but still appreciate male companionship, look for a place with a casino;
gambling affords opportunities for gamboling. Or try a lively
mountain resort or a spa. Many a romance has started over a
bridge table, while taking the waters or comparing the merits
of mud baths.

Go where your type is "in." If your hips are considered too
wide in the United States, they'll be pluperfect in Turkey;
Turks like their women Rubens style. If tweeds suit you,
consider Scotland or Ireland. Blondes go over big in Mexico
and any Latin country; brunettes rate in Scandinavia.

Do be practical. If you are seeking more than a passing
fancy, go where you will meet people from your home area.
For example, Easterners abound in the Caribbean; Westerners
head for the west coast of Mexico and southward into South
America. If you are stalking the Midwestern male and Cleve-
landers are grazing in Capri this year, don't be too bullish to
follow the herd.

Do consider the seasons. In summer, the world is overrun
by women in search of a mate. You'll have much more chance
of attention in winter, when there is less competition from
compatriots.

Do let the Army, Navy, and Marines come to your rescue;
establish your beachhead near a government base. (*Note:*
This works only if you are young.) The strategy may produce
only a shavetail who is already engaged to Mary Jones of Oshkosh or a sergeant whose chief claim to good looks is his

number of stripes, but either should be good for a Martini at six o'clock and a tour of the PX—plus the chance of meeting his friends.

Go where the men are. Males congregate in fishing camps and ski resorts, on golf links and tennis courts. Resort areas near mining and archaeological expeditions are a good bet; after hours, men prefer a live girl to a mummy. A little research beforehand pays off in dates.

Remember that the man who will entertain you is not necessarily the man with money. Often men with the leanest wallets are the most fun.

Don't turn up your nose at fellow Americans. That nice Antonio can be very good company for an evening in Rome, but his home is Rome and yours is New York. Whereas that accountant Bill Jones, whom you met in the hotel gift shop, may not have a charming accent, but he does live two miles across town. Don't give up Antonio. Just make sure that Bill has your telephone number—and that you have his.

MEN

Twenty Surefire Ways to Meet Them Abroad

Back home it is standard procedure for you to chase your quarry until he catches you. It doesn't work this way abroad. Once you manage to meet him, he'll do the pursuing with pleasure. To the foreign man, you are the new girl in town who won't be around long enough to be a threat to his freedom. He feels secure in this knowledge. The American man abroad is easily available; he's lonely and needs you just as much as you need him.

So the basic problem becomes that of the initial encounter. Here are a few methods that may not result in a permanent

twosome but should at least bring about dinner for two in
a local restaurant:

1. *Play Helpless.* The damsel-in-distress strategy works
much better outside the U.S.A. Standard devices: be unable
to understand the currency, cope with change, read the street
signs, get on the right bus, follow directions from the slip of
paper in your hand, or read your map. On ships you can be
confused by a life preserver, on buses by where to get off,
and on planes by how to hook a seat belt. All these dilemmas
make it necessary for you to ask help from a man. When
choosing your prospect, pick one who is not wearing a wedding ring. (Most Europeans do wear wedding rings, often on
the right hand, so in nine cases out of ten you are pretty safe
with the man minus the band; for the tenth case, proceed at
your own risk.) If at first you don't succeed, don't give up.
For example, you buy a large street map, unfold it while
standing at a busy intersection, and look puzzled. If ten
minutes later you're still puzzled, head for another corner
and try again.

Certain props support helplessness. Carry a large piece of
hand luggage when traveling and whatever your looks, age,
or degree of sex appeal, if you suffer visibly enough, some
man will offer to carry it for you. A friend of mine sports a
large hat bag. She reports that not only does a man always
offer to tote the bag, but that she scores dates with one out
of three of the self-appointed porters—in Europe, that is.

The dictionary is the most helpful prop I know—superior
even to an offbeat volume of Trollope, a James Bond thriller,
or the *Guide Michelin.* Possession of a Russian-English dictionary once brought me a dinner date with a Russian movie
star. Yalta-bound for a week's rest on the Black Sea, I was
taking the plane from Moscow to Simferopol, where the Intourist car would meet me. I got on the plane exhausted from
the difficulty of finding the one bound for Simferopol instead
of Sevastopol (the names look remarkably alike in Cyrillic

characters). What's more, I was scared. While the floor of
the plane was carpeted with Oriental rugs, there were no seat
belts. The motor, too, was suffering from nerves, and it sput-
tered alarmingly and asthmatically as we roared upward. The
only non-Russian on the flight, I resigned myself to six hours
of talking to myself, unless the plane disintegrated in mid-air
beforehand.

Several hours later, we zoomed down on a dirt airstrip.
Good, I thought, we've arrived early. Then I noticed that the
airport sign, whatever it proclaimed, did not say Simferopol.
Moreover, no one seemed to be looking for a lonely American.
We had come down somewhere in the middle of the Ukraine!
There was not even a real café at the field—merely a caviar-
and-coffee counter where flies were dancing cheek to cheek.
First I controlled my panic. Then I worriedly approached
various passengers and asked, "What is the matter? . . . Why
is the plane on the ground?"

No one understood me.

I grew desperate. This was a nightmare. Here I was stranded
in the wilds of the Soviet Union, somewhere in the middle
of the Ukraine, unable to make myself understood, cut off
from my own world—probably forever. Regardless of the fact
that I now had an audience, a planeload of passengers who
were watching me as though I were something out of the last
act of a Chekhov play, I burst into tears.

The friendly Russians clucked at me sympathetically but
futilely. They could not crack the language barrier.

Suddenly I remembered the Handy Phrase Book buried
deep beneath the flotsam and jetsam of my purse. I dived in,
came up with the little volume, and quickly turned to the
page that had the Russian translation of that all-important
sentence, "Why has the plane come down?" Immediately a
good-looking Russian, complete with wavy pompadour and
too-tight suit, stepped forward to help. Never again will I
make fun of phrase books with peculiar English sentence

structure. This one, picked up for fifty cents, turned out to be of enormous help.

My rescuer rapidly flipped the pages until he found what he wanted. He pointed to: "There has been a temporary delay."

I flipped pages, too: "Is anything serious the matter?"

A shake of the head. This time the book didn't produce the right word, so he pointed furiously to the internal workings of the Aeroflot plane and then picked out the word "trouble." Even I could guess that that meant engine difficulties.

"How long?" I asked.

"Three," he said by means of his finger; "hours," he noted from the dictionary.

Once we were airborne again, we both were pretty expert at dictionary communication. I learned that he was a Moscow movie star, unmarried, proud possessor of a *dacha* (country home) ten miles from the Kremlin, and that he was now heading for Yalta to take his annual holiday. For his part, he was delighted to know that I was familiar with Deanna Durbin movies (this was the first time in years I had admitted to remembering Deanna, but she certainly was the rage of Russia in 1959), that I liked caviar, and that I could hum the entire *Swan Lake* off-key. Our conversation was like a silent movie, but it was very soothing.

2. *Make Friends with the Hotel Employees.* The minute you arrive at the hotel, *tip the lift boys.* A few dollars' investment may result in much useful information. For instance, an attractive man gets off at the fifth floor with an encouraging smile beamed directly at you. As soon as the door closes, you might say, "That man who smiled at me—I suppose he's married with three children."

The answer may be a promise of things to come: "Oh, no, mademoiselle, he used to be married, but not any more. He's a widower from Milan with a grown son."

Always get acquainted with the concierge or hall porter. He's the best friend you can have. At major hotels in world capitals, he may be too busy to maneuver in your behalf, but at smaller hotels he can serve as an excellent accomplice. Ask him a few questions and explain that you are alone; maybe he'll succumb to your charm and introduce you to fellow guests.

Another important contact is the maître d'hôtel. Once a friend of mine was dining alone at her hotel in Oslo, Norway. She talked a bit with the maître d', asking him several tourist questions. When a stalwart blond Viking came in and sat down alone, the maître d' noticed my friend giving the man the eye. Soon the helpful maître d' reappeared at her table. "Miss, the gentleman at the corner table is a Mr. Olaf Olson," he explained politely. "I can vouch for him. He is from a good family and is a successful businessman. His wife died over a year ago. Mr. Olson has asked that you join him for dinner. Would you? You have my assurance that it is perfectly all right." She had a very pleasant evening. Never underestimate the authority of a headwaiter.

3. *Go Down to Breakfast.* It is a temptation to start the day in the solitary elegance of your room. Don't. Sip a cup of coffee in privacy if you must, and then head for the dining room. Go early. Men don't sleep late; they rarely have a tray in bed; and some of your best possibilities for the evening will be businessmen who have early appointments. As you eat, survey the scene, and smile at anyone who looks promising. At 9:30 A.M., this cannot be construed as an overture, but should you meet the gentleman in the lobby at cocktail time, he might return the smile, along with an invitation. After all, men get lonely, too.

4. *Talk in Hotel Elevators.* The lone man riding with you may have a wife, but you can take a chance in this nice impersonal atmosphere and make small talk. I once ventured, "I hear the *France* is going to leave two days late because of

the strike." The man turned out to be similarly becalmed in Paris. Two hours later we were dining together on the Left Bank.

5. *Sit in the Hotel Lobby.* From this vantage point, you can spy out just what possibilities are available. If you feel awkward, utilize props like the European edition of the *Herald Tribune,* a murder mystery, or the always-useful cup of coffee. Try to plant yourself in a chair with a color becoming to you; sallow-skinned brunettes should avoid hotel green. Don't relax at random; do your lobby sitting when there is something—and someone—to be seen—for instance, when the crowd from an ocean liner checks in, at the cocktail hour, or just after dinner.

6. *Go Places.* Your hotel may be your home away from home, but you didn't go abroad to feel at home. Get out and go places. Take a tour; your seatmate may turn out to be a fascinating man. Sporting events, such as a bullfight or rugby game, can be most productive. You can't be suspected of trying to pick up someone if you just turn to your neighbor and say, "I don't understand what's happening; perhaps you can explain." Don't restrict yourself to left and right maneuvers; there are people in front and back too. Through your hotel, you can gain admission to local sporting clubs abroad; it helps if you can really play tennis; if you can't, play a watching game.

Festivals are excellent for meeting men. Whether it's a music festival in Spoleto, a wine tasting in Burgundy, or the running of the bulls in Pamplona, walk in and you become a part. The same thing holds true for local dances given by societies. You'll find these advertised in the papers. Buy a ticket and go. You'll probably be the belle of the ball and you'll certainly be the only lady tourist to think of it.

Visit art museums. It may be difficult to launch conversations in vast institutions like the Louvre, but in the smaller museums, it is simple to make artistic conversation with the attractive man who is also inspecting ancient or abstract, medieval or modern works at the same gallery.

7. *Change Your Money at American Express, Not at the Hotel.* The walk to the office will benefit your waistline— and besides, you never know who will be in line with you. Don't go directly to the money-changing desk; read your mail until someone interesting appears.

8. *Remember the Way to a Man's Heart May Be Through His Mother.* Or through his father, sister, aunt. Don't feel you're wasting time talking to some grandmotherly soul from the Middle West; she may have an unmarried son.

Recently, a friend of mine toured Russia. In each city she kept running into a well-dressed, vibrant widow of sixty-odd who had returned to her homeland after fifty years in America. Proudly she boasted to Allison, "When I get back to Duluth, I'm going to lecture to all the women's clubs." Despite the difference in ages, they became friends. They shared cars, took tours together, attended the theater.

One night the widow asked Allison, "Do you like doctors?"

"Well, yes, except when I'm sick," responded my friend.

"I mean, do you like to meet doctors?"

"Surely, if they can talk about something besides operations."

"I've got five children," confided Mrs. Jones. "The four oldest are all happily married, but I worry about my baby. He's thirty-five now—and still single."

"Oh, lots of men don't marry until they're forty," sympathized Allison, wishing the statement were true.

Mama warmed to her subject. "With this one, I've had nothing but trouble. First Robert studied to be a doctor, but he wouldn't be an ordinary doctor. Not my boy. He's a psychoanalyst. It's difficult for me to find a girl for him. Oh, he's got plenty of women, but I want him to settle down. What can I do? I'm in Minnesota and he's in New York. That's why

I'm so glad I met you. You're such a nice girl. I'd be so happy if you liked my son."

They exchanged addresses, and Allison forgot all about the incident. A month later, back in her Madison Avenue apartment, the telephone rang. "Good evening," announced a masculine voice, "I'm Bob Jones. I think you met my mother in Leningrad."

9. *Get Friendly with a Married Couple.* This is the four-star way for a single woman to meet an eligible man abroad just as it is at home. Couples are usually delighted by a change of face, and they'll man-hunt for you. But don't sponge. Pay your own way.

10. *Take the Local Trains.* The compartment holds six people in first class, eight in second, and one of them might be a male headed in your direction. Even if he isn't a handsome stranger, he might know one.

Don't limit train exploration to your own compartment. I was going from Venice to Paris via the *Orient Express.* Bound for the diner, I passed an elderly man wrapping several oil paintings.

I ventured a timid, "May I see?" He showed; I saw—and ten minutes later we were eating scaloppini of veal together. The man was an Austrian art dealer who lived in New York, then en route to Paris for an exhibition. In Paris, he squired me to Maxim's and Le Grand Véfour.

Back in Manhattan, he ruefully confessed, "You're just a little too young for me, my dear"—and introduced me to his nephew.

One young woman succeeded on a European train without really trying. In Luxembourg for several weeks on business, she took the *Trans-European Express* to Paris for Christmas weekend. Anxious to see Metz, her grandfather's birthplace, she would ask her neighbor at each stop, "Is this Metz?"

Finally, the neighbor answered, in pleasantly accented Eng-

lish, "Now we are coming into Metz." The voice belonged to
a nice man of just the right age, and they made small talk all
the way to Paris.

On returning to Luxembourg the next Sunday, who should
be in her compartment but the same nice young man. By this
time, they were old friends. He, too, had business in Luxembourg, and they dated during her stay. When she returned
to the United States, he came along. Two weeks later they
were married.

Additional train tip: reserve or select the middle seat. You
may have a better view of the scenery from the window, but
you're in a better position to survey the cast of characters
from dead center.

11. *Make the Most of Your Language Difficulties.* A man
with a smattering of English will be delighted to come to your
rescue. If you can say, "Please," "Thank you," and, "How do
you get to the hotel?" in his language, he is bound to tell you,
"You have a wonderful accent. Where did you learn to speak
so well?" This technique brings top results in the Latin countries.

12. *Pick a Café and Make It Yours.* If you sit in the same
spot and have coffee every day at the same time, you will be
noticed by fellow habitués, usually male. Outdoor cafés like
the ones on the Via Veneto in Rome, St. Mark's in Venice, and
Boulevard St-Germain in Paris are prime spots for man-watch-
ing and -catching. In Latin countries, if a woman sits alone, it
signifies willingness to be approached.

13. *Look Up Everyone.* If Aunt Mollie, who is really a mess
by anyone's standards, told you to look up her dressmaker's
cousin in Paris, do it. You may end up with no findings at the
dressmaker, but she may send you to a friend in Bayonne
who knows a young man in Lisbon.

14. *Attend Conventions.* One of the newest travel gimmicks
is holding medical, psychiatric, legal, advertising, chemical,
and public-relations conventions in major European cities dur-

ing the summer season. If you are vacationing during July
and August and are going to Paris, Rome, London, or Vienna
anyway, why not adjust your schedule and stay in the same
hotel where men of a friendly and congenial profession are
convening? It's easy enough to find out where and when from
the professional societies at home.

15. *Speak Up.* One of the best things about traveling
abroad is that you don't have to wait to be asked. You can
make the first move. If you see an attractive man, do something, don't just stand there—or some other woman will act
first.

I met a perfectly marvelous man by speaking first and
thinking later. I was standing in line waiting to check into a
Riviera hotel and feeling like a social caterpillar instead of a
butterfly. Suddenly, I noticed a man signing the register. He
was slim, aristocratic looking, with eyes that absolutely proclaimed that Latins are good lovers. Furthermore, his fingers
were bare of rings. When he presented his passport to the
desk clerk, I thought, Take action! My conscious noted that
his passport was green, not the old American blue-green, but
a firm dark green. From the depths of my subconscious
emerged one of those curious facts that win thousands of dollars for quiz-show contestants: Uruguayan passports are green.

I plunged. *"Está Uruguayano?"*

"Ah, señorita, usted habla español," he responded delight-
edly, shifting his attention from the desk to my legs.

We had reached the end of my Spanish, but the impression
had been made. I furthered it by telling him Uruguay was my
favorite South American country because everyone was so
simpático. That did it. He was hooked—at least for three
lengthy dinner dates on the Côte d'Azur.

Why not learn one interesting fact about each country and
bring it into a chance conversation with a national. For instance:

PORTUGAL—"I just adore *fado*—especially when Amália Rodrigues sings." (*Fado* is a type of tragic Portuguese song, and Amália its greatest interpreter.)

SCOTLAND—"I just can't wait to eat scones."

HOLLAND—"Please tell me how to pronounce Scheveningen?" (It's *Skay-vah-nin-gun*, but if you learn, you're a linguist. During World War II, many a German was spotted, despite a flawless Dutch accent, by the way he mispronounced this tricky word.)

NORWAY—"Are you a Norwegian or a Bergenser?" (Proud Bergen residents want to be known as just that.)

FRANCE—"Why is the average Frenchman such an individualist?"

ITALY—"Do you really pinch strange girls on the street?"

TURKEY—"Does anyone at all still wear a fez?"

GERMANY—"How is it that German men are able to get so much done—and still have time for women?"

ARGENTINA—"Can you explain your political system to me?"

16. *Go to Church.* Do a little advance preparation in your reference library at home. Get the name of your church and its minister in the city to which you will be going. Write the minister (or priest or rabbi) and tell him when you will be arriving. Be sure to say that you want very much to attend services, and you might add that you "would enjoy meeting and exchanging ideas with some of the town's young people." He'll get the idea and may have a few of his own.

17. *Use the Hotel Bar.* Lots of men who hate to swim, skate, fish, or shoot ducks love to get their exercise from lifting a glass to their lips. Later I'll elaborate on the technique of bar-sitting at resorts, but here are three general rules to follow. (1) You can go alone into your hotel bar, but I find it better to sit at a table. A girl on a barstool is a clear come-on signal to any man in the room and he'll be annoyed if you don't come across later. (2) It is a good idea to introduce yourself to the bartender as a recent arrival. Then if someone bothers you, you can signal the bartender for help against a pest. You can

also enlist the bartender's help if someone interests you. (3) If you are uncomfortable about going into a bar alone, but feel you should, don't. You'll be so obviously tense that no one will dare to try to strike up an acquaintance.

18. *Practice Politeness.* Foreigners seem to expect very little from Americans in the way of courtesies, so surprise them. A little thing like "please" might stop a man dead in his tracks where "hey, Mac" will only spur him on. A heartfelt "thank you" can often cause a man to stop, look, listen, and notice you as an individual woman. So learn them all: *gracias, merci beaucoup, muito obrigado, danke schön, grazie, hvala, spasibo.*

19. *Wear Something Different.* If everyone at St-Tropez is wearing hip-slinger pants from Choses and you're wearing an adorable cotton dress, you will be noticed.

20. *Go by Ship.* You are bound to meet some men. You'll note I say men, not single men. Usually they are married, traveling on business, with a wife back in port. But you will have companionship.

Almost all the methods I've listed involve some form of the pickup—a technique that is sure to pick up your trip overseas if applied with judgment, discretion, and predetermined limits. With a sixth sense of what's right and what's wrong, you can safely meet some interesting people, enjoy delightful *apéritifs,* a good dinner, an evening at the opera, and dates back in the U.S.A. Nonsense pickups can result in trouble. You can lose your money, miss your plane connection, become involved with unsavory characters, and end up in the wrong hotel room.

Abroad, you can do things that you would never do at home and lose none of your self-respect. The woman alone must make social overtures or she will spend her time alone. She must respond when overtures are made to her. The pickup that you would reject at home with a shrug can be extremely pleasant abroad.

On one occasion, I found that my middle-class convention-ality ruined what might have been an exciting adventure. A

fan of French theater, I had spent several evenings watching
the Jean-Louis Barrault repertory troupe. At *Amphytrion* and
The Cherry Orchard, I was particularly intrigued with the
performance and personality of the blond leading man.

After this intensive exposure to the Barrault company, I
was going through the Galeries Lafayette one afternoon, when
I saw a blond gentleman whose face was familiar enough to
be someone from back home. I nodded a polite greeting.

To my surprise, the gentleman burst into words. French
words. *"Comment ça va?"* he hailed.

Startled, I looked again and realized that it was the repertory
company star. Only this time he wasn't Jupiter, just charm
personified. I had become so well acquainted with him from
the audience during the past week that I thought I knew him.
I was embarrassed.

He was undaunted. "Have you eaten yet?" he asked. "Perhaps you would care to join me."

To my amazement I heard myself saying, "Oh, I'm so sorry,
but I can't."

The moment I realized what I had said (a direct quotation
from my maiden aunt), I could have thrown myself into the
Seine.

The stage star, unaccustomed to such rebuffs, was already
heading in the direction of Men's Underwear. Some months
later he married his leading lady. I've always wondered what
might have happened if we had broken French bread together.

MEN

Vive la Différence

The very best thing about foreign men is that they are
there—and so are you.

What are you going to do about them?

Will you give up before you start because you're scared by the unfamiliar prospect of hand-kissing, pinches, oglings, and prolonged propositions?

Will the charm of the foreign accent beguile your senses so that you don't know a knight from a knave?

Will you be so unsure of yourself abroad that you're afraid to use the same discard system you'd apply to bores and boors on home ground?

Meeting men on foreign soil is only half the battle. The other half is understanding what makes them tick, and there's the rub. The differences of language, psychology, customs, and courting impose boundaries on what should be a simple matter of woman meets man, woman likes man, and vice versa —and woman goes back to the men at home.

You won't solve the mystery of mankind on a brief trip abroad, but you may be able to improve your dating rating if you have a little foreknowledge of the men you will meet. Here are some thumbnail sketches that should help while you are sparring for an opening:

The German. Brush up on your Freud, Jung, and Adler, girls. The way to a Teuton's heart is through his psyche. His opening maneuvers are through your mind. Instead of concentrating on moonlight and roses, like the Frenchman, or "love at first sight," like the Spaniard, he focuses on the inner meaning of love. "What does love really mean?" he will ask soulfully as his hand moves meaningfully up your arm. "Where do you feel our relationship?" he wonders as he stares into your eyes. If you meet his soulful and psychological standards, he will proceed to the physical plane.

Never judge a man by his clothes in Germany; you may pass up a rich Ruhr industrialist or a nonworking baron. Inverse snobbery is at work here. Germans regard shabby lederhosen and sloppy knapsacks as status symbols—even if you don't. The German male is assertive (that "master" complex at work), stingy (some even carry coin purses!), and often fat (his love of good food goes right to his stomach). A sure way to lose him is to appear ten minutes late or be too authoritative. The Teuton likes his women prompt and adoring. Try the "you-are-so-big-smart-and-wonderful" patter. You'll find that he believes every word.

The Italian. By his own admission, the Italian is a little like a *pavone* ("peacock"). Handsome and temperamental, he definitely expects to be admired and waited on from midnight to morn. Despite his storied unfaithfulness, Tony, Giuseppe, or Alfredo can be the most reliable of husbands and fathers. But in a wife, he definitely seeks a combination mistress-mother, preferably with a forgiving nature and a little money of her own. He delights in expressing his emotions by tears, tantrums, or tearing his wavy, pomaded hair. He likes women— to say an Italian can love only once is an insult—but an Italian woman I know analyzes his amorous exploits this way: "Italian men always talk about love, but never make it. Germans have unsatisfactory small talk, but they do make love. Some American women have been disappointed by the performance of Italians, but this volubility, rather than action, is really one of their charms for the tourist. Most tourists don't really want an affair; they just want to be flattered." (*Caution:* Married men feel especially free to flirt in Italy. Their religion makes divorce unlikely. The wife doesn't care about her spouse's extramarital affairs as long as she holds on to her wedding ring. The only person who can really lose out is the other woman.)

The Frenchman. Gallantry seems to lie in a Frenchman's attitude, not his actions. You can wait all day for him to open a car door, produce a *jeton* for a telephone call, or peel his own fresh peach. These are services that he expects *you* to perform for *him*. But when the subject is sex, he's delighted to take charge. He will go to enormous lengths just to provide such props as moonlight, candlelight, Degas etchings, Debussy preludes, and a delightful *pied-à-terre* overlooking the Quai

Voltaire. Despite his short stature, he is egotistical, sure of his manhood, and quite confident that he is the world's sexiest creature. Because of this confidence, he likes his women to be witty, talented, accomplished—and economical. Brag about your new purchases at Dior or Givenchy and you might scare him across the Seine in search of someone who buys bargains. He contemplates with horror the stag gatherings and hen parties of life in the United States.

He seizes every opportunity for action. Once when I was traveling from Cannes to Paris, a handsome lieutenant entered my train compartment. He looked with approval, ogled a bit, but said nothing until the train pulled into Marseilles. Grabbing his duffel bag with one hand and me with the other, he implored, "Kiss me, mademoiselle!"

"Are you crazy?" I asked.

"Oh, no," said he with all the aplomb of a general briefing his staff. "In France, we have the custom that a girl must always kiss an officer before he goes into battle. If she doesn't, he will die."

Far be it from me to have a soldier's life on my conscience. I complied with that request but turned down the one for my address in Paris.

Above all, remember that never, *never* does a Frenchman doubt his own attractiveness. Should you find him resistible, he will be convinced that you are frigid.

The South American and Spaniard. Unlike the Frenchman, he does not want his women efficient, practical, or dynamic. He prefers them fragile, feminine, and responsive to the arts of music, ballet, and, naturally, love. Customs of other countries appal him. He is shocked by the Englishman who prefers dinner at his club to a date with a blonde, astounded by the Scandinavian custom that lets a man lie inert on a steam table while a pretty girl gives him a massage. His aim is to conquer. Making you feel like a woman makes him feel like a man. Compliments, oglings, and lengthy propositions are his *taza de té.* His is the happiness of pursuit. The more he chases you, the happier he is, so the game is to prolong resistance as long as possible. However, keep this in mind: those same romantic speeches, the lovelorn poems, the "I-die-if-I-don't-win-you" attitude that he practices with you at cocktail time, he will be using five hours later with someone else.

One friend claims that Latin men are completely unable to make the distinction between, "You're a cute number," and "I love you passionately." Lonely and thirsty in Madrid, she gathered her courage and ambled into the Ritz bar. At the next table, a sleek Latin type dawdled over his sherry. Inch by inch, he moved closer and started talking. Attracted by his charm, good looks, and lack of a wedding ring, Judy encouraged the pickup. Soon he asked her to dinner. For the next four hours he progressed from, "You are so beautiful," and, "I love to look into your eyes," to, "I cannot wait until we are alone," and finally, "I want to marry you." He emphasized these expressions with knee action under the table.

At two in the morning, her problems began in the Ritz lobby.

"I will escort you to your room," said he.

"I'll just take the elevator," countered Judy.

"No, I will see you upstairs," he insisted.

"Please don't bother. We can just say good night here."

"No, it is not our custom. We always walk a young woman to her room."

The word "custom" called for tact. Not wanting to be rude, but having no intention of letting the moustached, romantic stranger into her room, Judy agreed. All the way up to the twelfth floor, the man gazed eagerly into her eyes, pressed her hand passionately, and murmured, "*Cara mía, yo te amo.*" Meanwhile, Judy was doing some fast thinking.

The elevator stopped. The pair emerged. Judy led her swain purposefully to the door *next* to hers. There she said good night so unyieldingly that the man acknowledged defeat and made a graceful exit to the elevator with a fervent, "*Hasta mañana, señorita.*"

Comments my friend: "If anybody's door was going to be knocked on in the middle of the night, it wasn't going to be mine."

Three days later she passed the gentleman in the street. He ignored her. He wasn't sulking; he was just too deeply engrossed in his search for more hospitable doors to remember her.

The Portuguese. To the Portuguese male, life is not a rhapsody, it's a dirge. Perhaps his outlook on the world has been colored by the despair and heartbreak of all the *fado* songs he listens to. Perhaps he has an inferiority complex because, on the average, he is so short. Whatever the reason, he has none of the virile fighting-cock quality of the other Latins. Consequently, you never have to worry about getting pinched on the rear—or anywhere else—walking the streets of Lisbon.

The Irishman. If you are hunting for a husband from old Erin, do your looking in Boston, not Dublin. The marriage rate is appallingly low in Ireland, and it takes a lot of luck and hard work to land a man. Irish men are mother-dominated; they look for a girl just like the girl who married dear old dad. A girl can start going steady with one man at seventeen—and find she's still doing it at forty. The slang for "courtship" is "lines," and the "lines" are long.

Despite all the talk about blarney, the modern Irishman rarely makes complimentary speeches. When he does, he might go as far as, "You're not looking bad tonight." He dances well, golfs, swims, plays tennis, is lively, amusing, good fun, but hardly rates the term "sexy." As one Irish girl put it to me, "You're more than safe ninety-nine times out of a hundred— that's why so many Irish girls leave home!"

The Scandinavian. If you are bound for Denmark, Sweden, Norway, or Finland, take a dark wig. With the abundance of fair-tressed females in these countries, gentlemen prefer brunettes. They are the world's most energetic men, and they love to display their Viking strength on the ski slopes, the mountain peaks, and in the fjords. Women do have a place in their lives; but on many occasions, Scandinavians are quite content to ski, drink *aquavit*, and take steam baths with an all-male cast.

Their taste in women varies from country to country. Danes prefer lively, jolly women who know how to cook. Swedes are inclined to be stiff and formal themselves, but they like their women natural. You won't get by with false eyelashes or falsies of any kind in Sweden. Driving a car is an asset. Swedish law says that you can't drive if you've had a drink for dinner, so the girl stays sober and plays chauffeur. Norwegians, according to one friend, are sexy twenty-four hours a day—as unflagging as the midnight sun in summer. Says she, "They're sexier than the Spanish. How can they not be, with all that solar energy!"

The Englishman. The over-thirty man is often still a bachelor, deeply attached to the Queen, his mother, his nanny, his club, and his collection of cricket bats. The prevalence of the Oedipus complex may stem from the fact that so many British youths go off to school so young that they spend the rest of their lives missing Mother. Whatever the psychological cause, on the Continent you're apt to see an Englishman and his white-haired mother touring together and having a wonderful time.

The English male has good manners. He fixes furnaces, lights cigarettes, pulls out chairs, and sends flowers. Always the perfect gentleman, he will make his pitch casually. For instance: "How about it, my deah?" over a cup of tea or a glass of warm beer. If rejected, he takes it with a stiff upper lip; there will be no scene. But the average Englishman is more on the make than most Continentals. (One friend insists that "every Englishman has the soul of a Profumo.") Legend has it that Englishmen are great lovers but terrible husbands. They certainly spend a lot of time at all-male clubs.

Englishmen like American women but are a little afraid of their energy, enthusiasm, and drive—in contrast to the average British female, who rarely excels at anything but gardening. It is much more fun to meet an Englishman out of England. Once away from the rigors of weather and the British caste system, he expands into the gayer, sophisticated human being that makes him a favorite with American women.

The Russian. Russian men are charming, vital, lusty, and absolutely sure of their masculinity. They possess a tremendous capacity for love and liquor, plus a talent for penning poetry. The Russian Don Juansky admires the intellectual woman, looks down on the frivolous female, and despises anyone who is *ne kulturny* ("not cultured"). However he is packaged (tall Muscovite; big, black-haired Georgian; short, stocky Ukrainian), he is hardworking, sexy, and wouldn't understand what a New England conscience is. Date a Russian and you're bound to have fun; the trick is to meet him.

Others. Brazilians like their women beautiful, but it helps if you have both a face *and* a fortune. The *Dutch* prize cleanliness and cooking; sport a shiny skin, talk about food, and you'll go over big in Amsterdam. The *Israelis* are independent, virile, attractive, and the bonds of matrimony are not too tight. They are a hardy breed, too, for they have been trained in warfare since the age of sixteen.

If you're a size 16, head for Turkey; both young and old *Turks* like their women pretty, pleasing, and plump. *Egyptians* like to bargain, so make sure you don't end up with the less-than-half share. *Viennese* men are charmers. Before they marry, they kiss your hand. If you marry one, you're apt to end up kissing his—and putting on his slippers when he returns from using his wiles on someone else.

In addition to classification according to nation, there are certain universal types that know no boundaries, to wit:

The Remittance Man. This type is not limited to Somerset Maugham novels or remote islands of the Pacific. You can find him also anywhere surroundings are picturesque and living is cheap. In fact, there is a new breed that abounds in Majorca, Ibiza, the lesser Caribbean islands, and other off-beat spots—American university graduates living on a pittance supplied by businessman Dad to keep Sonny out of the family business and the family's hair. Sonny supplements the remittance from home by doing occasional piloting, skin diving, or selling multicolored cork ash trays. Rarely does he need new clothes; his uniform is shorts, cotton shirt, and sandals. For women, he usually depends on local talent.

Doing the palm-tree circuit one winter, I arrived at Cozumel, Yucatán, and the first night there I felt I had walked into a Maugham short story. A nice-looking man, ex-Harvard, ex-playboy, invited me to have a drink. He seemed eligible, and I accepted. I couldn't have been more wrong. The expatriate had not one but *two* female roommates in his thatched hut. They were dark-skinned sisters, Nola and Lorna, who had come with him to Cozumel because life had become too hectic back home on Grand Cayman. It was a perfect design-for-living setup, with only two problems: the man had a wife and three children back in Connecticut, and the two sisters didn't speak to each other.

These remittance-man types can prove very useful for learning spear fishing while you're on an island, but don't expect to reform them and lure them back to a rose-covered Connecticut cottage.

The Gigolo. This type comes in two varieties, amateur and professional. The former is content with an evening on the town; the latter seeks a new way of life. Both expect you to foot the bills. Any lady in search of a gigolo can find one in any of the flashier hotel bars. From then on, proceed at your own risk, but know what you are doing. And watch your purse.

Acquiring a gigolo by choice is one thing; landing one through ignorance is another.

Doris was vacationing at the Excelsior Hotel on the Lido in Venice. While she was eating dinner alone the night of her arrival, the waiter presented a bottle of vintage wine.

"From the gentleman at the corner table, signorina." He smiled.

Doris saw that the corner table was occupied by a slim, distinguished-looking, gray-haired man with spaniel eyes. She nodded her thanks.

The next night a bottle of brandy arrived with the rum cake.

She learned the man's name from the waiter and left a note of thanks in his mailbox.

As she emerged, dripping, from the Adriatic the following morning, she collided with the handsome stranger. He was elegant in putty-colored trousers, striped shirt, and print ascot.

His pursuit was standard. He kissed her hand, introduced himself, and began a jet-speed courtship. He wined Doris, dined her, eventually proposed.

She weighed the pros and cons. "He is a little old," she reasoned. "But I could do worse. He is British but is descended from Polish nobility, owns a London town house, travels half the year." The prospect of this gay, international life was certainly appealing. And what a triumph to report to the girls back in Oshkosh.

On the night of the Excelsior gala, the Count made Doris feel witty, charming, and so beautiful that it didn't matter that her only jewelry was a string of pearls, a graduation gift from Grandma. They made a stunning couple. Admiring friends crowded around, and the Count bought drinks for everyone. He ordered bottle after bottle of champagne, for this was not only a hotel gala but also a special evening for the two of them. The Count was leaving next day. He expected an answer.

As the waiter asked for their room numbers, he smiled approvingly at the romance he had wrought.

"Why do you want my room number?" asked Doris suspiciously.

"Oh, signorina, tonight we must make sure that everyone is a guest of the hotel," was the bland reply.

That night the Count pleaded with her to leave with him for Switzerland next day. "We can be married there. I never dreamed anyone could be as beautiful as you. Come."

Doris was confused—drunk with the champagne and the glamour of the gala. "Give me time to think," she begged. They agreed to meet the next week in London.

The seven days passed quickly. Doris sunned herself and thought. Should a little girl from Oshkosh marry this rich and handsome Britisher? What would Mother think? Was twenty years too great an age difference? She hadn't answered her own questions before it was time to go.

The desk clerk passed the bill through the grille. Doris took one startled look and burst into tears. The whole evening of the gala—the dinners, the champagne, the drinks for the Count and his friends—had been charged to her. The total was more than $300.

"I can't pay it," she sobbed to the entire lobby. "All I have is my ticket home and enough money for four days in London."

A kindly American came to the aid of the damsel in distress. "Look here," he said to the manager. "This girl has been taken. You can't hold her responsible for that heel's debts."

The hotel canceled the charge.

Doris never heard from the "Count" again, but in December she sent him the bill as a Christmas card.

The Quota-Seekers. Many foreign men are eager to marry American girls—not for their charm or money, but because of the quota system of U.S. immigration laws, which limits admissions from some countries. It's up to the girl to decide whether her suitor is motivated by true love or by his desire to enter the U.S. outside the quota as the spouse of a citizen.

For example, I was once proposed to during the two-hour ride from Rome to Naples.

Vittorio sat next to me in the compartment. I spoke no Italian, he no English, so we communicated in our equally bad French. After an hour, he murmured, *"Je t'aime."* I corrected him to the more formal, *"Je vous aime."* But he knew just what he meant. As the train drew into Naples, he proposed marriage. I barely had time to decline with a polite *"Merci, mais . . ."* when he was gone with the Neapolitan wind. Maybe he *was* devastated by my charm, but the chances are he just wanted to come to America. And the Italian quota is filled for the next nine or ten years.

The Unwanted Male. In any country in the world, you will meet the man in whom you have no interest. Whether he is a missionary who wants to reform you, a crook after your good American dollars, a virile youth who aims to seduce you, or just an uninvited pest, the problem is to get rid of him. The solution is slightly more difficult on foreign soil than in the United States, because foreign men find it hard to believe that you don't find them irresistible. However, there are some time-tested techniques:

(*Wear a wedding ring.* A simple gold band from the dime store lends you authority when you say demurely, "My husband doesn't like me to go out with other men."

(*Use the "I'm-too-busy" approach.* Tell the unwanted gentleman that you're taking a tour and you've already paid for it. This works particularly well in big cities. Just as no New Yorker wants to visit the Statue of Liberty, no Parisian wants to spend hours tramping through the palace of Versailles.

(*Tell white lies.* You can always suffer from tourist stomach, be too tired, have a previous engagement with a friend from the ship, or have a job assignment you must do. Career-minded females scare foreign men.

(*Ignore him.* Traveling alone in Italy, I once took the over-

night train to the Riviera. Ensconced in my berth, I was reading, when in came the conductor. I produced my ticket.

"Oh, I do not come for that," said the attractive Romeo of
the *wagons-lits*. "You are a very attractive woman, and men
will probably annoy you, so I'll sit in the compartment with
you while you sleep."

I told him to offer his protective services elsewhere.

The elimination process can boomerang. On another occasion, a handsome Italian helped me with my luggage at the
Venice mainland, then asked me to dinner. Hoping to find
someone more interesting at the hotel, I refused. Nothing
turned up. As I sat by myself over an after-dinner coffee at
Florian's, feeling pretty lonely, the Italian passed—and paused.
I smiled and waited, but his pride had been hurt. Giving me a
baleful look, he *spat* furiously in my direction. Hell hath no
fury like a man scorned!

When your best efforts fail to get the unwanted foreign man
out of your life, stop fighting and put up with it. Leaving
Yalta, I bounded eagerly up the gangplank of the boat that
was to take me to Sochi. Carrying my overstuffed suitcase,
three volumes of Aleksei Tolstoi, and a net bag filled with
cantaloupes, I felt quite Russian in appearance and spirit. The
ever-present representative of Intourist was waiting for me on
board. He led me to a spotless cabin with two neat bunks and
left.

I started imagining my cabinmate. Perhaps she would be a
Czech lady with whom I could talk French . . . a girl
like myself on vacation . . . or, even better, a venerable Russian grand duchess who had survived the Revolution.

The door opened and in waddled my partner for the night.
He was bent, bearded, fat, at least seventy years old, and
emitted an aura of garlic.

"There's a man in my cabin!" I screamed.

The aromatic septuagenarian started to unpack his wicker
suitcase.

I went wild. "What kind of ship is this? The idea of putting a man in with a single lady!"

The man in question was stepping into his striped pajamas by this time.

The steward entered, took one glance at my face, and scurried for the Intourist agent.

By then I was in the corridor, attracting a crowd by emoting at the top of my lungs. "In America we don't do things this way!"

The Intourist representative looked at me as if I were a hysterical child. "It's only for one night," he said in tones of sweet reasonableness.

"That's one night too many!" I shouted. "I won't put up with this!"

Intourist tried again. "It is the custom here to mix men and women in cabins."

I started to cry.

Intourist capitulated. "All right, we find someone else. The old man goes."

Forlorn and bewildered, still in his pajamas, the old man went.

Ten minutes later Intourist was back with my new cabin-mate—a brooding, pimpled, gangly lad of eighteen. "You like?" asked the servant of the Soviet Union with a grin.

I knew when I was licked. But, thought I to myself, it's the same under communism as under capitalism. They're either too young or too old.

MEN

What Do They Think About You?

You'll have much more luck in attracting men abroad if you think about you—not them.

Understanding the faults and foibles of Juan, Giovanni,

Johannes, and Ivan across the seas is important, but it is imperative that you also examine your own shortcomings as a female. What can you do to better your own image and performance rating as far as manners, mentality, flirting, and femininity go?

To find out what foreign men think about American women, I talked with one hundred articulate gentlemen, married and single, representing twenty different countries. The interviews were carried on in such diverse locations as the Hotel Connaught bar in London, over *Kaffee mit Schlag* at Demel's in Vienna, at Tahiti Plage in St-Tropez, and in the Delegates' Lounge at the United Nations.

From serious Hindu to handsome Greek, they praised the "vitality," "honesty," "ambition," and "independence" of American women. They applauded the fact that "she looks young so long" and complimented her "cleanliness" and "the best-looking legs in the world."

On the debit side, they agreed that the American female traveler is "possession-minded," "bossy," "wears the trousers," "drinks too much." Even more serious is the charge that she leaves her manners at home.

Let's take a look at what they are saying about you—and what you can do in the way of corrective self-service:

"American women don't know how to flirt." If your education has been neglected in this respect, expose yourself to some personal tutoring abroad. Foreign men have the same old object, but a different approach—so relish all the flattery, love letters, hand-kissing, honeyed words, and gallantry in action. In Europe, you may expect flirtatious attitudes from all men, including clerks, policemen, and waiters. I once asked an Italian *carabiniere* for directions. After replying politely, he let traffic at the intersection get badly snarled while he tried to make a date to show me the Victor Emmanuel monument by night. Think of flirting as a game, and enjoy the sport. But be discriminating. Coquet too actively and you must be

prepared to deliver. Make eyes at a handsome stranger on the beach, along the street, or at the restaurant and you can expect a knock on your door in the evening.

"*American women want to be boss.*" The European woman, like the Oriental, is brought up with a mission—to be a companion to a man and to make his life as pleasant as possible. Her aim is not to emulate a man. Many a top French career woman doffs her lady executive mask at 6 P.M. and turns into a "yes-sir" soul. Try it yourself. Act like a woman. Let your escort pick the restaurant, order the food and wine, decide where to go after dinner. If he makes a romantic gesture, react properly. One man complained, "I told my date I was arranging a surprise. At midnight I sent three Neapolitan singers to her door. While they were chanting 'Come Back to Sorrento,' she was calling the hotel manager. Furthermore, she had her hair in curlers. How unfeminine can you be!" Let any man you meet feel that he is the most important thing that ever happened to you. You can always change your mind later.

"*American women don't know how to talk to a man.*" The trouble may be that you talk about your job, home-life, parents. The Continental has little interest in your ability to write headlines, prepare a beef stew, or get things done on time. He wants to know what you *think* about everything from people to Plato, politics to propaganda. Rid your vocabulary of "cute," "wonderful," and "lovely." Talk about life in an interesting fashion and maybe you will experience it more.

"*American women like only things that cost money.*" You give that impression when you judge a country by the hotels, restaurants, and shopping facilities. Far too many women chatter about "that wonderful bargain I bought this morning" and "that duck I ate at the Tour d'Argent" and forget the intangibles that make life overseas pleasant. To sport a mink stole in the daytime or talk about your Cadillac back home will not endear you to a civil servant who earns in a year what you make in two months. Don't judge a man by his occupation. A summer-tour guide in Rome may be a full professor at the university in winter.

"American women are standardized in looks and actions." No man wants to know just what he can expect in a female package. A Hollander remarked, "When you see an American girl come out of the water on a European beach, you know she will first comb her hair and then light a cigarette." Forget conformity; be individual in your clothes, your actions, and your reactions. Do what you want to do—not what you think the American woman should do.

"American women are all interested in landing husbands." No man in any country of the world wants to feel that the lady is out for his particular scalp. You should know that by now.

"They are always apologizing for being American." Don't look now, but your insecurity is showing. When a foreign man smiles and tells you how typical you are, it is a commendation. He is probably praising your neat appearance, forthrightness, and self-sufficiency. Accept it as a compliment—even if you think it's not.

"You can interest an American woman in sex only by getting her drunk." The way you conduct your love life abroad is up to you, but whatever you do, do it with dignity. Continentals have little respect for the woman who lets herself be seduced with a preamble of five Scotches and then excuses herself the next morning with, "I was drunk last night."

American male globe-trotters also have plenty to criticize about the actions and attitudes of their female compatriots:

"They always look for an angle," says a thirty-five-year-old bachelor from Milwaukee. "When they ask me, 'How long are you going to be here?' or, 'Is your family here with you?' I know that they really mean, 'Are you worth my while, or am I wasting my time?'" If you have a calculating disposition, try to hide it.

"American women abroad are always suggesting expensive places to eat," a successful Louisville lawyer gripes. "If I want

to go to a really fancy place, I'll take the initiative. They wouldn't dare force their champagne tastes on a foreign man, for fear of making a bad impression. With me they don't care." Gold diggers are never attractive. Americans abroad respect a woman who respects their wallets.

As you go man-hunting, international style, keep this basic point in mind: the foreign man's sex appeal, skill at flattery, and overall charm cover a multitude of sins—he can be just as neurotic as the man back home.

CHAPTER 7

Worldly Fashion

"Most American women try to look as unfashionable as possible when they go abroad."

This remark, made to me by the fashion-wise head of a New York cosmetics corporation, has been echoed by foreign storekeepers and innkeepers, couturiers, knowledgeable gigolos, men of the world, and women of the Continent, as they roll their eyes, shake their heads, and wave their hands in horror at the fashion fantasies of Miss or Mrs. American Woman abroad.

What does the American woman do to merit this damning with no praise?

How can she manage a good travel wardrobe that starts and stays in good condition—and that makes *her* look good, too?

What should she wear where?

Recently, my stepmother, who is in her sixties, looks fiftyish, and sometimes acts like a teen-ager, while packing for a European jaunt, asked me, "Do you think I should take these shoes?" She displayed a pair of faded, scuffed black ghillies that looked as if they belonged to Eliza Doolittle before Mr. Higgins took charge of things.

"Would you wear them here?" I parried.

"Goodness, no!" she scoffed. "I wouldn't even be seen in them at the supermarket, but they're so comfortable I thought they might be useful abroad."

This story typifies the major fashion mistake of the American female traveler. At home she is among the best-dressed women of the world, but abroad she spends so much energy dressing for comfort, she neglects to look chic. As a result, an army of carbon-copy drip-dry addicts can be seen everywhere from Bonn to Bangkok. Some pick the blue-and-white tailored-suit model; others elect the full-skirted black shirtwaist; but no matter which version they wear, the effect is one of sensibleness—without any real flair, fashion, elegance, or individuality. No wonder you hear such caustic comments as, "I think 90 per cent of American women look terrible."

Clothes make the woman—especially if she's traveling alone. The married woman adventuring with a husband can dress to suit him and her. You can't. No man is going to know what a sympathetic, fascinating soul you are if your image consists of oxfords and a nonmuss, nonchic travel suit, enhanced by a huge, map-filled handbag; he'll take off in the direction of someone else.

If you're smart, you'll be smart. Look your best and you can expect invitations; look like everyone else and you'll eat alone.

The American female traveler seems to fall into five categories of dress:

The Look-Alike. She buys special clothes for the trip right off the "perfect-for-travel" rack, the same mass-produced clothes available throughout the United States. Anxious to maintain a wardrobe of washables, she forgets that touch of individuality and becomes the "typical American tourist." She may be a tourist, but she doesn't have to look like one

The Caricature. To her, a trip abroad is a chance to show the world her wardrobe. She wears most of it simultaneously—especially that mink stole, her most expensive jewelry, and a flowery hat in the daytime. Since most women abroad can't even afford muskrat, this flamboyant show-off embarrasses not only herself but her country.

The Beatnik. Untidy, grimy, and funereal in her basic-black tights, she thinks nothing of sporting her North Beach or Greenwich Village attire in the heart of Rome. She should head for St-Tropez or other beachnik spots—or stay home.

The Nonwoman. Every curse can be an asset abroad, but this type prefers to camouflage her charms behind ill-fitting shirts and sweaters or an unbecoming tailored suit. Men look at her rigid, girdled back and think, "Ah, yes, there certainly is something about European women!" The man-tailored look is great—on men. Take a tip from French women. They wear *tailleurs,* but there is as much difference between their version and most of our tailored suits as there is between a chapeau and a derby.

The Ideal. She plans her travel wardrobe as carefully as she does her home-base ensembles, considering the countries she'll visit, length of her stay, and state of her budget. She plays Pygmalion to herself or consults people in the know. The result is a well-dressed woman who truly knows her own fashion type.

The most important part of a "going-places" wardrobe for the lady loner is chic. And you can have this without being rich, young, or beautiful.

Every woman traveling alone should try to look a little distinctive and not just like every other woman headed for Continental diversion. Select from current fashion only the clothes that belong to your style. Avoid clichés. Because everyone else travels in knits doesn't mean that you must, if fuller, softer fashions are more your type. The French, firm on the subject of originality, think American pursuit of "the latest thing" is quite amusing.

I found this out one dark day in Montevideo, Uruguay, when my "fashion originality" won me bold, black headlines on the front page of a local newspaper and the kind of publicity reserved for kings, queens, contest winners with 38-24-34 dimensions, and couturiers of Chanel caliber.

The night before my departure on a group expedition to South America, I realized that I had completely forgotten to acquire a new raincoat. The only one in my closet was a lipstick-red slicker, which I had worn so much on stormy Fire Island holidays that it could practically walk out in the rain by itself. The $11 slicker was the last item of clothing a high-fashion writer would designate as having the "new look," but it was becoming and practical.

"You are not going to take that old thing!" exclaimed the friend assisting with last-minute packing chores. "You've worn it for years. Those good-looking Latin women will be horrified."

"I like it—besides, it's the only one I own," said I, stowing the offending piece of outerwear, along with its worn matching hat, in an already bulging suitcase.

For the first part of the trip, to my great relief, there was no need to wear the coat. The three other females in the group possessed up-to-the-minute raincoats of black silk and pretty print. I clung to my cloth coat and began to have second thoughts about ever wearing the red slicker again.

We arrived at Montevideo in a downpour. To wear my cloth coat would be ridiculous, so I donned the oilskin slicker and descended to the crowded hotel lobby, where members of the press waited to interview our group of fourteen North American journalists in a small side reception room.

The questions covered everything from press censorship to dictatorship. I sat silently, feeling my relative unimportance.

Suddenly, I heard the interpreter announce, "Miss Baer, the reporters would like to know about your coat."

"My coat?" I stammered. "Well, this is what we call a slicker."

"A 'slicker'?" said one reporter, who knew a little English. "I thought that was someone who lived in a city."

"You mean a city slicker—that's a slang term. This is a raincoat made of oilskin. It's called a slicker because the material is oily and slick."

How the interpreter translated that sentence I can't imagine. The reporter didn't seem to comprehend but responded with typical Latin flattery. "It is very attractive, señorita. Do all women wear these in the United States?"

I assured him that women, men, and children from the age of two up liked this sort of coat, adding to myself that probably the only people who didn't were fashionable females.

"Where did you buy yours?"

"Best and Co., a New York department store. I got mine four years ago, but I think the store still carries them."

"May we take a picture?"

Everything came to a stop as I posed in true model stance.

The other American women began to whisper among themselves. They started buttoning their smart raincoats to show how much more fashionable they were, but the photographers packed up their equipment and the reporters raced off to meet deadlines. The press conference, which had begun on formidable matters of state, finished on fashion.

The next day the female contingent was even more annoyed. As we came downstairs, the inquisitive reporter was waiting. With a bow, he handed me a copy of his paper. There, in the right-hand column of the front page, was a headline, "The Lady in Red Comes to Montevideo," and underneath it a grinning picture of me in the well-worn slicker. The entire story, two columns, was devoted to the fashion originality of my coat and where similar ones could be purchased in the U.S.A. The story concluded with the sentence, "The other women in the group wore traditional rain attire."

One of my female companions couldn't stand it. "Well, dear, some people will wear any old thing to get attention, but if I were you I would throw that coat out when I got home."

A good travel wardrobe is simply a good wardrobe that

happens to travel well. To be worth its weight, it should not only pack well but unpack well, so that a dress emerging from the suitcase can go right out to dinner. Clothes must be adaptable, coordinated, limited, and practical. A mauve sweater may look divine on you, but it won't be much use if most of your dresses are red and yellow. You may love all your five cocktail dresses, but if you're planning on a series of two-night stands in different countries, you won't need more than two.

Organdy and starched muslin looked ravishing on Scarlett O'Hara, but they are out of bounds for today's woman traveler unless she is worth her weight in excess luggage. Concentrate on knits, ribbed-wool ottoman, silk twill, silk and wool jersey, challis, denim, seersucker.

Here is an eleven point program for a wardrobe that fits within a forty-four-pound weight allowance, yet will help you to leave fashion footprints everywhere from the Rue de la Paix to the Gobi Desert:

1. *Shop in Your Own Closet First.* Most people you meet while traveling have never seen any of your clothes before. New clothes for a trip are exciting and part of the fun of travel, but clothes that are already friends can be very comforting when everything else—people, scenery, language—is new. A run through your wardrobe will probably show that you have most of what you need. A desert safari by camelback or jeep calls for special clothes provisions, but a jet flight to almost anywhere demands nothing beyond the clothes that you wear all the time at home.

2. *Read the Fashion Magazines.* Let your neighbor play parcheesi, collect trading stamps, and peruse Jackson and Perkins rose catalogs. Spend your spare time studying what *Harper's Bazaar, Vogue,* and even the French publication *L'Officiel* have to say about style. Get acquainted with good clothes. Visit the better-dress department at the fanciest salon in your area. Try the "just looking, thanks" approach, and try on some of the dresses and coats from name designers. You

may be lucky enough during your trip to come across one of those "little French dressmakers" who exist everywhere from Tangier to Buenos Aires and can create models in three to five days. If you're prepared and know what looks good on you, you can take advantage of your find. A dressmaker in Majorca once made three satin shirts for me (the kind that sell for $40 here) for $2 each. In Tangier, a seamstress whipped up a coat and dress in silk pongee for $25, including material. I told her what to do, sketching a *haute couture* creation I had daringly tried on just two weeks before in a posh Manhattan specialty shop. Incidentally, if you don't have the name of a dressmaker, ask the concierge at your hotel; he knows everything.

3. *Practice Makes Perfect.* Give every outfit a tryout before an audience to check length, shoulder fit, loose buttons, split-prone seams. Never pack things directly from dry-cleaner bags; you're apt to discover yourself in Afghanistan, where they have camel supplies but no notions counters, minus a zipper that works.

4. *The Shoe Must Fit.* Comfortable shoes are all-important, so take plenty. Guidebooks always advise travelers that one pair of casual shoes, one daytime pair, and one for evening are adequate. They are not. European lasts are different from American, and if a shoe breaks, you'll waste precious hours trying to find a pair that fits. For sight-seeing, take whatever is comfortable at home, but be prepared for long uphill climbs and cobbled streets. You'll need smart walking shoes, as well as a pair of less-sturdy daytime shoes for short shopping trips and a gay lunch somewhere. If you take low one-and-a-half-inch heels for cocktails through evening, everyone will know you're an American. Continental women wear high heels when they're dressed up. They don't have long American legs, so they can't afford the comfort—or maybe they dress for men. Anyway, count on two pairs of evening pumps, sneakers to wear with slacks, and easily packable bedroom slippers.

Because I didn't always practice what I now preach, I once

had to come home from Mexico City in bedroom slippers. The
heels of my pumps broke; it was Sunday, and all the shoemakers were at the bullfights or taking siestas. It was my
last pair of wearable shoes, so I flew home, nattily attired from
the feet up, hoping no one would look more than twice at a
pair of faded pink scuffs.

5. *Consider Your Destination.* If you are heading for the
Hotel de Paris at Monte Carlo or the oh-so-swank Opera Ball
in Vienna, a Saturday-night gala at the height of the season in
Cannes or a Christmas party in London's Mayfair, you will
need an evening gown and all the props that go with it. But
for those who plan more sight-seeing than soirees, less formal
attire is the rule. You won't be going to the same places with
the same people, so two short dinner dresses should see you
through. You'll need many more outfits for daytime. If you
are crossing the ocean first class by ship, one or two formal
dresses are nice but not necessary. A cocktail dress is quite
practical.

6. *Watch the Weather.* No matter where you go, from
Leningrad to Lisbon, be prepared to frizzle or freeze without
warning. Russia is icy in midwinter—but so is the mistral that
sweeps down the Rhone Valley to the supposedly sun-drenched
Riviera. Continental trains are overheated, but the heating in
hotels and houses sometimes seems confined to the ground
floor.

I went to a dinner party in a twenty-room mansion in São
Paulo, Brazil, in my barest black. The meat was perfect, but
the steam was underdone, and the next day I came down with
a heavy head cold. An exceptional hotel, such as the Connaught in London, plants a heater in every room, but most
hotels and houses leave you to your own heating devices. So
be your own thermostat—take along a warm coat, extra sweaters for daytime dresses, a jacket for your sundress, and a warm
robe. Clothes in layers adapt well to fickle weather. A knitted
cotton dress could be the first layer of a costume that adds a

bright cashmere cardigan plus a top layer of an all-weather coat.

7. *Travel Light.* Excess luggage charges can ruin a whole trip, and you'll grow to despise that adorable little frilled white organdy that you toted around from Antwerp to Athens and never wore once. The fewer the clothes, if they are right, the better the time you'll have—and the more time to concentrate on people, places, and ideas.

8. *Do Be Prepared.* Have one breathtaking number for every occasion. This advice is not as formidable as it sounds. You should have a traveling suit that serves your looks as well as your comfort, a topcoat that is pretty as well as practical, two daytime dresses that make foreign women ask with envy, "Where did you get that?" and a really stunning evening costume. With these numbers, you can be a walking conversation piece, outshine the ladies in their basic blacks, and still stay within your weight allowance. A few eye-filling costumes are better than a rackful of clothes that add up to nothing except excess baggage.

To guide you, here are some average weights:

Suit (wool)	2½ lbs.
Dress	1
Sweater	½
Blouse	¼
Skirt (wool)	¾
Shoes	1
Swimsuit	½
Bra, slip, girdle, nightgown	1¼
Robe	1

9. *Choose a Basic Color Scheme.* Build your wardrobe around it. It doesn't have to be black. Navy, gray, beige, brown, green, or red travel equally well. I like to be seen in a crowd, so last year I toured Europe in yellow—yellow skirt

and sweater, yellow suit, yellow dress and coat. As the sunny days passed, the clothes became more taupe than canary, but I got my effect. I was noticed. One Parisian, leaning on his long-handled umbrella, stared at my yellow wool dress in one of the glove *boutiques* on the Rue de Rivoli and asked, "Balenciaga?" Since it was a $50 number off the rack, he made my day. Your basic color can be whatever you want it to be. Then get your effects with accessories. Travel offers many chances to pick up lovely and unusual accessories at bargain prices. They'll spark your basics while traveling and later set your friends at home raving.

10. *Don't Pack as for a Trip to the Siberian Wilds.* Paris, London, Rome, and Hong Kong boast some of the best shops and best-dressed women in the world. One of the delights of travel is buying clothes. A good point for the budget-minded to remember is that there are sales in Europe just as there are in the United States. The French word is *solde,* the Italian term *liquidazione,* and the Spanish *saldos, rebajas,* or *venta a rebajada.* Watch for them from June to August for summer things, December to February for winter acquisitions. You can pick up buys at the top *couture* houses for one-fourth the normal cost.

11. *Dress Down.* Nothing marks the amateur traveler as much as the woman who sails through the Excelsior Hotel in Rome on a balmy spring day covered from calf to collar in heavy mink or the woman who ambles along the Champs-Elysées in Paris in slacks and heavy costume jewelry. Keep it simple. Overdressed people are considered provincial. Some "don'ts" might include: see-through plastic handbags, too-teased hair, rhinestones in the daytime, ankle bracelets (in Latin countries they signify "I'm available" to men), rollers in the hair in city streets, mink stoles by day, dark stockings with light shoes, on-the-beach bareness in town, too-long sweaters if you are short. The French call the overdressed woman

clinquante; the Spanish call her *cursi;* even in Sanskrit, she is something to be avoided.

Other traveling fashion and grooming notes: STOCKINGS. Be sure you have enough. Get a dozen pairs all in one color. HANDBAGS. You'll need a large go-with-everything size plus an evening bag. Don't buy a new handbag for the trip. Take an old one, throw it away on arrival, and purchase a lovely piece of European leather at half the price you'd pay at home. UNDERCOVER AGENTS. Preferably two of everything—one black, one white—plus a strapless bra slip suitable for wearing with sunback dresses or low-cut evening gowns. A thin challis robe is useful for train or hotel corridors. If you're going to Paris, buy yourself a new bra on the spot. COATS. The ideal coat should be rainproof, reversible, and have a removable woolen lining for tricky temperatures. If you can't find the perfect one, pack a warm fleece (in a glorious color) with enough sleeve and back depth so that it can be worn over suits. If you are traveling first class or are planning much evening activity, you'll need a dressy full-length coat, too, or a fur piece. Why not try a raincoat in satin or silk that does double duty as an evening wrap? BATHING SUITS. Be sure to take along a becoming one. Most of the really pretty European models are available only in the United States. YOUR MAKEUP. You don't want to wear a mask, but neither do you want to look cosmetically naked. Your skin should look clear, alive, and believable, and improve on nature if you can. YOUR HAIR. A smart haircut, properly maintained en route, will add immeasurably to the total effect of the simplest, most inexpensive clothes. Stop worrying about getting your hair done abroad. Nearly every city has modern beauty salons. Many large U.S. salons have branches in London, Paris, Rome, Lima, and Australia. It's fun to get your hair done around the world, but keep two thoughts in mind: if you dye your locks, take a bottle of the right color with you; if you don't want to worry about your hair en route, this might be the time to buy a wig.

Now, let's take a look at a world of travel situations and see what you might want to wear where:

ENGLAND

I forget the name of the Englishman who once said, "We had a lovely summer last year—unfortunately, I was having a shave at the time." In England, you won't go wrong with a raincoat and umbrella at all times and a wool suit in mid-July. This is the country where the newspapers headline "heat wave" when the thermometer hits 79 degrees. Almost anything you wear is going to compete more than nicely with your English counterpart—particularly at night. Unless she's one of the Mayfair set, dressed elegantly by Norman Hartnell or Hardy Amies, or the Chelsea set, who buys her *gamine*-type attire at Mary Quant, or the new group of young pacesetters who acquire their "mod"-type clothes in Soho, she is apt to be beribboned, bowed, ruffled, and, often, just plain dowdy. At the theater, Covent Garden, or Glyndebourne, she might be straight out of an Angela Thirkell novel. But during the day, dressed in trim tweeds, she's at her best. So be sure to take a well-tailored suit to England. An invitation to a black-tie dinner in London doesn't mean that you should appear in a strapless evening dress. In winter, the women usually wear long-sleeved round-necked frocks (there's no central heating in most homes), and the men are the ones who look dressed up. So look smart, but underdressed. Take flat-heeled shoes for walking. You'll want to give England back to the Romans if you climb the Tower of London in spike heels.

FRANCE

Paris in June is delightful—and cold. You'll be happy in a wool walking suit or a dress with a jacket. The weather is unpredictable. Your morning stroll along the Seine may be sunny enough, but by noon a downpour may flood the red tile rooftops. So take a raincoat—and comfortable shoes. Strolling in

France is fun, and you'll bless the day you bought those stack-heeled loafers when you're ambling through the cobbled street leading to the Balzac Museum in the château country. If you are invited out to dinner, ask your hostess what to wear. You'll be embarrassed if you show up in something casual and everyone else is straight out of Dior. Hats are no longer necessary for every occasion, but proper Parisians prefer them for all official ceremonies.

ITALY

I was once asked to dinner in Rome in August. I wore what I would in New York—a simple, elegant black chiffon. The wife of my host wore a low-necked cotton print, bare, bouffant, and sexy. I felt like a servant at the manor house ball. In Italy, be as feminine as possible; you'll be competing with some of the most attractive women in the world. If you're going to the La Scala in Milan, to a fancy hotel on the Italian Riviera, or to a party in Rome, your evening clothes must go far beyond the "little black dress." Wear glamorous silks or satins, chiffon in heavenly colors, or pale, pale crepe. Be prepared for the afternoon heat in summer, but if you're dashing off to the Dolomites, take warm clothes, too. The scenery is magnificent—much better than spending your time in bed with a good book and a head cold.

SCANDINAVIA

Wear your English wardrobe. You won't need formal clothes unless you have connections. You'll wear slacks in Denmark, Sweden, and Norway if you go sailing in the fjords—which don't change models every year. Even in summer you'll need a warm coat every evening. In winter, wear woollies, as the sensible, glamorous Swedes do.

GERMANY

For that watch on the Rhine—by boat—take your sweater and skirt, plus a tweed suit. For the bus into East Berlin, you'll

need a plain cotton dress in summer, simple suit in winter.
If you're asked to dinner at someone's home, wear a basic
dinner dress. And when Germans say dinner, they mean dinner; pick a dress with room at the waistline. German opera
houses provide more Wagnerian sound and fury than warmth;
a dress with sleeves makes listening to *Tristan* and *Lohengrin*
more comfortable. If you're headed for festivities at Munich or
in the Austrian Alps, a simple cotton is best; or better still,
buy your own dirndl.

SPAIN

Spanish women love to show off their glowing dark hair.
Dinner hats are just as "out" here as they are "in" in Santiago,
Chile. If you go to Spain in summer, dress for the tropics. For
winter, take furs and woolens. Black is by far the smartest
color for evening.

AUSTRIA

Vienna is a charming city, but it hasn't the chic of Paris.
Any silk suit will do nicely for restaurant dining, and for a gala
evening at the Staatsoper followed by Sacher torte at—where
else?—the Sacher, you'll feel fine in a simple frock. Don't get
all dressed up for an evening of visiting the *heurigen* in the
Vienna woods. The same holds true for Salzburg and other
festivals where people go to hear Mozart, not to see or be seen.
A very simple dress is all you'll need for the best hotels at
Kitzbühel or Bad Gastein, but if you're headed for the swank
of Mittersill, take the proper attire to go with black tie.

PORTUGAL

Perhaps because the women so seldom get out at night that
they want to show off when they do, Portuguese female fashions can be the most elaborate in Europe. If you adore flowing
black lace, frilled organza, and bouffant chiffon prints, you'll
like it here. If you don't, just wear the coolest thing you can

find in summer and the prettiest in winter. This logical advice
doesn't hold at the beach. Bikinis are forbidden, and if you
wear a two-piece bathing suit, you'll be glared at, stared at,
and in some cases criticized by a Portuguese policeman.

GREECE

Unless you have royal connections, you'll need few dressy
clothes here. Concentrate on good walking shoes, so that you
can climb the Acropolis in comfort, and a suit and girdle that
will withstand a two-day bus trip to Delphi and back.

TURKEY

If you have a good bust line, here is the place to show off
your dimensions. Turkish men like their women plump. There
are some very nice dining-dancing places, so if you rate an
invitation, dress to the nines. For touring the Grand Bazaar
and going into Asia Minor, dress as simply as possible.

ISRAEL

Be prepared to wilt and collapse in the afternoon summer
sun. Everyone does. Take costumes that will make you look
and feel cool and collected. For evening, the simpler the
better.

EGYPT

People here (and in Beirut, Lebanon) know good jewelry
and *haute couture* with a French accent. For the rainy season
(December through February), you need a raincoat and
woolen suit. The rest of the time, the sun shines. You'll want
durable, smart—but never low-cut—cottons for daytime. Cu-
lottes are a good idea for that camel ride to the Pyramids.
Take a pair of flat shoes, a comfortable cotton dress, and a
visored sun hat for the trip to Luxor and the Valley of the
Kings. Dress up, not down, at night. And if you possess any
authentic jewelry, wear it.

RUSSIA

If you've watched Greta Garbo pine, sigh, and suffer in velvet and sables as the ill-fated Anna Karenina on the late, late show, forget it if you are headed for the U.S.S.R. Women in Russia are barely awakening to the importance of appearance; their clothes are strictly utilitarian, and you'll help Soviet-American relations by looking pretty but practical. Moscow and Leningrad in summer require simple suits and cotton dresses for touring the Kremlin and shopping at Moscow's leading department store, Gosudarstveni Universalni Magazin, popularly known as GUM. Even for a gala evening at the Bolshoi Ballet, a simple black crepe or the equivalent will do. Many Moscow women go straight from their jobs, in their working garb, to the opera, ballet, or theater; don't embarrass them. In winter, be prepared to freeze. The temperature reaches 20 below, and you'll want the protection of a fur coat, fur-lined boots, and woollies. In Russia, it is customary to check your coat in public places, so save the sleeveless look for warmer climes.

INDIA

Wear comfortable, cooling cottons for sight-seeing, sandals for sport—and be prepared to take off your shoes in the temples and mosques. English tradition is still strong in Bombay, Delhi, and Calcutta, and there are many black-tie dinners. So you'll want a really stunning short evening dress for fancy dinners in private homes or dinners at the hotels. In the cool months (November until the hot weather begins in March), you'll need a light coat for evening. It is hot in the sun, but the minute you step into the shade, you'll need a sweater. During the monsoon rains (June through September), you'll need a raincoat if your schedule unfortunately takes you to India then. Re saris: unless you're one of those rare people who can feel like yourself wearing one and not like someone in costume, don't.

CRUISE GARB

If your entire vacation is to be spent on a cruise ship, do *not* travel light. Take every becoming costume you own. Free from the worry of excess baggage, enjoy the luxury of spur-of-the-moment choice. You should have two to three bathing suits, a beach robe, plus shorts, sports skirts, and sports tops for daytime wear. For shorts, most people should stick to Bermuda or Jamaica lengths and avoid the really short shorts that are so beloved on the Riviera. Pack plenty of chiffon scarves to hold your hairdo in place, a lightweight coat or fur stole for evening, and a white cardigan. For evening, dress as if you were going to a country-club dance—a soft pink linen or a floaty green chiffon. For shore excursions, you'll need comfortable cottons and low-heeled walking shoes. Aboard ship never dress up the first or last night or when your ship leaves port late in the afternoon.

PLANE WEAR

I have a pet jet-age trick. I board the plane in my nicest suit, but once airborne I change into a pair of slacks and hang up my suit skirt. That way, I arrive with a well-dressed, well-pressed look. I usually carry an extra sweater; sometimes the air conditioning aloft works too well.

The well-organized wayfarer takes two suitcases—one marked "Hot" and one "Cold" if she is headed for a variety of climates, or "Daytime" and "Night," or "City" and "Country." However, unless your luggage has been made especially for you in your own dazzlingly different color, adorn both cases with green or red masking tape so that you can be sure that the bags you collect in different cities are really yours. It can be pretty demoralizing to take what you think are your two green-plaid bags at the Paris airport, check into your hotel, bathe, and get ready to unpack and do the town, only to discover that your baggage contains a blue-serge suit, some drip-dry shirts, and a selection of men's underwear.

A travel agent once advised me, "Take twice the money and half the clothes." It's a sage rule. And for the woman traveling alone: the smart woman takes smart clothes and wins twice the beaux.

CHAPTER 8

En Route

Travel has many advantages, but rest and relaxation are not high on the list. The minute you purchase your plane ticket or steamship passage, you have added new complications to your life. Sometimes, the problems you leave behind are minor compared with packing and unpacking, making train connections, checking in and out of hotels, getting through customs, finding your way around strange cities, knowing how much to tip. At home, you usually can consult friends. Abroad, you are on your own, facing your own decisions, exasperation, exhaustion, fears, and the need to get to the next stop. You may wonder sometimes why you ever left the peace and comfort of Main Street.

HOW TO ACT ON THE BOAT

Brochures always describe the transatlantic liner as "a floating resort hotel." It is an accurate description, but in order to have a good time, you must act as if you were at a resort. Unless you plan to spend your time in your cabin writing the great American novel, you must swing into action the second you get on board.

As a matter of cold fact, you should have been in touch with your steamship line before sailing. Go to your travel agent and say, "This is my first crossing. Would you ask the purser to invite me to one of his parties?" Or you can write directly to the French Line purser and tell him your family has been traveling with the company since Lafayette gave Washington a helping hand at Yorktown. If the Italian Line is your host, write the chief purser and tell him you are the leading lady of the Podunk dramatic club, as well as the mayor's daughter. It's how you present yourself that counts, so concoct a missive on business stationery or your best engraved personal note-paper. If you make the steamship company think you are important enough to rate an invitation to the purser's cocktail party first night out, you will meet at least twenty-five of the nicest people aboard almost immediately.

Lady loners should make sure to dine at the second sitting. No matter if your stomach aches for food at exactly 6:30 every evening, for the duration of the crossing forget your cravings and concentrate on your social life. The minute you have seen your cabin, run to the chief dining-room steward and wheedle yourself a seat at a big table for eight at the second sitting. Sharing a small table with a charming French couple will improve your accent but not your chances of an after-dinner partner. The advantages of eating late are obvious: you have a chance for a predinner drink, an opportunity to see easily who's who without worry about where (most of the men automatically head for the bar), the chance to go to and to give cocktail parties.

Don't sit back and wait for people to introduce themselves. At home you pour drinks for people who might do you some good. Do the same on board ship. If your letter to the purser has not brought results, give a party of your own. The ship will supply the hors d'oeuvres. Drinks for ten to fifteen people cost little when you consider the possible dividends. Ask your deck-chair neighbors, your tablemates, and anyone else, male and female, who might be worth knowing. You'll make friends for the voyage.

Choosing a Deck Chair. Don't be in a hurry to pick your place in the sun. There are always good seats left. Look over the seating situation, then pick a chair near people who look promising. Be a nomad until you decide on a permanent spot.

Meeting People. I spent my first transatlantic crossing waiting for Romance. I had been reading too many women's magazines. I sat silently on deck chairs, sofas, and the cold side slab of the swimming pool with my muscles tied into knots, waiting for that handsome stranger to propose in the moonlight—or even sunlight. No one did anything more than nod briefly. I didn't have a chance, because I didn't create the climate.

Now I know better. To be a shipboard success, you must circulate. You have a wide choice of opportunities—from breakfast to Bingo, lunch to movies, tea to horse races, dinner to dancing, bar to a community sing, shuffleboard to contemplation of the sea from populous vantage points.

Sitting all day long reading a book may improve your mind, but it won't improve your chances of finding a group to sit with after dinner. Carrying a current best seller may. If you haven't brought one with you, take a copy from the ship's lending library as a possible conversation piece.

No Plans for the Evening? Don't worry if after that last heaping of *meringue glacée,* you face an empty evening. Instead of fleeing to your cabin, try fortitude. Ask the floor captain for a table near the dance floor. Try, "Could you hold a table for me? I'm alone. If someone else comes in, you might want to place him or her at my table." Smile, even if it kills you. If you get tired of sitting, join in the Paul Jones or other dances with changing partners. Sooner or later, someone will sit at your table—even if it's because there is no room elsewhere.

Make Friends with the Purser. Just as the head porter is

your best friend at a hotel abroad, the purser can be your best
ally on board ship. Get to know him. His job is to please. Tell
him about yourself and your hobby—whether it's collecting
eighteenth-century maps, raising orchids, or studying Moslem
architecture around the world. He may know someone else on
board who shares your interests. Consult him for information
about your destination; he may delegate one of his handsome
assistants to help you.

Getting acquainted with the purser really scored for one
young American. M. Joubert, the chief purser of the *France,*
told me about a pretty girl on the *Île de France* twelve years
ago. She complained to him that she couldn't sleep because of
the terrible noises overhead. M. Joubert not only changed her
cabin (which was beneath the kitchen), but married her.

People aboard ship live in a small world of their own between ports. Winning a ping-pong game becomes a matter of
tremendous importance and missing the chance to see a passing
vessel, a major tragedy. The successful traveler must feel the
same way. Otherwise, blame only yourself for a lonely crossing. If you really don't want to talk to anyone, don't. You can
be sure that few will break the silence barrier.

EN ROUTE

Dining Alone

One of the saddest sights abroad is a waiter bearing a tray
of tea, toast, and a lonely lamb chop to a frightened lady who
prefers dining alone beside a silent hotel telephone. Room
service is convenient in the morning, a delightful luxury at
teatime, and sometimes a necessity at midnight, but it can be
a blow to your psyche if you prefer it at dinnertime rather
than face the ordeal of walking into a strange restaurant.

There is no doubt about it, dining alone takes strength,

nerve, and a certain spirit of adventure. Only the most confident woman of the world could walk alone into Le Pavillon in New York and order a meal. You can't go to the equivalent of Twenty-one abroad any more than you can here—unless you have an inner strength that I certainly don't possess.

If you want to go to the really elegant dining spots of the world, like Lasserre in Paris, cash a traveler's check and go for a gala midday meal. Otherwise, find a woman friend and venture at night. If you never get to go, console yourself with the thought that it is mainly the *nouveaux riches* and tourists who dine there, anyway.

On the other hand, you might want to consider the advice of M. Pierre Jammet, proprietor of the Hotel Bristol, Paris. "When a woman is anxious to dine at the very best restaurant and is afraid to go alone, she should consult the manager of the hotel—not the concierge or head porter," he counsels. "He will telephone the maître d'hôtel for her. He will arrange to send her there in a car. As a result, she will be given a warm reception on arrival and not be banished to that table directly in front of the kitchen."

Many of one's fears about dining alone grow out of loneliness. If you know you are alone by choice, the fears vanish. Once, in Paris, I had planned to join a group of friends for the evening, but canceled the arrangements when I developed a bad headache. But when, after a two-hour nap, my head felt fine, it was my stomach that ached from hunger. Secure in the knowledge that I could have had a date, I went straight to Prunier's and dined on *langoustines, filet de sole à la Normande,* and *soufflé aux pralines.* Not once did I think about being alone.

Here are some good rules for the woman dining alone:
(Do what your mood tells you. Be honest with yourself. If you're in Rome for just one day and you know that you should go to some marvelous restaurant, but you don't feel like it, *don't go.* Head for the corner café for some *pasta* and red wine.

❨ Search the hotel lobby for another single woman. Say to her, "I see you are alone, too. Would you like to join me for dinner?" She probably will be delighted to have company.

❨ Ask the manager of the hotel for the name of a place where you will be comfortable.

❨ Hotel restaurants may not serve four-star food, but you will be at ease there. Look around the room for someone else alone who might be a companion for the next day.

❨ The rule about dining alone at the big-name restaurants at night applies only to the big cities. Apply the same standards you would in Manhattan, Chicago, or San Francisco. But if you are in a small city and there is a top restaurant, go without hesitation.

❨ The "little restaurant around the corner" that serves regional specialties is a good bet for the woman alone. Italian espresso houses are excellent places for quick snacks sandwiched in between shopping and sight-seeing. If you want a *gemütlich* atmosphere and good food combined with beer, go to the *Bierstuben* and *Weinstuben* in Germany and Austria. You'll be able to wander into the kitchen and take a look at what's cooking on the stove before ordering in many of the colorful Greek *tavernas*. English pubs are fun. The food is not anything to write home about, but it's cheap, and you'll have fun trying the different types of bars—public bars, private bars, and saloon bars. All charge different prices, and all are open to the general public. You'll find *smørrebrød* and *smörgåsbord* restaurants all over Scandinavia. In Portugal, there are many restaurants where *fado* singing is the specialty of the house. Waiters alternate between chanting torch songs and serving *fofos de bacalhau* or *carne de vaca*.

❨ If you're in a town for more than a few days, find a place you like and stick to it. You'll become a friend of the management, and the owner might even ask you home for dinner. That's what happened to me in Biarritz, where I started eating seafood nightly at a small restaurant. On the second night, the proprietress sent me a cognac, compliments of the *maison;* on the third, she sent me her thirty-five-year-old bachelor nephew who promptly took me off to a fair at St-Jean-de-Luz. ¶ Stop thinking so much about food, anyway. It's bad for your waistline. Intelligent tourists concentrate on people. The least important part of your trip is where you eat. It's whom you meet and what you see that count.

EN ROUTE

Eating Abroad—Without Gaining

Many a woman lies awake nights figuring out how to avoid excess-baggage charges. But she forgets all about weight where it matters most—on herself.

No one wants to diet on vacation. Everyone wants to try the delights of foreign food. Must you dine on carrots and self-discipline in order to face that moment of truth on the bathroom scale when you get home?

Here are some ways to hold that waistline:

Save calories for a month or two before the trip starts. Eat lightly, so that you start the jaunt a few pounds under your normal weight and have calories as well as cash to spend.

On the trip, hoard your calories to spend on meals that count. Avoid eating two or three full meals a day. You will come home pounds heavier if you stick to an American-style ham-and-eggs breakfast and then pad your intake with two daily dinners. Have a light Continental breakfast (coffee with milk and one *croissant*), a light lunch, and a big dinner—or the other way around. The lunch can be a grilled fish, cheese, and wine. Then you can go wild at dinner.

If you travel by ship, scale your appetite to what the scale will report. Many people gain six pounds, an average of one a day, crossing the Atlantic. Just because the food is there doesn't mean you have to eat everything on the menu.

Stop drinking Martinis for lunch. Each one has 150 calories. The average European rarely has an *apéritif* before lunch. You might also pass up the straight liquor on board planes. Stick to a drink before dinner and wine with meals. Champagne is comparatively inexpensive abroad and makes any meal taste better. So does the *vin ordinaire*.

Make a friend of the waiter. Instead of blurting, "I'm on a diet," tell him you have an upset stomach and want something simple—no rich sauce and nothing sautéed in olive oil. Waiters are frustrated internists; they love to prescribe.

Or consult the restaurant owner. Tell him you've heard wonderful things about his restaurant, and ask him to suggest something that is not too rich. Have a meal to remember—without prompting by your hips.

Avoid what Americans call table d'hôte dinners (and the French call *dîners à prix fixe;* in France, table d'hôte means mass service, boardinghouse style). You don't need to eat that much. Order à la carte.

Order sauces, mayonnaise, and salad dressing served separately. You decide how much hollandaise sauce you want on your fresh asparagus. Just because the sauce is there doesn't mean you have to eat all of it.

Don't make the mistake of thinking everything foreign has to be rich. The pressed duck is wonderful at La Tour d'Argent in Paris, but so is the poached sole. Enjoy the clear soups (homemade and not from a can), the fresh seafood, roasts, and vegetables raised to the art of Lucullus. Some nonfattening specialties for traveling and tasting:

FRANCE: *Bouillabaisse* (skip the toasted, buttered bread); *pot-au-feu* (boiled beef)

RUSSIA: *Ikra* (caviar); *kavkaski shashlik* (skewered lamb barbecued in one piece)

AUSTRIA: *Rindfleisch mit Meerrettich* (boiled beef with horseradish)

BELGIUM: *Waterzooï de poulet* (Belgian chicken in the pot)
SWEDEN: *Kort lax* (poached salmon prepared with dill)
TURKEY: *Doerner kebab* (slices of roast lamb)
GREECE: *Kotta avgolemono* (lemon-flavored chicken)
ITALY: *Bistecca alla Fiorentina* (plain, tasty steak)

Wherever you go, try to find items on the menu that are good for diet hunters. A Chateaubriand sounds deceptively simple, but it is a tenderloin of beef sautéed in butter on both sides and then cooked slowly another fifteen minutes in the same.

Some additional tips: In France, go easy on that delicious bread; one *brioche* for breakfast is plenty, and you don't need to smother it in strawberry jam. In England, dine on roast beef and Stilton cheese, the best of English cuisine, and don't go dashing around London looking for French and Italian restaurants. In Holland, Switzerland, and the Scandinavian countries, half portions will be enough. Soufflés are an international favorite and are calorically economical. An asparagus soufflé adds up to a minor 200 calories.

Remember that exercise provides you with calories to squander. An hour's brisk walk entitles you to 250 calories; an hour's rowing, 450; a half-hour of table tennis, 123. A fast Viennese waltz burns up 171. Mountain climbing for sixty minutes earns you a whopping 600.

Make up your mind to forgo fancy desserts most of the time. The pastry, chocolate mousse, and *marrons glacés* will be in your mouth for minutes and on your hips for months. In almost every country in the world, you can order fresh fruit or a simple ice for dessert.

This advice does not mean that you cannot splurge every now and then, but keep your objective in mind—to come home weighing about the same as when you started. If your skirt still fits, you're fine.

EN ROUTE

Loneliness

Every woman traveling by herself must face up to the fact that she will be lonely at times.

Loneliness en route has various causes: dining alone in a roomful of pairs; the melancholy of seeing wondrous sights with no one to share the experience; the simple desolation of making your own way thousands of miles from familiar places.

Lonely moments like these from time to time are normal. But if you let them go to your head and come down with a chronic case of deep-blue doldrums, you are an incipient neurotic.

No one can say to you, "Stop feeling lonely," but you yourself. Concentrate on the new sights and surroundings, and stop playing the melancholy baby. Misery may love company, but company does not love misery. You'll have a much better time if you preserve a bright exterior. This is not Pollyanna talk. There are ways to avoid getting in a funk. Here is a blueprint for understanding, avoiding, and overcoming the lonesome-traveler blues.

❐ *Stop feeling sorry for yourself.* It's natural to think, if you are the only person alone in a crowded dining room, that people are looking at you pityingly. But these diners are complete strangers, and their opinions, even if they have bothered to form any, cannot affect you—unless your imagination takes over. So stop moping; enjoy what you paid good money to enjoy.

❐ *Make the unfamiliar more familiar.* Loneliness breeds in a strange place, so attack the feeling of strangeness. Go into the local bookstore and buy books in English about the country.

While you're at it, chat with the proprietor. I did this once
during a vacation in St-Tropez and ended up at a cocktail
party. Try doing what you would do at home with an empty
evening confronting you. Wash and set your hair, for example.
If you would normally sip a drink at exactly 6:30 P.M., sip
that drink—but do it in your hotel lobby. Play seek instead of
hide. Tears in the privacy of your hotel room will only make
you feel worse.

❲ *Make plans.* Evenings are always a problem for the lone
lady. There is always plenty to do in the daytime; but before
dark, read the English-language newspaper, consult the hotel
porter, inquire at the tourist office for after-nine-o'clock ac-
tivities. Attend a concert. It doesn't have to be a leading
violinist or a famous pianist; a local folk-dancing troupe will
do. Go to something culturally interesting. If you can't find
anything typical of the country, attend an American movie.
Almost every city, unless you're in the wilds of Tibet, will be
showing one—even if it's one you've seen before. I remember
going to see an old Cary Grant film on the Greek island of
Mykonos. Depressed when I went in, I felt great when I
emerged. Furthermore, I saw other American tourists alone,
and the next day when we passed on the island's one street,
we greeted each other and stopped for a companionable *ouzo.*
The movie and a common language were our introduction.

❲ *Walk.* This is one activity that it is almost more fun to do
by yourself. Walk for thirty blocks and you'll be so tired that
pleasant dreams will come easily that night. Your promenade
should be in an area that is not full of American tourists
toting cameras. You might take a bus out to the end of the line
and get off and explore without any sense of direction. You'll
feel adventurous just looking at the shops and comparing
prices of familiar cuts of meat.

❲ *Indulge yourself.* Substitute buying for brooding. Buy
a fancy face cream. Order a complicated, caloric, and expensive dish from room service. Purchase something extrava-

gant, for the good of your mind and psyche—a new hat or an
antique luxury. Once in Paris, with a hot summer day stretch-
ing endlessly in front of me, I took myself off to the Flea
Market. After two hours of looking at articles that fitted my
budget, I rejected them all in favor of a breakfast set of
antique Sèvres porcelain. "This belonged to a French mar-
quise," announced the wizened old salesman as he grabbed
for my hard-earned traveler's checks. I decided to believe him.
When I got back to my hotel, nothing seemed desolate any
more. How could it, when I was drinking steaming *café au
lait* out of an aristocrat's old Sèvres cup, now mine? Now
when I drink ordinary American coffee out of its blue-and-
gold brightness, I never think of how much like a lady hermit
I felt on that July morning. Instead, I remember the fun I had
strolling the aisles of the Flea Market, feeling like a real
Parisian.

❲ *Think "you"—not "I."* For the shy person, traveling alone
can be hard going. It is understandable that being the aggres-
sor in social relationships can be very difficult if you cannot
make small talk easily. But you have to realize that there are
travelers, also alone, who are just as shy and equally lonely.
So make a social overture to a fellow American who might be
in a gray mood too. Here are two stories—one of the girl who
didn't and one of the woman who did:

Janet Jones, a copywriter in a major New York advertising
agency, was alone in Paris on New Year's Eve. Instead of trying to find someone in the same fix at her hotel, she elected
to go to a famous restaurant for dinner. The management,
unenthusiastic over a lone female on a gala evening, sat her
in front of the kitchen door. All around her, people made
merry, and she grew progressively more miserable. Anxious
only for the anonymity of her hotel room, she gulped down
the elegant, expensive meal. When the doorman wished her a
bonne année as he opened the taxi door, she was so grateful
for the sound of a human voice that she burst into tears.

Contrast that with Lucille's behavior. She also was alone on New Year's Eve. She was in Tokyo. It was 10:30 at night, and she was lying wide-awake in her hotel room feeling ready to hurl herself into the imperial moat. But Lucille has sense. To herself, she said, "Well, girl, here it is New Year's Eve, and here you are in Japan. Do you go to bed, or do you go out and do things?"

The answer was obvious. In five minutes, she had donned a little black dress, left her unpretentious hotel and embarked for the Imperial, where she was sure to find many fellow Americans. Wandering into the coffee shop, she collided with an American man of forty-odd wearing the same unhappy, "what-am-I-going-to-do-with-myself?" expression.

"Happy New Year!" exclaimed Lucille.

"Happy New Year! Will you join me for coffee?" said he. Coffee turned into midnight supper. There was no forced intimacy, no romance, no promises of ever getting together back in the U.S.A. They were just strangers who wanted to wish someone a happy new year. "I went back to my hotel and slept like a baby," said Lucille.

⟨ Remember, "This too shall pass." No mood drags on forever unless you let it. Some years ago, I spent ten days at the Hotel Victoria on Majorca. No one spoke to me, and I was too timid to talk to anyone but the waiter. By the third day, I was so blue that I looked longingly and speculatively at the blue Mediterranean. To my friend Joan back in New York, I wrote, "I'm so lonely that I want to die. And I can't even leave. There's not a single reservation available out of here." On and on I detailed my misery. Toward the end of the letter, I stopped writing about myself long enough to note, "Would buy you some gloves if I knew your size."

Three days later, as I was lying on my brass bed staring stonily at the ceiling, a cable was pushed under my door. It was from Joan, and the message was succinct: "Size 7. Get out of that hotel room."

I laughed so hard that suddenly my depression departed. I went down to the lobby and became so joyfully and actively gregarious that when I asked for my bill at the end of the ten-day stay, the manager shook his head.

"No, señorita, no bill," he announced.

"But I don't understand."

"It is such a pleasure to see a girl enjoy herself so much that we want you to be a guest of the house," he said.

So my Majorcan holiday, which started so disastrously, turned out to be fun—and free.

As well as analyzing the psychological aspects of loneliness, the solitary woman traveler should take note of three practical notions:

❴ *The more offbeat places you go,* the less lonely you will be. It is impossible not to talk to people in a safari lodge.

❴ *Loneliness comes from thinking only of yourself,* but having moments alone can be the most memorable part of a trip. Thoreau said, "I never found the companion that was so companionable as solitude."

❴ *Prepare abroad for homecoming.* Write postcards to all the men in your life. Be specific. Say, "Trip terrific, but coming to an end. Home evening of July 16. So much to tell you." That is what is known as trip insurance. Your phone should ring shortly after your arrival. You'll feel welcomed and wanted, and soon you will remember only the good moments of your trip and forget the occasional lonesomeness.

EN ROUTE

Conquest of Vexations

There are thousands of guidebooks that are filled with everything from an erudite analysis of prehistoric cave paintings to the frank candor of, "The third-class hotels in Russia are rotten," but there are very few books that tell you how to solve the common problems you meet daily abroad.

There is no such thing as a new travel problem. Every woman about to suffer a nervous breakdown from wrestling with unfamiliar vexations and seeming catastrophes should realize that hundreds of thousands of lone females have faced the same difficulties before. Arriving in Paris to discover that all your baggage has gone on blithely to Nice is irritating. Losing a whole day in an airport because your plane is late is infuriating. Coming down with a virus abroad will make you long for the comfort of your own bed at home. But a tactical solution exists for every one of these quandaries.

Here are some suggestions for handling common problems with a minimum of fuss and irritation:

KILLING TIME AT AN AIRPORT. Learning how to play that balalaika you bought in Moscow takes talent, but keeping your sanity after that first multilingual announcement, "Flight 600 will be delayed indefinitely," takes technique.

The best kind of airport to be stranded in is one with a large, luxurious shopping arcade. Shannon is perfect, but for some reason, the flights I choose never seem to stop there any more. I always land at airports where the shops are filled with toy reindeer, models of the Eiffel Tower, and copper coins of the realm made into hideous charm bracelets. However, if you are lucky enough to be stuck at a field with a free port (where duty-free items from many countries are sold for what they would cost in the country of origin), do your Christmas shopping early.

Listening to inquiries over the loudspeaker is better than a language course. It's much more fun hearing, "Will Mr. Gonzales please come to counter number nine?" in Spanish and actually seeing Mr. Gonzales in the flesh than listening to Spanish-language discs at home.

One time-consuming trick is to haunt the ticket counter of your airline—the "just looking, thanks" approach. You might find a passenger waiting for the same flight. If male, perhaps he will treat you to a cup of coffee or something stronger. If nothing masculine turns up, you could share a cup of tea with a fellow female passenger, but don't let her outfumble you for the check. You can meet interesting people this way. Once, during an eight-hour stretch at Orly Airport, I started talking to a well-dressed woman of sixty who turned out to be a Virginia horse breeder. I learned all about dressage, the care and feeding of horses, and why women don't wear pink coats for fox hunting.

Under no circumstances read the paperback you have been carefully hoarding for the flight, for English-language reading matter is scarce on anything but American and British carriers. Instead, buy a newspaper at the airport newsstand. Or if you have any books ready for discard, offer them to someone who is on page 300 of a book he might like to exchange.

No amount of complaining will make the plane leave sooner, so try to use the time to your advantage.

SICKNESS. If you become ill abroad, don't worry yourself into a feverish state. Excellent doctors, many trained in the United States, are available all over the world. Large hotels everywhere have doctors on call. In principal cities, an excellent place to seek aid is the American embassy or consulate —if you get sick on a weekday; our Foreign Service officers take Saturdays and Sundays off. You also can ask for the name of a doctor from the local office of your travel agent, the manager of your hotel, airline, or steamship company, any nearby American military installation, branches of the Red Cross, and local police or clergy.

The American Hospital, situated on the outskirts of Paris, has an English-speaking staff. Other hospitals on the Continent, for instance in Italy, have many doctors who can diagnose your symptoms in understandable English. The Far East is filled with British doctors, holdovers from the course of Empire, and South America offers handsome Latin physicians who did their internships and residencies in such top hospitals as New York–Cornell and Bellevue. Great Britain is the ideal place to fall ill; not only are there no language difficulties, but foreign visitors are entitled to the benefits of socialized medicine—hospitalization and medical care at no, or very little, cost. Your hotel will give you the name of a doctor registered under the National Health Service scheme or one who will treat you as a private patient for a fee.

Before you decide that you're dying of some dread disease, you might memorize the simple method for converting centigrade, standard on Continental thermometers, to Fahrenheit. Then you'll know if you really have a fever. The formula is simple: double any centigrade figure above zero, subtract 10 per cent, then add 32 and you have the equivalent temperature in Fahrenheit. If this formula is beyond you, carry along your own Fahrenheit thermometer.

Incidentally, you don't have to empty your entire home medicine cabinet into a suitcase. Many common items can be bought abroad. But there are some things that should be part of every traveling medicine chest. These include: an antacid for indigestion, antiseptic, a mild tincture of iodine, aspirin, burn-and-bite ointment, a motion sickness remedy if you're prone to air- or seasickness, paregoric or Kaopectate for diarrhea, sunscreening or tanning cream. You also might take some simple first-aid notions, such as adhesive bandages, packaged sterile gauze pads, and safety pins. If mosquitoes love you, take some portable 612 cans. Carry enough of any prescription drug you may be taking to last through your trip. If you wear glasses, it is foresighted to carry an extra pair, as well as a copy of the lens prescription.

Travelers who have suffered from any serious illness might want to take along a special pocket-size document (twenty-two pages) that records details of your health. This new "Medical Passport" (abridged) is filled out by your physician and immediately gives any doctor or hospital essential information on the state of your health and your medical record. This document is published by the Medical Passport Foundation, Inc., 35 East Sixty-ninth Street, New York, New York, 10021. Write to this nonprofit organization for full details.

Don't deliberately court illness abroad. If you feel sick before you start, stay home. To defer the trip for several weeks is much simpler than being sick alone in a strange country. Don't count on feeling better once you get away. A vacation in a foreign hospital is no treat.

LOSING YOUR PASSPORT. I once escorted a teen-age contest winner to six European countries. At least once a day, I would advise, "Joan, whatever you do, do not lose your passport." So, of course, I lost mine. The fact that it was stolen on the Brussels railway platform, while clearing me of carelessness, did not change the end result. When the customs official at the French border demanded, "Passport, please," I dug into my purse—and discovered that my wallet, containing $80 in cash and the passport, had disappeared. Somehow the French admitted me to their country, a fact which I credit to my charm, but which probably was due to some Franco-Belgian border agreement. Instead of spending the next week enjoying Paris, however, I scurried back and forth between police, embassy, and photographer in my quest for a new passport. So to all travelers, I caution:

1. Each time you show your passport, put it back into an inside section of your bag. Never hold it in your hand for convenience's sake at an airport, railroad station, or hotel. When it's not in use, put it away.

2. If you should lose the passport, don't have a heart attack, for you won't go to jail or stay stranded forever. Report your loss to the local police immediately. Don't wait even five minutes. Then drop everything and rush to the nearest U.S. embassy or consulate. You can expect a new passport within

a week or less. Naturally, it is much pleasanter to lose your
passport in Paris than in some desolate outpost like Bokhara,
U.S.S.R., where a week among the Oriental rugs will seem
endless.

3. Memorize the number of your passport, date and place
of issuance, or write these basic facts down in a little black
book. This will save time in getting a new passport. Better
take two or three of those unbecoming passport pictures along
with you also. Finding a photographer in a strange country
can be exasperating. By the time you locate his studio and
climb the five flights of stairs, it is depressing to find a sign
reading, "Closed for lunch—back at four," or, "Away on vacation."

LOSING YOUR VACCINATION CERTIFICATE. This can be annoying but not disastrous. Write immediately to your doctor in
the U.S.A. and ask him to send you a new card, signed and
validated. If the loss occurs at the end of your trip and you
have no address to which the card can be sent, cable your
doctor and have him notify the health authority at the airport
where you will reenter the U.S. Otherwise, you will have to
be revaccinated upon arrival—a boring delay after a long trip
home.

LOSING YOUR TRAVELER'S CHECKS. Report the loss immediately to the nearest American Express office or First National
City Bank branch (or whatever agency issued your checks).
The checks will be replaced or refunded within twenty-four
hours—if you have been a good girl and have kept a record of
your check numbers and the place of purchase. Always keep
this record separate from the checks. I always travel with three
separate books of checks. For instance, if I take $700 with me,
I carry $300 in one book made up of $10 checks and divide
the rest into two books of $20 checks.

HELP, THIEF! Should something be stolen from your hotel
room, notify the manager and, if necessary, the local police
and the American embassy or consulate. Try not to make a

fuss unless you've lost something as valuable as jewelry. Don't waste the time of busy officials for two nylon slips that you may have left in the hotel room of your last stop.

LOSING YOUR LUGGAGE IN TRANSIT BY AIR. If this happens, don't lose your temper, too. Calmly report the loss to the airline's representative at the airport. The airline will put a tracer on your baggage and will usually deliver the luggage to your hotel within a day or less. Keep the claim checks handy. As insurance against having to wear the same clothing for twenty-four hours, I carry a fresh blouse, sweater, panties, bra, and slip in my flight bag. If you are headed for a resort, you might take your swimsuit in the bag, too.

FINDING THE LADIES' ROOM. Knowing the words for "ladies" and "gentlemen" in the language of the country to which you are going may save embarrassment. If you think *uomini* is Italian for "women," you'll find yourself walking into the wrong john in Rome. (*Uomini* means "men"; "women" is *donne*.) In France the word is *dames,* in Germany *damen,* in Spain *damas* or *mujeres*. Remember, the initials WC (for water closet) are used generally throughout Europe to designate toilets, and often the same toilet serves both sexes. In Japan, too, the plumbing is often sexless, and you probably couldn't read the ideographs, anyway. The phrase, *"Onna-no-benjo-wa doku des'ka?"* should get you to the right place. Don't be discouraged by the sanitary conditions of some of the WC's. They serve their purpose.

EATING ON TRAINS. Do not expect to go into a dining car on the Continent or in Great Britain and blithely demand, as you would in the United States, "A steak and salad, please." In Europe, extraordinarily good soup-to-nuts meals are served on trains, but only to those with reservations. There are two, sometimes three, sittings. Go to the dining-car steward as soon as you board the train and tell him which sitting you want; he will give you an appropriate slip. The meals are not cheap, but they are good. Coffee, mineral water, and wine are extra.

YOUR FIRST DAY IN A STRANGE CITY. It is not a tragedy if you don't see all the famous landmarks. I've lived in New York all my life, consider myself an authority on Manhattan, and yet have never been to the top of the Empire State Building or to the Statue of Liberty. An ideal plan for getting the feel of a foreign city when you don't know a soul is to take a tour in the morning, lunch at the most atmospheric restaurant in town, look at the one point of interest that most appeals to your soul in the afternoon, shop briefly and buy something that strikes your fancy, purchase a ticket to the opera or theater, and skip dinner. Rest instead. If you are hungry after the performance, you can always nibble some local specialty. By touring, walking, and just looking on your first day, you won't feel a bit strange on the second.

HOW TO DIVIDE YOUR DAY. Like Gaul, the tourist day is divided into three parts—morning, afternoon, and evening. If you have exhausted yourself from 9 A.M. to 6 P.M., dine leisurely and go to bed early. If you're headed for a gala night at the opera, sleep late, breakfast in your room, and do nothing more exciting than apply makeup and write letters until noon. In other words, always save one part of the day for rest.

HOW TO BOLT. As every single woman knows, there comes a moment when you just can't stand being single. This can happen abroad as well as at home.

If you are in a hotel occupied, except for you, exclusively by couples, if you feel so lonely on a Paris weekend that you want to jump into the Seine, if you just can't bear London without an escort—don't stay. All the cathedrals, towers, tours, and tourist trappings won't make up for that lonely feeling. The technique of departure is simple. Decide where you'd like to go, change your ticket, tell the desk clerk you're leaving, and cable another hotel that you're coming. If you've paid an advance deposit for your room, forget the $10 or $12. Changing your state of mind is worth much more.

EN ROUTE

How to Budget Yourself While Traveling

Someone once wrote, "Poverty is no vice but an inconvenience." This is never more true than when spoken of the traveler who wants to be a Big League spender on a Little League budget. My personal theory is that every woman traveling alone should try some Big League ventures while abroad—stay in a deluxe hotel for a night or two, purchase one extravagant something or other, indulge in a superlative dinner at a grand restaurant. This is being pound wise, and it is well worth it. At the same time, you must adopt a little dollars-and-sense strategy to avoid the miserable feeling of having figured everything down to the last penny—and finding that you don't even have a penny.

On my first trip to Europe, I spent my last day in Amsterdam with exactly fifty cents in my purse. What I would have done if the plane had not left on schedule, I don't know, except that even in those neophyte travel days, I had enough intelligence to realize I could probably throw myself on the mercy of the U.S. consular staff. Now I keep one $10 bill hidden from myself during the whole trip, to be used as "mad" money at the end.

To be treasurer of your own exchequer, you must organize your funds in advance. If you are on a personally conducted all-expense tour, you will not require money for anything other than extra wines and liquor, laundry and pressing, entertainment, shopping, getting your hair done, and tips on the ocean liner if you are traveling by ship. If you are going via prepaid independent tour, you will need cash on hand for meals and gratuities.

If you are managing your own arrangements, how much money will you need to take care of your necessities and your extravagances? According to a spokesman for American Express, the average woman should count on expenses of $22 to $28 a day. The student who stays at youth hostels and eats a bread-and-cheese lunch in the park can cut this to the bone; so can the budget-Baedeker type, who will be content with a $10 daily minimum that includes third-class hotel rooms, simple restaurants, and entertainment limited to free museums, parks, and people-watching.

In budgeting, count the essentials. Usually breakfast is provided by the hotel. Lunch will run from $1.50 to $2.50. Dinner will cost from $4.50 to $8 in a big city, $2.50 to $4.50 in a small town. Hence, in a major capital, you should allow $10 a day for meals, $5 to $7 in a small town or village. Hotels can be as low as $3, zoom to $25 nightly for hostelries deluxe, such as Claridge's in London or the Lancaster in Paris. But there are many decent, clean, and often charming, second-class hotels where you can stay for $7 a night.

Once you've worked out what kind of spender you will be, divide your money four ways: American cash, foreign currencies, traveler's checks, and the money you leave in the bank at home. I suggest you take $100 in cash—half in $1 bills, the rest in $5 and $10 bills. These U.S. bills come in very handy for last-minute buying at airports when you don't want to use up a new traveler's check.

Most traveler's checks will cost $1 per hundred. Unless you plan to spend a long time abroad, take them in $10 and $20 denominations. You can exchange these virtually anywhere in the world—always at a bank, usually at the hotel, sometimes in shops. Most stores in France provide a 20 per cent discount for all purchases made by traveler's check. Worldwide institutions such as American Express, First National City Bank, and Thomas J. Cook & Son are known everywhere, but a clerk in some village may be afraid to cash a check bearing a less familiar name. A letter of credit is not as convenient as traveler's checks—it usually has to be cashed at just one bank in a particular city, and if you arrive on a Friday night and are leaving early Monday morning, you are out of luck.

There isn't much saving any more in carrying a lot of foreign currency with you. Take at least $5 in foreign currency for each country on your itinerary so that you will have tip money for porters upon arrival.

My pet budget trick is to estimate how much I expect to spend in each country before I leave home. I mark the country on the back of each traveler's check. It provides an automatic budget. If you do overspend, you know it. Furthermore, you plan in the quiet of your own home, when you are still rational.

Take your personal checkbook with you, so that if you run out of money or have an unexpected expenditure, you don't have to panic. Most hotels will accept a personal check if you are dressed in something quiet and becoming and if you flash either an impressive piece of jewelry or a smile.

Even this routine has to be organized correctly. On her first European trip, my friend Irene limited her traveler's checks so that she would be sure not to overspend. But her capital flowed like wine, and soon she was several hundred dollars short. At the American Express office, she found that she had her passport and identification, but no personal checks. Her bankbook showed her married name (she had just been divorced); the passport, her maiden name. The American Express man was totally confused.

Irene turned on the charm. "Well," she smiled, "please give me $200 on a blank check. I'll turn it into traveler's checks right in front of your eyes."

The man must have liked her big black eyes, for he agreed, with an "I-shouldn't" shake of his head. "This is so complicated that you couldn't be passing yourself off as someone else or making up the whole thing."

Moral: Carry your personal checks with you, but make sure that they bear the same name as your passport.

Here are some Minor League ways to fight the battle of the budget that should enable you to indulge in a little Big League spending on a few occasions:

⟨ Don't insist on a bath with your hotel room. It won't kill you to walk down the hall.

⟨ If breakfast isn't provided with your bed, don't order it from room service. Have a roll and coffee at a little café down the street. It will be more fun at less money.

⟨ Buy your cigarettes on the plane or ship, where they are duty free. When you run out, purchase American-type cigarettes abroad, but not American brands. A pack of Pall Malls costs sixty-seven cents in France, but you can buy Gauloises for twenty-eight cents.

⟨ Never enter a restaurant that doesn't have a menu in the window. Stay away from restaurants with music; you will pay for the strolling violinists. The set menu for lunch is often one-third cheaper than a similar dinner menu.

⟨ Look for restaurants crowded with local people. They know their way around town, and they know values.

⟨ Don't be intimidated by waiters. Their job is to serve you, and it is perfectly all right to order just one dish and coffee. In Denmark, you may eat only a sandwich; in Austria, just a dish of goulash. Spend your dollars on a specialty of the house instead of on two or three courses that you really don't want.

⟨ Don't overtip. If the bill includes "service" at the restaurant, that's it. You don't have to show off by leaving more just because you feel so insecure. Local residents resent Americans' overtipping.

⟨ Drink local drinks instead of demanding bourbon in Yugoslavia or a Martini in Russia. Local wines are excellent in France, Italy, Spain, Portugal, Chile, and even Russia. The Yugoslavian 100-proof plum brandy, called *slivovitz,* is delightful. You may even acquire a taste for Greek *retsina* (a wine flavored with pine resin) or *ouzo* (a sort of Athenian Pernod). If you want something nonalcoholic in Spain, try *horchata de chufas* (orgeat with sedge tubers); for something a little stronger, sample the lovely wine with fruit called *sangría*.

⁅ Carry local money with you. Cash a traveler's check each day before leaving the hotel. It will pay off in convenience, and local retailers won't pad their prices to match your fat wad of checks.

⁅ Ride the local transportation. Subways and buses are fun and much less dear than taking taxis everywhere out of fear and ignorance. Even the wealthiest French—the kind with private houses off the Avenue Foch—ride their handy Métro; in their thrifty way, they think it is nonsense to spend hard-earned money on cabs that take longer, cost more. If you are going to be in town for a while, investigate buying a special tourist ticket instead of paying individual bus fares.

⁅ For a short haul (for instance, between Amsterdam and The Hague), travel third class by train. Sitting on a hard seat for an hour will make you appreciate first class.

⁅ If you arrive in town and don't have a hotel reservation, shop around and compare rates before you check in. Check your baggage at the railroad station.

⁅ Travel with two bags at the most. You'll spend less on tips for station porters.

⁅ Realize that the fewer places you go, the less it costs. The expense of moving from place to place can be considerable with all the tips at each end.

⁅ Cut down on your letter writing. Those airmail stamps cost money. Send off your postcards to friends by regular mail the minute you arrive abroad, and let it go at that except for letters to People Who Matter. Never buy writing paper; you can get it free at most hotels.

⁅ If you are staying *demi-pension* at a hotel and have the

choice of eating lunch or dinner on the premises, eat dinner. Dinners are more expensive out, and chances are you won't want to be around the hotel at lunchtime.

⟮ Try to buy all your souvenirs in one country, so that you don't end up continually cashing traveler's checks for $1 items.

⟮ Take advantage of what you can get free. Go to the tourist office for free maps and literature. Look in the local English-language newspaper for events that cost nothing or very little. Investigate folk dances, dog races, Sound and Light festivals, concerts, which are fun but inexpensive.

⟮ Most important of all, try to meet men who will spend their money on you.

EN ROUTE

More Helpful Hints

Traveling abroad will not guarantee all the comforts of home. Only a daydreamer expects to find her favorite soap in every bathroom, a Martini made just the way John makes it at her favorite New York bar, and dry cleaning done in twenty-four hours.

Just as Marjorie May found out on her twelfth birthday, there are certain things every woman should know before she takes off.

DRINKS. Never try to tell a Continental barman how to make a Martini. Directions such as "Four-to-one ratio," "Make mine a Gibson," or "A twist of lemon, please," will probably produce an unrecognizable concoction. The word "Martini" will probably get you Martini vermouth, a sweet *apéritif*, in many parts of Europe. If a nightly Martini is a must, patronize tourist haunts like Harry's New York Bar in Paris, the Excelsior in Rome, or the Savoy in London. While you're abroad, though, why not sample the local *apéritifs*?

LAUNDRY. If you don't object to excess weight, fold-up travel irons can be purchased here or in Europe. These have three-way plugs that allow them to operate on 110, 160, or 220 volts. But why iron your way through your trip, when you have much more pressing things to do, such as seeing four-teenth-century cathedrals and crown jewels? On a series of one-night stands, it's much better to rinse your Orlons and Dacrons in the bathroom and save your other laundry and cleaning for a longer stopover. Don't forget that time-tested trick of hanging a dress over the tub, letting hot water run full blast, closing the door to keep in the steam, and waiting for wrinkles to disappear.

When you do hand a bundle of laundry to the hotel maid, be sure to smile sweetly and immediately offer a tip. Words like "as quickly as possible," although potentially effective, will probably cost you three times as much. As for dry clean-ing, I have heard too many stories of coats coming back but-tonless and smelling of gasoline fumes. I just let my yellow coat turn mustard and my black coat turn blacker—and wait until I get home.

THE NECESSITIES. Take along a cake of soap in its own case. Yes, you can buy soap locally—along with toothpaste, deodor-ant, and cleansing cream—but even the best hotels seldom supply free soap. Other useful possessions: a handful of Kleenex, an extra lipstick in your favorite color, a workable flashlight, and if you are going into remote areas at all, a supply of toilet paper. We are so accustomed to our soft-as-silk variety that the rugged habits of other lands may produce quite a shock. In the Soviet Union, back numbers of *Izvestia*, *Soviet Woman*, and the Russian English-language equivalent of the *Daily Worker* are cut into six-by-eight-inch squares to stock some hotel bathrooms. After a month of touring Russia, I had no idea of what was going on in the world. In the provinces, I had been without a newspaper I could read, and I had heard no accurate news of the world outside the Iron

Curtain. Even the toilet paper was unrevealing. When I returned to Moscow and checked into the Ukraina Hotel, the squares of newsprint looked different. Before putting them to use, I discovered that the pieces had been torn from a two-day-old copy of the Paris newspaper *Le Figaro*. By laying the pieces on the floor, jigsaw fashion, I was able to find out what Nixon and Khrushchev had really said to each other at their "kitchen" debate.

When my friend Soni, on her maiden voyage to Europe, got off a Cunard liner at Southampton, boarded the train for London, and headed straight for the ladies' room, she found what seemed to be a fresh roll of toilet paper and began taking off the wrapping. She had unraveled half the roll before she realized that it wasn't wrapping.

Take your roll of toilet paper squashed flat to save space, but do take it.

Another useful prop is a purse-size tape measure. Most women can't resist buying something, whether a linen tablecloth or a woolen dress, and if you whip out one of these tape measures, you can prevent endless discussions about feet, yards, and meters.

Certain reading props will work to your personal profit. A hotel guide is essential, either as part of a general guidebook or as a separate publication, to give you a range of rates before you demand the best room in the house. Tourist bureaus provide hotel guides, and bookstores sell them for a small fee. They list hotels by location, class, and price range throughout a country.

The *Guide Michelin*, one of France's most respected institutions, uses various symbols to tell you everything you want to know about the hotels, restaurants, and facilities of various cities. A *Guide Michelin* also is available for Italy.

Major oil companies, which also sell their products abroad, give away maps and handy guides to every European country. Almost every city puts out some kind of directory to its own attractions, listing everything from horse racing to cinemas. Some are given away; others are sold for a small amount. A cheap folding map is a necessity and can be acquired from the concierge or the corner newsstand.

Choice of other available booklets is up to the traveler's own tastes. You can generally buy guidebooks to major galleries, and these are fun to have on the spot and after you get home. Institutions like the Comédie Française sell booklets detailing their history.

TICKETS. Travel abroad is complicated, and you should never throw away, lose, abandon, or misplace any permit, declaration, bill, form, ticket, or any other printed paper given or forced upon you abroad until you are safely home again. Then throw it out—or save it for income-tax purposes.

FIGURES THAT COUNT. Learn a few quick facts about the metric system. A kilogram equals about two and two-tenths pounds, and kilos can be converted to pounds by doubling the figure and adding 10 per cent to the doubled amount. A kilometer is equivalent to about five-eighths of a mile (roughly 60 per cent), so kilometers can be converted to miles by multiplying by six and moving the decimal point one digit to the left. Remember that airmail is weighed by the gram abroad and not by the ounce (one ounce equals about thirty-one grams) as in the United States. Rates may be high. Never let your friends deluge you with self-addressed envelopes stamped with U.S. airmail stamps. They are just useless.

DATES. Dates are written differently on the Continent. Continentals put the day first, then the month. For instance our 12/8/64 becomes 8/12/64. One young lady I know cried her eyes out because she thought that a handsome Spaniard had stood her up. They had made arrangements by mail to rendezvous in Majorca. She showed up on the date she thought he had set, was lonely and forlorn for three days, then went home to mother. Later, she received a "Dear Jane: I came, but where were you?" missive.

CHAPTER 9

How to Be a Hotel Guest Abroad

Despite the invasion of four continents by the Hilton, Shera-
ton, and Intercontinental hotel chains, there are still fine
foreign hotels that are superior because they are different. If
you cannot live without the American trademarks—lobby news-
stands, superb message service, a lively cocktail bar, a coffee
shop with orange juice and griddle cakes, and studio couches
that turn into beds—go Hilton and pay American rates. If you
can forgo these supposed necessities in favor of the personal
touch, register at a Continental hotel that boasts elevator
operators who smile and mean it; service that is precise and
good-natured; a comfortable, homey atmosphere; a worldly
hall porter (concierge in France and in most Continental
countries) who is never baffled by *any* problem; and, best of
all, tender loving care.

Lady loners should never dismiss the hotel-room choice as
"unimportant—after all, I'll only be changing my clothes
there." The right hotel room can be both a panacea for loneliness and a setting that improves your social life.

What sort of selection system should you use?

You do *not* listen to your travel agent. He is a busy man,
and the easiest hotels for him to recommend are those with
U.S. representatives. He can pick up the phone and confirm a

reservation for you instead of making the effort to write abroad. Unfortunately, most—not all—of the hotels represented in the U.S. are the real "tourist-type" places.

Therefore, do your own research. Ask someone who has been there and whose advice you trust. Or write someone who lives where you'll be going. As for government tourist offices, they will supply you with the names and prices of every hotel in their country, but they hesitate to make decisions. If you can talk a tourist-office representative into picking for you, he is apt to suggest a slick, modern, Hilton-type spot, full of American convenience, but short on charm.

Examine your budget. If you are poverty-stricken, you have no choice. You must stay in a small hotel that doesn't offer much except lodging for the night. If you have money, you should never hesitate. Give yourself the best. It is foolish to travel first class on the boat and then bury yourself in a nondescript hotel abroad. There is nothing like a truly elegant European hotel, a fact which I learned only after years of economizing and a case of mastoiditis.

Even though today no one is supposed to come down with this disease, I did. It involved weeks of illness, extensive doctors' bills, cancellation of a long-planned European trip, and general misery. When the specialist finally announced, "You can leave next week," the last thing in the world I could face was a second-class or even first-class hotel room. I wanted deluxe, with all the trimmings, and decided to treat myself to three days at the Hotel Bristol in Paris.

The experience was as I imagine heaven must be. A doorman, garbed in magenta and green livery, welcomed me at the door. Manager Pierre Jammet treated me to a Burgundian *kir* (white wine and cassis). In my room, I discovered a dozen roses, fresh fruit, and a toilet seat that bore the inscription: "This seat is refinished and rewaxed after each guest's departture." All the help greeted me by name, and I began to think that they had mistaken me for a visiting princess. Knowing

I was alone, M. Jammet introduced me to visiting Germans, Frenchmen up from the provinces, and American *cognoscenti*.

Feeling a little like Cinderella, at the end of the third day I counted my cash, found myself a new, less-expensive haven on the Left Bank, and returned to the Bristol to pack. But to my amazement, I found that all my belongings had been moved into a suite fronting the Faubourg-St-Honoré, complete with eighteenth-century antiques and a grille guarding the bed.

Luxury didn't matter any more. All I could think of was the bill.

Holding my head high, I confessed to the proprietor, M. Jammet, "I'm afraid I'm here under false pretenses. I can't even afford your regular rates, much less a suite. As a matter of fact, I'm moving today."

"Nonsense," said this hotelman *extraordinaire*. "We have plenty of people here who can afford it. We have few who really enjoy Paris the way you do. The suite is vacant. So you can stay here for the price of our cheapest single."

Who could resist?

Most women travelers fall into the great in-between of the economy-minded. Therefore, alternate between luxury and budgeting on your trip abroad. Whether the name is Bristol, Ritz, Claridge's, Connaught, Savoy, or Imperial, spend a few days at one of these really elegant hotels. It is an experience not to be missed.

It is a reassuring feeling to follow a doorman into the hotel, announce to the desk, "I'm Mary Jones of Peoria," and have the man say, "Yes, Miss Jones. You are expected. Boy, please take the lady to Room 712." Unfortunately, at the height of the season, you may find that the hotel is overbooked and that you have been farmed out, that you have to wait hours in the lobby for your room to be vacated, or that, despite your reservation and $10 deposit, there is no room. Many hotelkeepers prefer to give a double room to a couple for double rates than rent the same space to a lady traveling alone. That's why the woman alone should always provide her own room insurance by writing ahead to the hotel manager specifying exactly when she will arrive. A note sent from Rome to Paris saying that you will be at the hotel at midnight on June 21 assures you that the room will be kept.

Of course, all the precautions in the world can't keep you from making a mistake. I remember arriving in Naples one night around eleven o'clock. I was determined to get to Positano that evening so that I could wake up next morning and swim in the Mediterranean. I took the one-hour streetcar ride to Sorrento, then hired a cab to take me to Positano. The driver agreed to go for $10 provided he could take his girl friend along. Off we went into the night, the handsome Neapolitan driving cheek to cheek with his girl, and I clutching the seat nervously as we careened around the sharp turns.

When we finally got to Positano, all the town lights were off, the driver had never been there before, and neither he nor I had the vaguest idea where the Hotel Montemare was. It took longer to find the hotel than to get from Naples to Sorrento, but finally we saw the sign "Montemare." I got out of the car and strode into the lobby, where a withered old Italian was sleeping peacefully at the desk. A little irate at being roused, he asked my name. I gave it. "No reservation, signorina," said he. My protestations did no good. There was no room.

I didn't know what to do. More than anything else in the world, I wanted to sleep. I had always fancied myself something of a Spartan. The frills and furbelows of Park Avenue–type hotels always filled me with eloquent contempt. Suddenly I was no more a Spartan. I wanted not only a bed, but a plush bed with all the trappings.

To the driver, who was also eager for bed, I said firmly, "Take me to the Hotel Sirenuse." This is the very best hotel

in Positano, and, luckily, I had the name because a smarter
and wiser friend had given it to me in New York. When we
got there, I walked in and said to the manager, "I can't sleep
in the street. Please put me up somewhere, anywhere for the
night." Five minutes later I was in a beautifully furnished
room. Top hotels are used to demanding ladies who can pay
and do. Later I found out that the Montemare was still holding my room; in my fatigue and confusion, I had walked into
the hotel next door.

If you ever arrive in a strange country and have no reservation, go to the best hotel. If they have room, you can check in
for a night, and then, if you can't afford it, you can make
other reservations next day.

A single woman never has to accept no for an answer when
it comes to hotel rooms. If you are on the spot and want to
stay at the hotel that wrote, "Sorry, no reservations," when
you were back in Tennessee, see the manager. You probably
can get a room the next day.

Some other notes on hotels abroad:

(The American term "first class" becomes "deluxe" abroad.
Continental "first class" is American "second class." In big
cities, you can always be sure of decent accommodations at
the second-class hotels, but if you leave the beaten track, be
careful. All hotels in Germany, Austria, and Switzerland are
clean. Better stick to first class in Spain, Portugal, and South
America.

(There is no point in worrying about the lack of fire escapes
in most foreign hotels. The firetraps rarely seem to burn. For
your own peace of mind, you might plan your escape route—
just in case.

(When you register at a foreign hotel, a simple "Mary Jones,
U.S.A." won't satisfy the clerk. When you fill in all the spaces
on the form, the hotel will know more about you than your
best friend. As long as the desk clerk is going to find out all
your vital statistics anyway, get him to fill in the form while

you're unpacking upstairs. If he keeps your passport more than twenty-four hours, ask for it back.

¶ Lost your nightgown? Look under the pillow or the sheets, where chambermaids delight in hiding nightgowns and pajamas. Slippers usually can be found in the bathroom or even in the desk drawer.

¶ That shallow, oval, or kidney-shaped apparatus with faucets at one end, which comes with every European bathroom, is a bidet. It was devised for certain intimate hygienic functions before the bathtub came into use. It is not to be used as a water closet. One of my friends brought one home and now uses it as a flowerpot in her bathroom.

¶ If you are not in a deluxe or first-class hotel, you probably won't have your own bath. Let the chambermaid know when you want to take one, and she will make the arrangements. In most cases, you'll be expected to furnish your own soap, and there will be a small charge. Also let the telephone operator know that you will be incommunicado for fifteen minutes; that call you've waited for all day always seems to come through when you're in the tub.

¶ Many Continental hostelries offer the *pension* plan, somewhat similar to our American plan. You usually have your choice of full *pension* (room and meals), half *pension* (room, breakfast, and lunch or dinner), or bed and breakfast. Find out what is included as soon as you check in, and don't take full *pension* unless it is absolutely required or you have paid in advance. Give yourself a choice of food, particularly if you are counting calories.

¶ If you've always dreamed of pressing buttons to summon help, you'll have your chance abroad. In hotels built before the telephone came into style, you'll find three buttons—for chambermaid, valet, and waiter—beside your bed. For guests unable to read a foreign language, some hotels provide a silhouette of each functionary beside the proper button. Another delight of foreign hotels is the free shoeshine. Leave your leather pumps outside your door at night; they'll be all freshly polished in the morning.

❡ If you've a choice of rooms, take one on an upper floor with a view.

It is more important to stay at a top hotel in the big cities and economize in the small towns. It can be difficult to meet people in large cities, and a hotel provides a good base of operations. You won't turn up much in the way of eligible gentlemen or productive contacts in some shabby little hotel with forty shabby guests who depart daily on prearranged sight-seeing expeditions. Also, if you have letters to unknowns, it makes a much better impression if you telephone and report, "I'm Jane Jones, and I'm at the Connaught for a few days." You'll find that the money you spend on your room comes back in the form of dinner invitations. On the other hand, if you are heading for the châteaux of the Loire, it doesn't matter too much where you sleep. You are there to visit castles, and you will automatically meet other sightseers as you tour the turrets.

Another rule of thumb: if there is a world-famous hotel in town and everything else is new or nothing, treat yourself to the celebrity spot. For instance, the Raffles in Singapore, the Imperial in Tokyo, and Shepheard's in Cairo. Hotels like these are virtually legends.

One of the joys of foreign travel is to discover a "little gem" of a hotel. Little-gem hotels vary in size, location, and rates. What they have in common are real charm, comfort, good value for your dollars, atmosphere, character—and few vacancies. For example:

PARIS

The Family Hotel, 35 Rue Cambon (I), features a Left Bank atmosphere on the Right Bank. It is very conveniently located —across the street from the bar entrance to the Ritz and up the street from Chanel.

Pont Royal, 7 Rue Montalembert (VII). For upper Bohemians. A Right Bank-type hotel on the Left Bank, with a clientele composed of successful artists, art dealers, literary and musical figures.

Montalembert, located next door, is similar and a little less expensive.

Quai Voltaire, 19 Quai Voltaire (VII). Noisy, old, the bathtubs are uncomfortable should you be lucky enough to have one, but there is an unparalleled view of the Seine, and a lively bar.

Vendôme, 1 Place Vendôme (I). Old-style elegance complete with velvet seats in the elevator. No restaurant, but room service. Located in the heart of fashionable Paris, the Vendôme is the haunt of international sophisticates.

San Régis, 12 Rue Jean-Goujon (VIII), a quiet street around the corner from the Champs-Elysées. A quiet, slightly plush place for international types who would not be found dead at the George V.

France et Choiseul, 239 Rue St-Honoré (I). This is hardly an unknown hotel, and it is full of Americans, particularly in summer, but it is convenient, comfortable, and maybe you will be lucky enough to stay in one of the old-fashioned rooms filled with lace curtains and furniture upholstered in red velvet. *Caution:* There are few singles, and in the top tourist season, no matter what arrangements you have made in advance, a woman alone is apt to end up in an attic room. This hotel is where FDR and Eleanor spent their honeymoon.

Castiglione, 40 Faubourg-St-Honoré (VIII). A modern hotel, short on charm, but located in the heart of the shopping district and right across the street from the British Embassy.

St.-Simon, 14 Rue St-Simon (VII). Old-fashioned *pension* transformed from a Directoire mansion. You must stay on the half-*pension* plan, and this can be a comfort to lonely ladies who know no one in Paris.

ROME

Inghilterra, 14 Via Bocca di Leone. Near the Via Condotti shopping section, this hotel has a good bar, no restaurant, but an interesting cosmopolitan clientele. Reasonable.

Massimo d'Azeglio, 18 Via Cavour. Located in the business section of Rome and convenient to the CIT travel office in the Piazza della Repubblica, this completely modernized three-hundred-room old-timer offers 100 per cent air conditioning, cheerful bedrooms with bath, an excellent dining room, and a delightful sidewalk café. Owned by the noted Maurizio Bettoja, it gives extra value for your lira.

La Residenza, 22 Via Emilia, was once a private villa and still looks like one. Small, filled with antiques and rare books, it is conveniently located across the way from the Excelsior, Rome's liveliest hotel.

Dinesen, 18 Via di Porta Pinciana. The building used to be the monastery of a Syrian religious order, and what used to be its small cloister is now a dining room. A friendly, homelike atmosphere. Reservations are difficult to come by, so book well ahead.

Caprice, 38 Via Liguria, is a twenty-five-room hotel that shares its entrance with the well-known Capriccio Restaurant. You'll get breakfast in bed, have easy access to the American Embassy and the liveliness of the Via Veneto, and low prices.

Internazionale, 79 Via Sistina, is full of character and characters, Victorian atmosphere. Catacombs are located directly under the dining room.

Villa Borghese, 4 Via Giovanni Sgambati, is a charming second-class *pension.* There are about twenty-five rooms, and about one-third have baths. It is located in the heart of the Borghese gardens, and the clientele is international.

Hassler Villa Medici, 6 Piazza Trinità de Monti. Deluxe, delightful, and difficult to book. There are 119 rooms—some with balconies that overlook the Spanish Steps. For those who like true elegance and can pay for it.

LONDON

Dukes, 35 St. James Place. A less-expensive Connaught, complete with white-haired doormen and waiters and a delightful atmosphere of old-time elegance. A reservation from a friend who is a habitué may be necessary.

Stafford, 16–17 St. James's Place. Small, expensive, and filled with the kind of people who would commit suicide rather than stay in a commercial-type hotel. Perfect for young or old elegants who like the Carlyle in New York.

Brown's, 21–24 Dover Street, is a Victorian old-timer that has been famous for decades. A good resting place for New England types—if you can get a reservation.

Rembrandt, Thurloe Place, is an old-fashioned, pleasing hotel located directly opposite the Victoria and Albert Museum in Kensington. Modern touch: an excellent bar.

Goring, Grosvenor Gardens, offers one hundred rooms (all with bath) and a location near Buckingham Palace. A good choice for the woman of fifty and up.

Grosvenor, Buckingham Palace Road, is a lush, old-fashioned hostelry, directly on top of Victoria Station. It features a lobby usually filled with hydrangeas and has one of the oldest elevators in London (run by rope and a man in white gloves). Clientele: mostly traveling English; you're apt to run into lawyers from Liverpool and manufacturers from Manchester.

Meurice, 16 Bury Street, is a quiet, old-fashioned "veddy-English" hotel, located near Piccadilly. Best feature for lady loners: two nightclubs, Quaglino's and L'Allegro, where an unescorted woman who is a guest of the hotel can sip a Scotch and feel comfortable.

Garrick, 3–5 Charing Cross Road, has enormous, high-ceilinged rooms and a location that is tops for convenience—

a few steps from the National Gallery, the legitimate theaters of Trafalgar Square, and the movies of Leicester Square.

Pastoria, Leicester Square, is a charming small hotel that caters to chic, in-the-know travelers. A very comfortable bar. Try to get one of the rooms at the top; they have dormer windows, chintz draperies, and the perfect atmosphere to make you feel at home.

Hyde Park, 66 Knightsbridge, is stiff-upper-lip British to its core. Austere surroundings, excellent cuisine, and service that you can't get on our side of the Atlantic. For Americans who like a first-class formal hotel filled with English and Continentals with class, this is it. If you do stay here, better have connections; you are not likely to make new friends in the lobby.

The Georgian, 87 Gloucester Place, has central heating, twenty-five rooms (all with private bathrooms), a friendly Irish owner who has lived in the United States, and a completely unstuffy atmosphere. Rates start at $6.30 for bed and breakfast.

Carton Court, 32 Gloucester Place, is a simply decorated thirteen-room Georgian house with a small dining room and bar. Bed and breakfast from $4.20. The owner, J. Rust, sees that guests meet one another.

6 Sloane Gardens, has twelve pretty bedrooms (only one with private bathroom), a "b-and-b" rate from $4.50 per night. This Victorian guesthouse does not provide any meals other than breakfast, but it is a cheerful home-away-from-home for the lady on a budget in London. Supposedly, Greta Garbo has stayed there.

Selecting the hotel is only half the battle. You want to be welcomed and wanted when you arrive. Remember that when it comes to travel, diamonds are not a girl's best friend. The hotel manager is. Do not write him a letter which opens, "Dear Sir: I will be in Paris on December 19 and would like to stay at your hotel." Take the trouble to find out his name from the tourist office, and write him a letter that tells him a little about you. If he is any sort of manager at all, he will be awaiting you in the lobby and eager to please you.

Another good friend is the hall porter (he is equivalent to the purser on an ocean liner). He runs everyone but the dining room help and can help you with everything—postage, reservations, advice. Be nice to him. He can put you on a tour with nice fellow guests, include you on a special sight-seeing expedition. Be sure to tip him liberally, even though he probably makes more money in a year than you do in ten.

CHAPTER 10

Resourceful Resorting

"I'd like to give you a souvenir to remember St. Croix. How about a bed?"

The suggestion was made with the most honorable of intentions by a tall, dark, and definitely not handsome gentleman in his mid-forties as we walked along the main street of Christiansted during my Virgin Islands holiday.

The overture, in fact, had overtones of the highest respectability. It was a substitute offer, following a rejected proposal. Martin Wilson Salizar, undaunted by four successive divorces—from an English lady of means but no morals, a Spanish señorita who couldn't bear life away from Madrid, a Frenchwoman who missed husband number one, and an American who ditched him when he gave up big business for beachcombing—found bachelor life in St. Croix lonely. All his dividends from AT&T couldn't keep Martin warm. He wanted me to be wife number five.

It all happened because I had changed jobs and, before taking over my new desk, had treated myself to a ten-day holiday. A series of circumstances led me to my first out-of-the-country winter vacation, and a letter of introduction produced Martin. It was an immediate case of boy chases girl, and girl gets bed. For gentleman that Martin was, he insisted

he wanted me to have a "wonderful remembrance" of St.
Croix. This was 1953, and the island was still full of old-
fashioned antiques from the great plantation houses. Our
dialogue went something like this:

"What do you plan to buy to remember the island?"

"Oh I don't know. Maybe a silver bracelet."

"How about a bed?"

I stared up in astonishment at Martin's crinkling face, his
wavy black moustache, and pixie-looking eyes. "A bed?"

"You see, I own a genuine 1840 mahogany bed with pine-
apple posts. But I really need a modern convertible couch.
You said you like early-American stuff, so I thought you
might like to have the bed to remember me by."

I had been reared strictly on the books-candy-flowers gift-
giving school, but with a new, completely unfurnished apartment staring me in the face back in New York, this offer was
too good to resist. I turned down Martin, but accepted the
bed. He accepted my turndown and also the $75 I insisted
on paying him for the four-poster. Six weeks later the bed
arrived at Hoboken. I hired a horse and wagon to cart it to
Manhattan, paid my superintendent $20 to assemble it, and
have slept in it ever since. Meanwhile, Martin found another
American lady tourist who was delighted to accept his offer
for board and convertible sofa in St. Croix.

Acquisition of the bed made St. Croix an unforgettable
experience, but it was memorable for more than that. It was
the first time I had ever had a good time at a resort hotel.
Everyone has a distorted self-image, and mine was always
that I was just like Melanie in *Gone with the Wind*. My
imagined picture: gentle, sweet, kindly, always looking to
help others, reserved, frail, quiet, frightened by large groups
of strangers. Naturally, this type of person always has been a
complete flop at a resort, and I did nothing to spoil the record.
Furthermore, the American resorts that Mother trotted me to
in search of eligibles were terrible: the girls wore mink

jackets over bathing suits; the whole day was spent searching for evening-date security; and instead of being a change from the frantic life of the rest of the year, it was more hectic.

When I found St. Croix, I discovered that resorts do exist that are agreeable, full of atmosphere, and comfortable for women alone. By that time, I had also learned that I wasn't Melanie at all. I was much more like Scarlett.

For the lady loner, a satisfactory resort is the hardest travel spot to find. You can't believe what you read in the brochures; the management may have changed since the last edition. You can't trust the word of a friend; her tastes may not be yours. Never place confidence in the honeyed words of travel agents; they proffer run-of-the-mill-type places and have little comprehension of your special needs.

To you, your wants seem simple. If you are anything like me, you search for a site with "interesting" people, enough men so that you are sure of a drink at cocktail time, comfort (if not a private bath, a convenient one, and if tropical, well supplied with mosquito repellent), and either a clean beach or a climbable mountain, depending on your tastes.

This Shangri-La does not exist. You should look for:

¶ *A destination that appeals to you.* If you're a sun lover, find a spot on the Caribbean, Mediterranean, Black Sea or Pacific Ocean; concentrate on sun and sand and forget about finding a lover. Nothing is worse than going purely for man-hunting.

¶ *A hotel that caters to between 50 and 125 people.* That size is just right for the single woman. There are just enough people to meet, yet not so many that she is submerged in a sea of couples. Avoid those darling little guesthouses, run by ex-copywriters from big-city advertising agencies. They are fine for marrieds, but you'll get "away from it all" so completely that you'll have no one to talk to but yourself.

¶ *A hostelry that operates on the American plan.* If you encounter the same people day after day at mealtime, eventually you make connections. I remember staying at the Casa

Rosa in Veradero Beach, Cuba, in pre-Castro days. I was the only person there alone, and there wasn't a meal that someone didn't come over and say, "Won't you join us?"

❲A place from which you can make your exit easily. Nothing is worse than going to some remote island, hating it, and finding yourself becalmed for a week because the once-a-week plane to the mainland left yesterday. Everyone had told me all about the offbeat wonders of Puerto Vallarta, Mexico, so instead of investigating as I usually do, I just went. I hated it. The place was swarming with bugs, married Mexicans on the prowl, and John Birchers from California in search of converts. It was offbeat all right, but filled with people drawn together by mutual unhappiness. It even had a very active Alcoholics Anonymous chapter. But I couldn't leave, because I was too tired by a year's work to do things in Mexico City, and I didn't know any other place to go.

One evening I was brooding in front of the Hotel Oceano when a bearded gentleman approached. His eyes drooped sleepily like Robert Mitchum's, and his voice was low and soft. A rope kept his pants up. His name was Joe, and he said to me, "What are you doing here in Puerto Vallarta? Man, you got to make the Yelapa scene."

Yelapa sounded like Greek to me, but anything was better than where I was.

"Yelapa is the swingingest town in the northwest southeast Pacific," Joe added as a clincher.

So the next day, I took the three-hours-by-slow-boat trip to Yelapa, a tiny beehive village on the beach that has been termed the Tahiti of the Americas. Joe came, too. He had come to Puerto Vallarta to pick up supplies and was terribly anxious to "get away from city life."

At Yelapa, there were a group of refugees from North Beach, San Francisco, a few artists, a collection of yelapas (thatched huts), and the Lagunita Hotel. From a record player, Billie Holliday was singing about her man who wore high drape pants and was so fine and mellow. Everyone was drinking *raicilla,* an alcoholic potion that tastes like low-grade gasoline. Just fifteen miles from Puerto Vallarta, Yelapa was a real island retreat. I finished up my Mexican stay there, where I had "interesting" people for friends; single men who supplied drinks; a comfortable room for $6 a day, complete with bath; and gourmet-type cuisine, highlighted by grilled fish, caught right in front of me by local fishermen, for breakfast, lunch, and dinner.

Like any other aspect of travel, the most important thing to consider in picking a resort is knowing who you are. If you've a taste for the swank, roughing it in a fishing village won't produce peace of mind. If you like to cavort with beatniks, Monte Carlo at the height of the season is not the place for you.

The resort world may be your oyster, but you've got to know what you want. Abroad, you will find basically eight different types of resort hotels.

1. *The Luxury "Snob Appeal" Hotels.* These are for the woman with cash, courage, or good looks. Any of these assets will do, but one is essential. Perfect examples of this type are the Carlton at Cannes, Hotel de Paris at Monte Carlo, La Réserve at Beaulieu. The best way to succeed at these places is to have connections along the Riviera or to look terrific in a bathing suit. If your social and physical credentials are nil and you aren't interested in making café society, go elsewhere.

A few hotels offer a "house-party atmosphere" that enables the lady traveling alone to live high and meet people. The Bürgenstock Hotel in Bürgenstock, Switzerland, has fabulous resort facilities plus nearby drop-in neighbors like William Holden and Audrey Hepburn. The Zermatterhof in Zermatt, Switzerland, is another fun-type hotel. A third spot is the Cantegril Country Club at Punta del Este, Uruguay. Two and a half hours from Montevideo, it is a favorite gathering place for all the playboys from Europe and South America—and a North American lady on the loose is much more of a rarity there than on the Riviera.

2. *Sight-seeing and Scenery Combined.* Every woman should schedule some resort-hopping along with sight-seeing. Make your headquarters at a resort hotel, so that you can have scenery-seeing days and gala nights. In Portugal, see Lisbon by day but make your residence at Estoril, the nearby seaside resort town with year-round good climate.

Or the blasé girl who long ago discovered the Greek islands and buzzed Hong Kong on a flight around the world might try Kenya or Tanganyika—if the political situation is stable—and a combination of safaris and resorts. Safaris to Treetops are organized at the Outspan Hotel, an inn of unusual charm near the town of Hyeri, ninety-four miles from Nairobi and a few miles south of the equator. Outspan is a retreat in its own right, with an outdoor pool, squash and tennis courts, accommodations for more than one hundred persons, and a view of Mount Kenya. From there, you can drive to Treetops, a strange structure built on stilts, with room for twenty-two guests, and a water hole that attracts animals from buffalo to rhinoceros.

An ex-Broadway producer runs the Desert Inn in the middle of Israel's Negev Desert, with daily sight-seeing jaunts to Beersheba, the Camel Market, and other points. He and his wife are sympathetic to lonely ladies and delighted to introduce you to fellow guests at the hotel—many of whom are male businessmen. Other sight-seeing-area resorts: the Kvikne Hotel in the town of Balestrand, Norway; the Blue Peter Inn on Blue Mountain Beach in Capetown; the St. George in Beirut, Lebanon.

3. *The Guests Are the Show.* In this type of hotel the customers make its reputation. For example, the Oloffson in Haiti is an old gingerbread house with a second floor like a Somerset Maugham setting, but it has a deserved reputation

of attracting upper bohemians. French Leave, on the island of Eleuthera in the Bahamas, is run by ex-actor Craig Kelly, who follows the practice of seating all the singles who so wish at a large communal table. If you can discover this sort of place, go at once—but it is hard to find.

4. *The "Discovered Island" Retreats.* There are little islands, big islands, near islands, far islands, accessible islands, inaccessible islands, tropical islands, fun islands, secluded islands, jazzy islands, and untouched islands. Don't go to any of them unless you are the island type. Islands are for the woman who is enterprising, resourceful, wants to travel her way—not for the type who would go to American Express and say, "Put me on a bus."

One of my best vacations was spent on the island of Cozumel off the coast of Yucatán. A friend, Nancy Hanes, who used to be a magazine promotion writer at a TV network, decided to give up everything in favor of silk-screen weaving. To David Zorman, the radio producer who wanted to marry her, she said, "No, I want to go and live on an island first," and off she went to Cozumel.

Some months later, I received a letter from Nancy. "This is paradise," she wrote. "Why not come down for your vacation?" Southward I went that summer, laden with pleated paper lampshades, cosmetics, nylon pants, and other necessities of life for Nancy.

At that time, there were twenty tourists ensconced in tropical comfort at the one hotel, run by the Barbachano brothers, and one (me) at the Casa Maya Luum, a pink house resembling a stage setting for Sadie Thompson, run by a former violinist in a symphony orchestra who had left the United States to avoid the discordant notes of too many creditors. For two weeks, I was waited on hand and foot by my retinue of servants, took afternoon siestas in a bright-blue hammock, watched the sunset with all the other tourists at cocktail time, and had a lovely holiday. I met an elderly couple from Canada who collected islands, a Columbia University professor who listened to people as if they were reciting, a couple from Philadelphia (he a handsome devil with his shirt open to show his beefcake, and she a quiet blonde minus a wedding ring). Nancy stayed for a year on Cozumel, then came home and married David.

5. *The Nouvelle Vague.* Islands like Ibiza, Mykonos, and Tahiti have long been discovered. Some of the new ones coming up are Ponza, Sardinia, and Sicily in Italy, Korcula in Yugoslavia, Kalymnos in Greece. These are for true island collectors. Don't go unless you know all about where you're going and don't mind primitive facilities.

6. *The Spas.* Top ones exist in Germany, Austria, France, Belgium, Italy, and Switzerland. Consult the respective tourist offices for details. These health resorts are primarily for over fifty's, and if you are that age, remember that lots of elderly gentlemen like mineral water and mud baths.

7. *The Stereotypes.* Spots like the Canary Islands, Positano, Lake Garda, the English lakes, Biarritz, and Portofino have been famous for years and deservedly so. Generally, when people keep going to the same place year after year, there is something there. However, you might keep one or two thoughts in mind. Stay away from spots with predominantly German tourists; they will be dull. The British are always the first to find a good bargain; follow their lead. Realize that these well-known, run-of-the-mill places may get a few interesting, egghead types, but for the most part they will attract typical tourists, with a concentration of older ladies who sit on rockers. This may be what you want, but you should know in advance what you'll get.

8. *The Ski Spots.* "We've met before," said the Madison Avenue account executive to the pretty blonde at Sugarbush during the luncheon break. "Was it at Squaw Valley?"

"No," she answered, shrugging demurely under the black parka.

"Nancy Jones's party?"

"I don't know Nancy."

"Verbier—last February?"

"That's it," cried the blonde, shaking the snow off her ski boots. "At the Hotel de la Poste."

Reunited in the U.S.A., the couple let no ice form on their friendship. Two weeks later, the advertising man from New York and the blonde from Canada were married and took off for their honeymoon—to Verbier in the Swiss Alps.

On another occasion, a widow of fifty-five was talking to her young niece.

"Where are you going, Aunt Mora?" asked the latter.

"Skiing," said the aunt firmly as she stowed stretch pants and sweaters into gay red-and-blue luggage.

"But, Auntie," said the teen-ager naïvely, "it's December now and you're going to Europe for five months. You can't be going to ski all that time."

"I certainly can," said the aunt. "The rent I get by subletting the apartment practically pays for the cost of the trip. But there's a more important reason. Here, I'm always the odd woman out, and if a hostess does dredge up a man, he's usually an invalid who's looking for a nurse instead of a wife. In Europe, lots of older men ski. I have a date every night."

At still another time, a thirty-year-old secretary waited at Kennedy Airport for the flight to Munich to be announced. She was taking a seventeen-day vacation that would encompass a week at Kitzbühel, a night in Munich to see the Fasching Carnival, and a week at St. Anton—all for under $600. "It's no more expensive to ski abroad than in the United States, and it's even more fun," the young lady informed me. "Besides, I prefer a winter vacation—I can always be a weekend guest in the summer."

With excursion fares, airline packages, and the inexpensiveness of lifts and lessons, more and more women on their own are developing the rage to ski abroad. Skiing isn't the only lure. You can ski and eat *sukiyaki* in Japan, ski and buy a bottle of Femme at Chamonix, France, ski and take the thermal-bath cure at Bad Gastein, Austria, ski and live like a queen at Cortina, Italy. *Après ski,* you can listen to the zither and the jukebox. And all day and all night, you can set your cap for Yugoslavian diplomats, South American playboys, French television stars, or fellow Americans who, like yourself, have the urge to *schuss* out of the country.

Skiing abroad offers benefits that American resorts do not. It's much more casual. You don't start early in the morning. The accent at noon is on food. Instead of a hamburger and a half-hour for lunch, you take three times as long to dine on everything from *escargots* to *scampi,* washed down with plenty of wine. People don't ski until the lift closes, American style; they quit early to get ready for the tea dance. There is much more emphasis on after-ski life. People are more concerned with having fun than with becoming expert skiers. It's a great way to meet men, for there are always more males than females.

⟮ *Your ability.* For your first time on skis, pick a place with easy slopes and a lively bar. There's no point in going where the experts go if you're basically a snow bunny.

⟮ *Your background.* If you are of Italian descent, you might find an Italian resort more fun. "My grandparents came from Venice," is a grand opening wedge at Cortina. If your Spanish is fluent, you might want to try Guadarrama, just twenty-eight miles from Madrid. If you can't fracture a word of French, stay away from Megève and Chamonix.

⟮ *Your time limit.* If you have just time for a two-week vacation, make a limit of two resorts. Spend a week in each place. It's silly to scurry around. You scarcely learn the ropes before you have to catch a train for somewhere else.

⟮ *Your needs.* No single girl wants to ski in isolation. Pick a place with a good ski school, where you can get a pair of stretch pants made, where there is one hotel that is the central gathering spot. A place like St. Moritz, with its many hotels, is too big for comfort.

Because skiing has become such big business, many of the airlines have special ski advisers. I grouped skiers into eight classifications and asked pretty Mickey Roodhouse, holiday consultant specializing in skiing for Pan American Airways, where each type should go for good results. Here is her good advice:

The Top Ski Pro: Val-d'Isère, France; Albona, Austria; Pontresina, Switzerland

The Novice: Kitzbühel, Austria; Davos, Switzerland; Garmisch-Partenkirchen, Germany

The Social Skier: Megève, France; Kitzbühel, Austria; Chamonix-Mont-Blanc, France; Zermatt, Switzerland; St. Anton, Austria; Klosters, Switzerland

The Man-Hunter: Cortina, Italy; Zürs-am-Arlberg, Austria; Davos, Switzerland

The Transient Who Wants Weekend Skiing and Weekday Sight-seeing: Innsbruck, Austria; Interlaken, Switzerland

The Girl Who Speaks English Only: Zermatt, Switzerland; Kitzbühel, Austria

The Adventuress: Bled, Yugoslavia; Geilo, Norway; Cedars of Lebanon, Lebanon; Shiga Heights at the Maruika ski area, Japan

The Summer Skier: Portillo, Chile; Hotham Heights, Australia; Mount Ruapehu, North Island, New Zealand

Finding the resort that suits you is one thing; being a success while you're there, another. All the planning and plotting beforehand won't help if you don't know how to act on the spot. It is never easy to go alone to a resort, but here are some of the basic rules:

❡ *Look as if you are enjoying yourself.* Nothing scares people away faster than an unhappy female alone. I once arrived at the Oloffson in Haiti—alone. By the time I had changed and was descending the steps, everybody in the bar was comfortably guzzling rum. I wanted to die—or at least to take my murder mystery and flee to the isolation of the swimming pool. But I made myself walk into the center of the combined living room–bar, forced myself to smile and say good evening to the assembled twenty people. That was all I had to do.

A man immediately said, "Won't you sit down." Another offered a welcome drink, and a woman asked, "How long will you be here?" I started to relax. Soon I noticed a group of men eyeing me with a special kind of look. Not the glance that proclaims, "I like you, girl; I'd like to get to know you," but the look that says, "I like you, girl; I'd like to know you for special reasons."

Soon one of the men came over and introduced himself as Norman Jones of Pan American Airways Commercial Films Division. "I wonder if you'd like to take a day out of your vacation to pose for a commercial? We'd use you as the typical American girl."

I hesitated.

As a lure, Mr. Jones added, "You'll be paid, you know."

That did it. I spent a day posing as a typical American tourist in Haiti with my "real-life" husband, a typical red-blooded American male, portrayed by a Frenchman living in Pétionville. The commercial was so good, despite the fact that they cut out my best scene, that I collected $500 in residuals and even made the Ed Murrow "See It Now" program. Later, the Pan Am man informed me, "We liked your smile. You looked as if you were having such a good time." So when you arrive, don't hold back. Say good morning or good evening, but say something! And smile!

◖ *Wear comfortable, attractive clothes and don't think aloud about your hairdo.* Make sure you possess a few marvelous outfits in becoming colors, and then forget your wardrobe. And forget your hair. Let the place go to your head and keep

your hands off it. The beautiful mannequins with a look that
says, "Don't come near me—I'll spoil," have rotten times.
◖ *Sport an air of approachableness,* so that someone will want
to cross a crowded room to talk to you.
◖ *Make the best of rainy days.* They may not help your sun-
tan, but they are much better than sunny ones for making
friends quickly. On bad days, people generally congregate at
the hotel. Why not play hostess at a get-acquainted cocktail
party? Ask anyone appealing.
◖ *Lobby-hop after breakfast and at cocktail time.* You can
leaf through the magazines at the newsstand, read your paper
in full view, and talk to fellow guests. At St-Tropez, I started
making conversation with a blonde who was at La Pinède
with her husband. She insisted I call her when I got to Paris.
I wasn't going to do it, feeling that it would be presuming on
too brief an encounter, but one day I felt lonely and did. The
maid who answered said, "Oh, the American miss. Madame
has been waiting for your call since three days."
◖ *Do things.* Lying on the beach all the time won't get you
anything but dry skin. You can visit famous local sites. You
might want to organize a group. Ask the manager, "Is there
a group going to the caves?" Either an expedition will be
formed around you, or you'll join one that has already been
formed. Make use of the hotel's facilities. If guests have
privileges at the local golf course, take advantage. Don't look
around with an imploring "tennis, anyone?" look. Act. Speak
to the man at the desk and say that you want a partner for
tennis, golf, or skiing.
◖ *Don't feel left out.* At a resort, there are always people who
have been there three days longer. To you, they may look
like high-school cliques, and you may feel like the new girl
in town. Some may have been there two months. But that
girl who looks so at home probably just arrived yesterday,
had a date with the hotel's one bachelor last night, and now is

wondering what to do with herself tonight. Realize that if you feel excluded, you will be.

❡ *Don't judge people too quickly.* A resort is quite different from a cocktail party, where you accept or reject on sight. These people have traveled thousands of miles to get to a resort and are entitled to consideration by standards other than the superficial basis of clothes or accent.

❡ *Make the most of the hotel bar.* This is tough at the very large hotels, such as the Negresco in Nice, but in almost every other type, the bar at cocktail time is the place to meet and be met. Wear something pretty and, preferably, low cut. Stand in the doorway for a minute before you enter, so that you can see who's where and what's what. Pick your seat carefully. You do not have to sit next to the best-looking man in the place. You might even prefer to sit next to a girl who is your type and might prove to be good company. If nothing pans out fairly soon, leave the bar and go in to dinner. Under no circumstances be a Poor Pitiful Pearl desperately looking for someone. Act as if you merely want to have a drink in pleasant company before dinner. That technique leads to introductions.

❡ *A female friend* is helpful if you're staying in a place for a few days and encounter a kindred-soul type. Make it very casual, but you might meet for a drink before dinner. Don't commit yourself too deeply. You don't want to turn into a twosome.

In Antigua, I once met a charming woman, also from New York. The conversation turned to men, and after several days, we were cooperating to the point where we each racked our brains for suitable men to introduce to each other back home. She was tall and blond, with a penchant for sophisticated men-about-town. I am short and dark and prefer eggheads with Harvard degrees. I knew someone perfect for her, "a handsome businessman who loves nightclubs, a divine dancer."

She knew one for me, too, "an intellectual, reads all the time, fascinated by politics." We got more and more excited about these prospective heartthrobs, and it wasn't until the very last day that we discovered we were both talking about the same man.

❰ *At ski resorts*, the opening gambit is, "Where are you going to ski today?" Join a ski school. Don't consider a private instructor if you want to meet people; join a class and you'll have ten new friends immediately. Attend the tea dances, where you will meet everyone from fellow Americans to Australians on world tours. Sit down at a table and people will sit with you; often, you'll meet your dinner date at tea. Eat in your hotel at night; you can always join people from your ski class or the girl with whom you share a room. The waiters get to know you at the hotel. And so will fellow guests. Often, after-dinner coffee will be served in another room. Join the group.

❰ *At beach resorts, haunt the pool.* Action always centers there, even if a beautiful sandy beach lies just yards away. Girls have done everything to attract attention at midafternoon from walking with a heavy book to walking a Great Dane. The pool is *the* "meeting-people" place at the seashore.

No one can tell you where to go, but here are ideas that either I or friends who can be trusted have found to be special:

1. *Schloss Mittersill Club.* If you want to mingle with viscounts, baronesses, occasional dukes and duchesses, café-society figures, princes and princesses, without a pauper in sight, head for the swank Schloss Mittersill Club in Austria. You may go to the club as a nonmember guest just once, and your minimum stay is two days, maximum fourteen, and you should be recommended by a member or some authority known to the club. For $18 to $28 a day (single), you'll have a room with private bath, three meals with wine and beer; afternoon tea, the opportunity to play golf, steam in a sauna, practice lake swimming and water skiing, go glider flying and

partridge shooting. At night, you'll get dressed up in your flossiest, sexiest best, for everything is black tie during the club season, from May to October. Once you've been a guest, you must either fork over $1,000 for a life membership or never darken the doors again. For information, write: Manager, Schloss Mittersill Club, Mittersill, Land Salzburg, Austria.

2. *Le Manoir de Bécheron, Saché, France.* Have you dreamed of staying in a real château and yanking an antique bellpull to summon breakfast in bed? That's just what happened to me when I was a paying guest at Jacques Davidson's Manoir de Bécheron, two hours south of Paris. Jacques, an American history grad from the University of Wisconsin and former Office of War Information writer, is the son of Jo Davidson, famous American sculptor. He inherited the château from Dad, and to make ends meet, Jacques and his wife, Zabeth, started to take in PG's. You'll dine *en famille* with Jacques, his wife, and their kids; meet French journalists, broadcasters, and diplomats. A letter of introduction helps, but if you make yourself sound interesting enough, you may be accepted on your own. In defiance of European customs, you pay a flat rate to which no charge is added for mineral water, wine, *apéritifs,* or after-dinner brandy. Nearby neighbors are artists Alexander Calder and Max Ernst. You not only dine on gourmet cuisine, but are conveniently near all the castles of the Loire.

3. *Mount Kenya Safari Club in Africa.* From the manorial main house to the open, heated swimming pool, with the enormous hulk of Mount Kenya rising 17,040 feet behind it, this resort is pure swank. Screen actor William Holden is one of the men behind it. There are swans, peacocks, elegant villas, white telephones, a seven-thousand-foot altitude. There are more modest quarters, too, and it is possible to encamp at the club for as little as $15 a day, meals included. Big-game hunters can join the Mount Kenya Safari Club, which keeps

ten white hunters on call and promises to arrange instant
safaris. Hunters can go out in search of leopard, bongo, forest
hog, buffalo, and rhino in the nearby woods from 9:30 A.M.
to 5:30 P.M. and, after "working hours," return to the Holly-
wood-like luxury of the club grounds.

4. *The Club Méditerranée*. If you'd like to spend your vacation at an adult co-ed camp on foreign soil, complete with bar
and no chaperons, join the Club Méditerranée for a cut-rate
sporting vacation. Launched just fifteen years ago by a fun-
loving Frenchman, the Club Méditerranée has made travel to
distant places possible for thousands who could otherwise not
afford it. Today, there are 230,000 members, and the motto is
"Total Escape." The club has bases in such varied places as
twelve French beaches, the Italian mainland, Sicily and Sardinia, the island of Corfu, Yugoslavia's Dalmatian coast,
Greece's Peloponnesus, Israel, Tunisia, and Tahiti. Winter
facilities of the club are available from December through
Easter; in the summer season, from May through October.
Most of the club members are French-speaking; last summer,
360 Americans tried it. Members live in villages. Telephones,
radios, newspapers, and stiff collars are barred. Vactionists
indulge in sports once reserved for the wealthy—sailing, water-
skiing, deep-sea diving, skiing. From the moment a member
pays for his trip, he doesn't have to put his hand in his pocket
again. For bar expenses, he just buys a necklace of multicolored plastic beads to use instead of money. Average cost
for two weeks is $220, including plane fare from and return
to Paris and *vin ordinaire* with all your dinners. Don't expect
top comfort or VIP's. Most of the people will be secretaries,
clerks, lawyers or Minor League diplomats on vacation, and
it may be difficult if you can't speak French. For further information, get in touch with Hall-Ross Travel Groups, Ltd., 342
Madison Avenue, New York 17, New York.

5. *The Robert F. Warner Company*. When a travel agent
says, "The Robert Warner office represents this hotel," you can

be sure that the hotel will be elegant, expensive, and good. So be smart. Acquire the booklet "Distinguished Hotels of Europe" from your travel agent, read through it, see what you like, and then write to the Warner office (630 Fifth Avenue, New York, New York, 10036) for further information on the Schloss Fuschl near Salzburg, Austria, a dream castle in a fairy-tale setting that offers horse-drawn sleighing in winter and riding, swimming, and the festival itself in summer; the Miramare Beach Hotel on the Greek island of Rhodes, where you can blend resort life with Byzantine antiquities; the modern Santavenere Hotel in Potenza, Italy, where you can find your place in the sun south of Naples; or for those who seek the international set, the Regina Isabella on the isle of Ischia, Italy.

CHAPTER 11

The Lure of the Offbeat

Should the woman traveling alone venture off the beaten track?

What can she expect to find when she gets there?

Is the risk of discomfort, irritation, and loneliness worth the reward?

Thousands of female travelers ask themselves these questions annually as they weigh the glories of the grand tour against the charm of little-known curiosities, the assurance of seeing what they expect to see against the challenge of the unknown, the trouble-free comfort of European capitals against the frustration of finding—and getting to—a truly exotic locale.

If you are traveling alone and think it would be "fun" to get off the Main Line of travel and into the hinterland, you must realize that this type of adventuring is not for everyone. Essentially, it is for the *traveler* rather than the *tourist*.

There is nothing wrong with being a tourist. But a tourist is passive. She goes to the Louvre because it is the thing to do. She weekends at Capri because "everyone does." She dines at France's La Pyramide in Vienne because it is the top three-star restaurant in the *Guide Michelin*. She takes the advice of tour operators, travel agents, and guidebooks.

The traveler is active. Sometimes her derring-do has been acquired by the confidence that comes from travel experience, but just as often she has been born with the need to make things happen to her. She searches strenuously to encounter new people, adventures, experiences. She can be any age, for the need for the unusual and the bizarre involves attitude, not arteries. She possesses courage and curiosity—topped with a dash of craziness. She craves made-to-order travel—not assembly-line touring.

These psychological characteristics of the would-be adventuress are not enough to ensure success. If you are a woman traveling alone who wants to get away from the security of big cities, deluxe souvenir-mill resorts, and commercial tourist sights in favor of the unself-conscious picturesque, you must possess certain traits:

❬ *You must be hooked by geography.* There is no point in going two thousand miles out of your way to see a wonder of the world if you'd really prefer to wave hello to fellow Americans in the Ritz bar.

❬ *You must have the time, interest, and inclination to read beforehand.* Just plain curiosity is not enough to make the adventure worthwhile. It's senseless to see the ruins of Angkor Wat in Cambodia if you don't even know that a *wat* is a temple.

❬ *You must be able to live easily and beautifully with yourself.* Often, that's the only company you'll have. I once took the boat from Piraeus, Greece, to Poros, a get-away-from-it-all spot two hours from the mainland. I went just for the day, equipped with only a bathing suit and a dress for dinner. Off the boat I stepped at Poros, prepared for I-didn't-know-what. Two little boys asked, "Where to, lady?"

"I don't know," said I truthfully.

"Hotel *première classe?*"

"Why not?"

So the two little Greeks put me in Daddy's rowboat and

rowed me to the villa of Mme. Dragoumis, an eighty-year-old Athenian gentlewoman who took paying guests. The hotel, a Victorian house fronting the Aegean, was charming; the library was filled with nineteenth-century classics and thrillers, and there was even an eighteenth-century mahogany library stepladder. But neither Mme. Dragoumis nor the ten "guests" from Germany, Italy, and Austria spoke English, French, or Spanish. As a result, everything was pure Greek to me. But I liked it so much that I stayed for three days—rereading Wilkie Collins, sunning myself by the sea, and nodding pleasantly to my dining companions as we consumed *moussaka* from separate tables. I might never have left this island Shangri-La if I had not been still paying room rent at my Athens hotel.

❰ *You must be prepared to be stranded.* If your boss will greet you with a "Susan, you're fired" when you show up four days late, don't make your final stopping place an offbeat spot that has a single means of transportation out. For boats and planes to out-of-the-way areas have a way of not sticking to schedules. I spent four extra days in Cozumel, Yucatán, waiting for the supposedly daily plane to bear me back to civilization in Mérida and thence home.

❰ *You must be willing to eat anything.* Well, let's say almost anything. You may not have to dine on flaming sheeps' eyes at a Bedouin feast, but certainly no urbane headwaiter is going to bow low and say, "Will madame have the pressed duck or the *filet en croûte?*" in the middle of Mongolia, where the standard drink is *koumiss*—fermented mare's milk. If you can't take shark fins, bird's-nest soup, or fried grasshoppers, better stick to the steak spots on the Champs-Elysées and Piccadilly.

❰ *You must be ready to give up standard luxuries.* Maybe you'll be the one in a million who rates an invitation to stay at a prince's palace, but far more likely your room in some remote outpost will be bathless, the mattress will be lumpy, and the nocturnal insects may be bigger than the lizards put in your room to eat them. The new Desert Inn, which brings luxury to the middle of Israel's Negev, is an exception. For the most part, hotel beds, lighting facilities, ventilation, heating, and plumbing in offbeat areas are not in the style to which we Americans have grown accustomed. If you are looking for air conditioning and a Hilton Hotel atmosphere, go where you can find them.

❰ *Expect primitive sanitary facilities.* In many areas of the world, a U.S.-style toilet would be a miraculous object that the local people wouldn't know how to use. Once, between Delphi and Athens, my Greek host stopped his car at a low pink-stucco house bordered by an elaborate garden and said with understanding, "Perhaps you would care to wash your hands here." A well-dressed woman led me past polished antique furniture, ancient icons, and Oriental hangings to the bathroom. Behind the locked door, I spent what seemed like an eternity hunting for a toilet, until I realized what the grille in the floor was really for. Even after I had used it, I wasn't sure.

Years ago, before the Greek island of Mykonos had achieved its present popularity, I arrived there to find the hotel full. A village family rented me a large, dark room devoid of electricity and plumbing. The only light came from a small oil lamp that was either constantly running out of fuel or threatening to explode. The privy was outside the street door and very open to the public.

On still another occasion, I was stuck on an island, which shall be nameless, where there were no facilities whatsoever, and half my day was spent running from pillar to post in search of privacy. Taking a bath was simpler. I walked along the seashore carrying my cloth and soap until I found a piece of deserted beach.

❰ *Pick up a few words of the local language.* This technique works well all over the world. It can win friends for you, influence people, and help you get where you want to go. In tourist-traveled areas, it isn't necessary. Some helpful soul will always come to your rescue. But in a remote Turkish village where no one speaks English except the schoolteacher, who's on vacation, it helps if you can say a few necessary phrases like "How much?" and "Too much," and "Thank you."

Now that you are prepared for a hinterland holiday, let's talk about what you will get in the terms of personal rewards: ¶ *You'll mix with natives.* The typical tourist has contact with hotels, nightclubs, railroad stations, customs officials, foreign-exchange windows in banks, guides, and shopkeepers—all intrinsic parts of a country and its people, true, but very special parts, managed by very special people. They are Frenchmen, Englishmen, Japanese, and Indians, but they are Frenchmen, Englishmen, Japanese, and Indians who have been trained to deal with visiting Americans, Italians, Argentines, and Mexicans. When you go to a country or a city or a remote village where tourism as a business is practically nonexistent, you are bound to get a totally different impression. Even such a simple thing as purchasing aspirin in a strange language can be an adventure. You become a temporary part of the country. You'll have firsthand travel experience.

¶ *You'll see an untouched world.* The American way of life has spread all over the world. Cities throughout the globe show Hollywood movies, blaze neon lights, and build embryo skyscrapers. In Tokyo, pretty Japanese girls wear black tights; in Paris, signs advertise "Quick Lunch." When you leave the beaten track, you see life indigenous to the country instead of an elaborately contrived indirect experience designed just for the tourist. Furthermore, you are welcomed as a visitor instead of being wooed for your cash in hand. You become an object of curiosity, the answerer of questions. In parts of Japan where the "honey wagon" is still the only sewage system, people will ask whether it is true that in your country "such things" are carried off in iron tubes.

¶ *You don't have to worry about being alone.* When a woman

goes to an offbeat place, her single status is an asset. Enjoyable as Paris, London, and Rome may be, they can be difficult without introductions or other means of meeting people. You can't have a good time in a strange city just seeing sights— unless you are an architect or have a beau back home. But in a remote area, you don't have to fret about what you'll do at night. Usually there is nothing to do. If there is, everyone does it together. Seeing another American in the hotel lobby is just like bumping into your college roommate ten years after graduation. And unless you are a gorgon, local males will automatically turn their eyes in your direction. They may never have seen a blonde, a woman without a burnoose (the Arab all-enveloping cloak), or a female strolling alone. And you *can* talk—even if conversation is of the "Me Tarzan–You Jane" variety.

❨ *You'll meet kindred souls from home.* If you're the type of individual who will make a special trip to the Caspian Sea to see where caviar comes from or who will venture from London to New Delhi by bus, chances are the compatriots you meet on these expeditions will share your interests.

❨ *You'll dine out on your hegira for years to come.* Ever since Scheherazade, men have loved women who can tell tales. Casual sentences such as, "When I hired a houseboat in Kashmir . . . ," "That reminds me of the time I was paddling a canoe in Bora-Bora . . . ," and, "I had such fun hunting tigers in Bengal," guarantee you social success at dinners, dances, receptions, teas, housewarmings, confirmations, christenings, brunches, and office Christmas parties. You'll achieve the reputation of being interesting. And you will be, too.

In my search for the offbeat, I have skied in the Andes and fainted away from the altitude, slept in a Mexican hammock for a week because I missed the mainland boat, and caught my own fish lunches in a Chilean sea resort. But my most unusual off-the-beaten-track adventure came when I took the road to Samarkand.

As a matter of fact, Alexander the Great and I have a lot in common. He went by horse in 329 B.C., and I by jet in A.D. 1959. He camped in a tent en route, and I stayed in third-rate hotels. He wore kingly robes, and I sported natty cottons. He wanted to conquer the whole world, and I just wanted to see the world. But we both got to Samarkand the hard way.

I went because I remembered a poem from Miss Brower's English class at A. B. Davis High School. By James Elroy Flecker, the poem had the haunting lines: "For the lust of knowing what should not be known . . . we make the Golden Journey to Samarkand." When, in the spring of 1959, I had a chance for a free trip to Moscow, I found that more than anything in the world, I lusted to go to Samarkand, the onetime "Queen City of Asia."

My difficulties started when I began trying to find out how to get there.

Mr. Sherimagaze, the Red Star travel agent in New York, rotund, rosy, and with a few tufts of blond hair combed over his Khrushchev-like scalp, frankly thought I was crazy. "Why you want to go to Samarkand in August? Much too hot. You like it better in Estonia."

I told him all about the poem, but he wasn't interested.

"We Russians go to Samarkand for exile," he added stonily. "Why not a nice trip to Kiev and a ride down the Volga?"

It took effort, but finally Mr. Sherimagaze and I worked out a mutually attractive expedition: work for a week in Moscow; three days in Leningrad; fly to Yalta for sunbathing on the Black Sea; boat trip to the resort of Sochi and more tanning; fly to Tbilisi, Georgia, so that I could get a look at the country where Stalin came from; on to Tashkent, then Samarkand, and back to Moscow.

My first feeling of impending disaster came when he handed me the bill. My twenty-three days on my own in the Soviet Union, at the top tourist rate of $30 a day, totaled up to the whopping figure of $690, padded further by the $284 Moscow-

Samarkand round trip. My "free" trip was costing me $1,000 before I even left New York. Samarkand is in the Soviet Union, but it is two thousand miles south of the Kremlin, just above Afghanistan, and "practically touching" Tibet. My youthful fancy was turning into very costly fact. *For contrary to popular belief, offbeat traveling is expensive.*

It can also be difficult, uncomfortable, annoying. I'm sure Alexander had a much more comfortable ride atop that pet horse of his than I did in the special charter flight that took me to Moscow.

In high spirits, all of us participating in the fashion show at the American Exhibition in Moscow gathered at the airport for the takeoff. We were a collection of bleached blond, no-hipped models, second-echelon business leaders (the first-string people were all going first class or staying home in the comfort of the country), reporters, fashion authorities, and the frenzied men and women who were actually producing the show. Eight hours and some drinks later, we were still at the airport as the loudspeaker boomed, "There will be an additional delay on Flight 897 for Moscow." For the authorities had forgotten an all-important detail—to get permission for the plane to land in the Soviet Union.

As soon as that situation had been resolved, another problem arose. There was a seat for every passenger, but no room for the 150 changes of costume that had to go along. The passengers had to arrive the next day or there would be no fashion show, but how could there be a fashion show without fashion?

Resourceful authorities took space away from the passengers to give to the clothes. By cutting inches off the normal distance between the knees and the back of the seat in front of the knees, there would be room for clothes *and* people.

Have you ever tried spending twelve hours in a space half the size of the average airline tourist seat? Don't. Roaming the aisles was impossible, and getting to the ladies' room was

as difficult as fighting your way through Yankee Stadium
crowds for a hot dog in the seventh game of the World Series.
The aisles had been taken over by the vice-presidents of Bergdorf Goodman, Mahara Knitting Mills, Wear Forever Stocking
Company, and Allison Dress Corporation. Their six-foot
frames, padded by profits, were managing much better prone
than upright. I kept wishing that my two seatmates, a managing editor of a Manhattan trade paper and the promotion
director of a West Coast dress firm, would follow their examples.

Thirty hours later, following a change of aircraft in Copenhagen to a plane that did have permission to land, we arrived
at Moscow Airport. My first five minutes on Russian soil were
spent doing standing-up exercises.

From the inefficiency of the trip over, everything suddenly
became terribly organized. Two by two, just as in Noah's
Ark, we cleared through customs via Intourist and were
herded into long, sleek Russian limousines. I had dreamed of
staying at the National Hotel, across from the Bolshoi, with
its elegant Czarist décor and a view of the Kremlin. But
my fate was the Ukraina, a shoddily built tower that might
have been the illegitimate offspring of a skyscraper and a
cathedral. The lobby was spacious and empty, for it was 2
A.M.

Wearily, the managing editor and I plodded across the
marble floors and up to the desk, where a tired, worn woman,
with the map of Russia on her seamed face, was waiting.

"Passports," she demanded.

Wordlessly, we handed them over. I remember wondering
whether I would ever see mine again.

"Married?" she asked, pointing to the two of us.

Smiling awkwardly, we shook our heads.

The registration clerk brought out two keys and motioned
us to the elevator.

Tired as I was, I realized that I was in town to get a story, and I conscientiously made a move. "May I see the telephone book?" I requested, thinking it might give me a head start in the morning if I got the desk clerk to find a few numbers for me now.

She shook her head.

"Why not?" I demanded, wondering whether this was a sign of things to come.

My companion was more help. "There is no such thing as a telephone book here."

"What do you mean, no telephone book?"

He declared it to be an absolute fact. "They don't have telephone books in Russia. The commissars may have directories, but not the people."

I gave up for the moment. Wearily, we walked slowly toward the elevator. Ten minutes later, we were still waiting. The elevators at the Hotel Ukraina seem to move on a time schedule of their own. Finally, I got to my room and to bed.

I felt more at home the next morning when I went down to the Intourist office in the lobby. It was filled with Americans wearing sport shirts and carrying cameras. The American Exhibition in Sokolniki Park had brought out antibiotic specialists, a delegation of Florida schoolteachers, a group of American governors, thirty Indiana farmers, the complete cast and crew of the "Ed Sullivan Show," and Richard Nixon.

For the next week, I fought officialdom. My assignment was to talk with a typical Russian teen-ager. Intourist, the government press agency, the fair heads, and the local teen-agers themselves seemed to be united in their joint determination to send me home to get fired. Nobody would let me talk to anyone. My only consolation was that Vice-President Nixon was having his troubles with Khrushchev at the same time. By the time I got the interview, found a photographer to take pictures of my seventeen-year-old interviewee, and sent my material back to New York with a personal friend, I was a nervous wreck. All I longed for was to get to the peace and history of Samarkand.

The Hotel Europa in Leningrad was much more what I thought a Russian hotel would be like. My room had a sofa upholstered in red plush, the windows were hung with gold-velvet-and-lace curtains, and on the bed was a white-linen envelope through which you could see a colored blanket. The final stuffy touch was a big round table in the middle of the room covered with a red cloth and holding a large glass compote—in which was my room key.

By then I had learned a few things about getting things done *à la russe*. The minute I unpacked, I hurried to the Intourist desk in the lobby to meet my daily guide and to check on reservations for my trip to Samarkand.

My guide was introduced only by her first name, Nita. Her face was pale, with no trace of makeup or lipstick; her eyes, somber brown, and her hair, which she wore in a tight bun scooped to the nape of her neck, was auburn red. She had a figure like a Coke bottle.

I got straight to the point. "My schedule says I leave Friday for Yalta. Is that all set?" I asked.

Willingly enough, she looked through some papers on the desk. "Everything is fine. Friday you fly to Yalta."

Reassured, I set off on a sight-seeing expedition to the Hermitage, the Winter Palace, and the Museum of Non-religious Art. But I couldn't really enjoy the palaces, museums, department stores, monuments, and green grass along the banks of the Neva. Some inner feeling of disaster, probably prompted by my red-tape experiences in Moscow, kept warning me that there was trouble ahead. For three days, every morning when she arrived and every evening when she took off for home, I would check with Nita. "Are you sure everything is all right on my Yalta flight?"

"Stop worrying," she would say.

The day of the flight, I made one final check. "I leave to-night," I reminded her. "Is everything all right?"

Nita went to the desk and her face puckered. "They say they have no reservation for you," she reported sadly.

I panicked. "What do you mean? I've been checking for three days."

Summoning my fighting mood, I strode up to the tough-looking Intourist boss, a hefty female dressed in cheap voile and open-toed sandals.

She regarded me with stony eyes. "I am sorry, but there was an error in your reservations. There is no seat for you on the Yalta plane."

It was too much. I had never really wanted to go to Russia in the first place.

The Intourist chief's lower lip curled in dislike as she sniffed at me. "In two weeks we can get you a seat on the Yalta plane," she offered.

Suddenly, I heard myself speaking fishwife fashion, threatening all sorts of disasters if I didn't get on the plane that night. "How can I wait two weeks?" I shrieked. "I'm due back on the job then."

My sobs didn't move her, but maybe the mention of the job did. All Russians are work-oriented.

She suggested: "You go to Moscow at five o'clock in the morning tomorrow. Lots of planes go to Yalta from Moscow; Intourist there help you out. You give me your ticket and I fix."

Wordlessly, I handed over my elaborate ticket to Samarkand and stops in between. At that point, my spirits were lower than Gorki's lower depths. I had come to Russia for a month—not as a permanent guest.

At seven o'clock next morning, I was back in Moscow. The airport was deserted. No one from Intourist was on the job, and no one else understood English. I was ticketless and terrified.

Finally, an Intourist representative showed up. He was a personable, intelligent-looking young man, with fair complexion, broad cheeks, and a short, bristling crew cut.

I briefed him.

"Where is your ticket?" he interrupted efficiently.

"I gave it to the girl in Leningrad."

His blue eyes viewed me skeptically. "No ticket? I can do nothing for you."

I was lost. Suddenly, I longed for the security of Rome or Paris.

I screamed at the helpless official. "Look, you get me out of here somehow! Your people took my ticket. It's your responsibility to get it back. I want it now. I want to get out of here!"

He shrugged. "There is nothing I can do."

It was too much. I thought I could cope with any travel experience, but being stranded forever in Moscow without a ticket brought on the first fit of hysterics of my life. Grabbing the guide, I started yelling, "You can't do this to me!"

A crowd gathered, mouths open, eyes bulging.

"Be quiet, please," pleaded Mr. Intourist.

I couldn't. Oblivious of the people looking at me, I flung my arms about, sobbing, "I want to go home."

The sympathetic, noncomprehending onlookers muttered to themselves. The Intourist representative stood in stony silence.

Without thinking of my words, I declared wildly, "Things must have been better under the Czar! They couldn't have been worse!"

That did it. The Intourist man took one frightened look over his shoulder to make sure that the ghost of Lenin had not overheard me, then disappeared. In a few minutes, he was back, smiling. It was evident that many things had happened quickly.

"Everything is all right now," he stated cheerfully. "Here is your ticket. You go to Simferopol on the eleven-o'clock plane.

A guide will meet you and escort you to Yalta. Your guide, Gallya, will come soon to accompany you to Samarkand."

I looked up through my tears. "I thought you said you didn't have the ticket."

The representative almost split his face smiling. "Now I find. Come. We go have some vodka and caviar. We want you to like Russia."

My evocation of the Czars had accomplished a minor revolution. From then on, I never had a moment's trouble in the Soviet Union. Every day, fresh fruit arrived in my hotel room. Desk clerks hailed, "We are so glad to meet you." A capitalistic challenge had aroused communism.

In Yalta, I had a chance to meet the people. Every night, the women of the Black Sea town would gather in front of the Intourist Hotel to question the guests. In my case, they were mostly interested in my shoes, which were red, thin, and pointed. One woman remarked, "Our feet are not pointed like yours." She seemed surprised when I yanked off my shoes and showed her that my feet didn't come to a sharp point either.

I started asking questions of my own. We found a common interest in cooking. I had always wanted to learn how to make chicken Kiev. Soon the local women and I were exchanging recipes every night. For string bean and mushroom casserole, I got shashlik; for chicken with white wine and grapes, I got the top-secret recipe for chicken Kiev.

Surprisingly, I was starting to enjoy myself. One of the women took me to the beach. "Take your bathing suit; we will change there," she directed. When we arrived, I looked in vain for a bathhouse. Suddenly, my companion took off her clothes —in full view of the entire beach—and donned her bathing suit. I did likewise. To my surprise, not a soul—male or female —even glanced in my direction.

When I arrived in Sochi, my next stop, the desk clerk gave me a hearty welcome. "Your guide is here waiting for you."

Having a guide of my own was pretty special. Intourist used to give all first-class, $30-a-day tourists full-time guides, but with the recent influx of tourists, this had become impossible. Only a hysterical outburst could have produced a guide to travel around the country with me.

Gallya Guskova was certainly different. She was tall, slim, blond, animated, and the prettiest girl I had seen in Russia so far—until she smiled. Then I saw that she had three front teeth made of steel. She was certainly more frivolous than most young Moscow women I had met. She immediately wanted to try my lipstick, and she asked me how I set my hair. "Come to my room and I'll show you," I offered. She was delighted, but puzzled by the wire rollers. She had never seen one, and I knew then what my gift to Gallya would be at the end of the trip.

Off we went to the fancy private beach at Sochi. There were several sections—one for men to swim nude, one for women to swim nude, and a co-ed beach for bathing-suit wearers. I chose the latter. Gallya immediately deserted me in favor of a basketball game (Russian girls are terribly athletic). But I didn't lack for company. Three Czechoslovakian men approached. They tried me in Czech, Russian, and finally hit on French. When I answered, they were delighted and launched into a long discussion about politics. I kept thinking, Is this really me, sitting on the Sochi beach in the Crimea, criticizing Russian ideology in French with three Czechs?

As soon as they left, a young woman came over. "I noticed your English book," she said, "and I wanted to talk to you." She was a Moscow secretary on a month's paid vacation at a local rest home. She insisted on buying me a watermelon, so that "you will like us." Away from officialdom, the Russians were certainly a different people.

My next stop, Tbilisi, was fun. Tbilisi (now the official name for what was formerly called Tiflis) is the capital of Georgia, high in the Caucasus Mountains. The minute I arrived at the hotel, three Americans jumped up from their chairs. "Welcome, compatriot!" they chanted. They were a socialite schoolteacher from Philadelphia and a globe-trotting doctor and his wife from Los Angeles. Gallya immediately adopted the group, and I practiced the Russian philosophy by sharing my wealth. United only by the fact that we were all in Tbilisi together, the teacher, the California couple, and I became fast friends.

Another nice thing about Tbilisi was the men. That overworked adjective "gorgeous" is the only way to describe these tall, dark, and handsome gentlemen, who looked as if they should all be at least princes. We had no difficulty in communication; liquor was our common denominator. I had learned the Russian toast *"Mir i drujba"* (peace and friendship), and I found it an open sesame to friendship. At dinner, we tourists and Gallya sat at one table; three stunning Georgian males at another. First they sent over a bottle of wine. *"Mir i drujba,"* said I.

We drank. We waved glasses. Soon the three Georgian gentlemen were at our table. The dialogue went something like this:

"Amerikanski?"

"Yes."

"Tbilisi—gut?"

"Wonderful!" This with a happy grin.

"You," said one, pointing at me; "me," pointing at his heart. Then with a great effort, "Marry."

I had received my first and only proposal on Soviet soil. He was so handsome that for a moment I was torn between id versus ideology. Ideology won, and Gallya and I went on with our journey.

Finally, we arrived in Samarkand. First mentioned in 329 B.C., Samarkand, long known to the Greeks as Maracanda, was conquered by Genghis Khan in A.D. 1219. Tamerlane (or Timur) the Mongol took the city in 1369, built most of its

famous monuments, and made it the capital of his kingdom.
Samarkand was opened to Western tourists just a few years
ago. All of them, including Mrs. Eleanor Roosevelt, Adlai
Stevenson, and Eric Johnston, until recently stayed at the
dingy, doddering old Registan Hotel, which rates third class
even in the Soviet Union and is equal to the worst in the
United States.

The minute I took a look around the city, I knew that all the
expense and exasperation in getting to Samarkand had been
worthwhile. Through the streets parade masses of Asiatic
peoples—Uzbeks, Tajiks, Tartars, Cossacks, and Armenians—
plus a sprinkling of Russians. From low adobe houses in the
brown, rolling hills walked Moslem women in white sheets,
their faces covered with stiff, black horsehair veils. They come
out only during the daylight hours; at night they stay at home.
The men wear a quilted long-sleeved cloak of many colors
with their *tubeteikas* (skullcaps). In the bazaar, the Uzbeks,
with their black turbans and flashing black moustaches, sit
cross-legged in the teahouse, nibbling skewered meats, sipping
bitter green tea. Behind the bazaar is the Bibi Khanum
mosque, a memorial to Tamerlane's favorite wife, for whom it
is named.

Legend says Bibi Khanum was a bad girl. She had the
mosque built as a surprise for Tamerlane when he was away
on one of his military deals. But the architect was in no hurry
to finish the job, for he had fallen in love with Bibi Khanum.
He finally agreed to finish the mosque if she would kiss him.
She offered him many other women, telling him that all women
are alike. To prove the point, she sent him forty varicolored
eggs. "Taste them," said she, "and you will see that they will
taste the same."

For this, the amorous architect had an apt answer. He
showed her two jugs, one filled with brandy, the other with
water. "They look the same, but they taste different," he explained. "One is hot and one is cold. So do women vary, and

I want to kiss you." He won his point, and he kissed Bibi Khanum so hard that he left a mark.

When Tamerlane got back home, exhausted from his hard wars, he saw the completed building, but he also saw the mark on his wife's face. Enraged, he chased the architect, who climbed the minaret and disappeared into the sky. At that point, the now-wise Tamerlane ordered all women to veil their faces.

"A nice story, but not true," scoffed the Intourist guide who told it.

I knew I was in the center of Central Asia when dinnertime came at the Registan Hotel. Gallya and I were the only women in sight; I was the only tourist. Unbothered by the flies that were dining happily on the same skewered lamb, the Uzbeks ate with tremendous appetite. We couldn't. It was seven o'clock when we left the hotel. As we walked the streets, drunken Uzbeks breathed in our faces what I'm sure were proposals to join their harems. Gallya was frightened. "I don't like this country," she declared. "I want to go back to Moscow."

We found a bookstall, and since I had run out of reading matter, even a battered copy of *The Five Little Peppers and How They Grew*, in English, looked as good as a new best seller to me.

Bored, Gallya left me to my own devices. As there was nothing else to do, I went to bed in my tiny bedroom with the overhead bare ceiling light, the mattress stuffed with straw, the grimy bathroom with clumps of raw cement patched around the fixtures, and huge cockroaches walking the floor.

I was reading all about the five little Peppers when I heard a strange wailing sound. For a minute, I thought I was hearing Uzbekistan fire engines, but when I rushed to the window, I realized that it was Oriental music. The orchestra made me feel that I had suddenly landed in the middle of the Arabian Nights. At least fifty men, lying on pallets, were busily tooting

away on peculiar Oriental reeds that gleamed in the starlit
night. Looking closer, I started. Each of the musicians was
stark naked!

They looked up and saw me peering out from my third-
floor vantage point. The noise grew louder. One or two of the
men waved. I realized that they were Uzbekistan wayfarers
who couldn't afford the bed-and-board charges at the Registan
and who were sleeping in the open, just as their forefathers
had done in the time of Alexander the Great and Tamerlane.
But there was one modern touch foreign to those days when
women stayed home and sent their men off to war. These men
were serenading me!

Routing Gallya out of bed, I made her come to my room.
"Look," I said ecstatically, "isn't it the most romantic thing
you ever saw?"

Gallya regarded me with scorn. "Silly girl!" She shrugged.
"I do not understand your psychology. You did not like our
wonderful new buildings in Tashkent, but these poor people,
who probably have no education, you think are interesting.
You are a child!"

When I first arrived home from Russia, my feelings were
mixed. A year later, I attended a rerelease of the Russian film
Ten Days That Shook the World, based on the classic by the
American convert John Reed. Suddenly, I was tense with excitement. As the camera focused on the Kremlin, I thought,
"I was there." Even Moscow was beginning to look good to
me. I was forgetting the annoyances and remembering only
the good things.

To all offbeat travelers, I caution, *don't make an immediate
judgment.* Give the trip time to settle. It's rather like shaking
a cup of stagnant water. The things that come to the surface
can be observed with delight, surprise, amazement, or indif-
ference.

I sometimes look back at the foolish girl who went to the

Soviet Union expecting to find the gaiety and charm of Czarist days, looking for real-life characters straight out of Tolstoi, and skipping thoughtlessly over the psychological changes of revolution. It is like looking into one of those triple mirrors in department-store dressing rooms. I saw the things in myself that usually only a stranger sees—and I didn't like it.

Samarkand may not be your cup of tea. But there are many underexplored areas, or even unusual things to do, in spots nearer to familiar capitals. For example:

⟪ Go to Lambaréné (Republic of Gabon) and stay at the Relais Hotel (fifteen rooms, thirty beds). You can probably succeed in watching Albert Schweitzer at work even if you don't meet him.

⟪ If you've strong legs and a yen to rough it, travel to Beirut, Lebanon, and take a walking tour. It takes two to four weeks and can be arranged through the local tourist office. You'll travel in a group with other tourists—and donkeys—and stay in little villages that turn the clock back hundreds of years.

⟪ Venture to Machu Picchu, Peru, and see the awe-inspiring, centuries-old ruins of a pre-Incan city with houses, temples, and a cemetery. These ruins, high in the Andes, have not been restored, but remain as Dr. Hiram Bingham of Yale found them back in 1911. You can travel by train from Cuzco to Machu Picchu, the former ancient capital of the Incas, 11,207 feet above sea level.

⟪ Fly to Addis Ababa in Ethiopia. Try to arrange an audience with Emperor Haile Selassie through USIA. If you're an ophthalmologist, he may send for you.

⟪ If your pockets are lined with gold, go on a shikar (big-game hunt) in India. Cost runs about $200 a day. The Maharaja of Cooch Behar conducts one annually in Assam; so does the Nizam of Hyderabad. The shikars take from one to two weeks and are limited to eight to ten persons. You live in luxury, sleep in white tents plunked down in the middle of the

jungle, with dozens of servants. If you like this sort of wild
life, try to wangle letters of introduction to other maharajas
and you can have a whole new social life.

⟨ If you are a culture-seeker, take one of the popular high-
brow "odyssey" cruises run by Swan's Hellenic Tours of London. Swan's has little interest in American trade, the cruises
are "something one hears about through friends," and they are
booked up years in advance by British who want to see the
Greek end of the Mediterranean the classical way. Ships of
the cruise are Spartan, and the food is indifferent, but lecturers from Oxford give daily briefings on everything from
Mycenae to the treasury of Atreus. Prices are fairly high, accommodations are not luxurious, and the boat is filled with
elderly spinsters and intellectual professors. It is the only trip
I know of where a questionnaire asks you to list your degrees.
Lecturers have included Lawrence Durrell and Sir Maurice
Bowra. My informant says, "The most interesting trip I ever
took." Don't worry about preparation. Swan's supplies you
with a bibliography before the trip.

⟨ Travelers in France looking for a sporty way of seeing the
countryside in summer can take tours by horseback. Organized
in 1961 by one of the world's most famous riding groups, the
Cavaliers Arvernes, the unusual trotting tours include visits
to many historic towns in the Auvergne region of central
France. Trips vary from eight to ten days; $16 daily covers
hotel accommodations, all meals, and, of course, the horse.
You ride ten miles a day for two consecutive days, rest the
third. To qualify, riders must show certification of adequate
riding ability from an acceptable source. For further information, write to the Cavaliers Arvernes, Place du Mas, Ceyrat
(Puy-de-Dôme), France.

⟨ Ireland isn't all bargains at Shannon, pubs in Dublin, and
haute couture at Sybil Connolly. See what's worth seeing in
the center of Ireland on a "Floatel." This is a small, comfortable riverboat that takes twelve passengers—no children. The

"Floatel" cruises the whole length of the great river Shannon, starting from Athlone, one week up- and one week downriver. It always starts on Friday. The upriver cruise takes you through a string of romantic lakes (you can go swimming in some) plus a stop at Lough Key. The tour also throws in a coach tour to Galway City and part of Connemara. The downriver cruise goes through Lough Derg to Killaloe, features a visit to Limerick and to the strange monastic ruins called Clonmacnoise. Cost is about $80 for a week—plus the bar check. Reserve through Irish River Floatels, Ltd., Athlone.

⟨ Go to the "rose-red city of Petra, half as old as time," in Jordan. Now alive with lizards and blossoming with oleanders, Petra was lost for six centuries until its rediscovery by the Anglo-Swiss traveler Burckhardt in 1812. You'll feel just like Lawrence of Arabia as you ride on horseback through the narrow track called the Siq, the rock-scooped passage to Petra, a city carved from rock mountains, a half mile wide, a mile and a half long. In the shadow of the temple, there is a camping site, run by the Philadelphia Hotel of Amman, where guests may spend the night. You can also bed down in some of the tomblike, rock-cut dwellings that are arranged as bedrooms. Petra is accessible from September 15 to October 30 and from March 15 to May 31. The trip to Petra from Jordanian Jerusalem costs about $55 for everything.

⟨ Follow the route first navigated by Magellan in 1520. This unusual and beautiful voyage, little known to North Americans, takes the tourist three thousand miles from Buenos Aires down the Atlantic coastline of Argentina through the Strait of Magellan to Punta Arenas, Chile—the southernmost city in the world. The trip takes you through the narrow channels of the hundreds of islands of Tierra del Fuego to scenic Chilean ports and finally to Valparaiso. The whole trip can be made in a month on the clean, comfortable ships of the Compañia Chilena de Navegación Interoceánica. Consult your travel agent.

❬ If you have time and little money, take the bus trip from London to New Delhi.

❬ Climb Fujiyama in Japan. Although many women are among the thousands of Japanese pilgrims who make the climb every year—some of them seventy and over—the 12,400-foot altitude makes it a stiff day's walk, and the accommodations en route are hardly deluxe. Like Popocatepetl in Mexico, the beautiful snowcapped cone of Mount Fuji is an old volcano, but it hasn't erupted in more than 250 years. The trip can be arranged in either Tokyo or Yokohama. The starting point is a forty-mile drive from the latter.

❬ Go to Mount Sinai, where Moses received the Ten Commandments. (Make arrangements in Cairo.) The trip takes you across the Red Sea, where the Children of Israel passed on their flight from Egyptian bondage. You stop overnight at a guesthouse on the Red Sea. You carry your own food and water, and two cars must travel together in case one gets stuck in the desert. At your destination (you'll find a Greek Orthodox monastery), climb Mount Sinai and look out over desert. You'll find no golden calf when you come down.

CHAPTER 12

Tours

"Guided tours are only for innocents abroad. Once you've been overseas, you can always manage better on your own."

"Too much herding. I want to go where I want, when I want."

"No one sophisticated, interesting, or enterprising would ever take a tour."

These three statements by three different women would seem to condemn the package tour. All three are wrong. Pre-packaged travel can be pleasant and productive, but only if the woman who tries it knows what to expect and gives attention to *who else* is going as well as *where* she is bound.

What are the pluses of tour travel?

How can you find the group expedition that suits your needs?

What should you expect to happen en route?

First of all, the advantages:

❡ *It's a beginning.* For first-time travelers, the group tour offers a bonus if only because it starts them on the trip—they're not sitting at home in Peoria nursing their travel insecurities. They can acquire an overall view of several countries—and return later independently to those they like best.

❡ *You are relieved of all decisions and details.* The organized

211

tour eliminates problems of hotel reservations, transportation, baggage handling, itinerary, sight-seeing. Nothing is left to improvisation. When you arrive in a city, you have a hotel room, your meals usually are provided, and you are coached on such matters as converting currency and what to see locally.

❮ *You're sure of company.* You may not like what you find, but you never have to be alone. Evenings are no problem. Tour conductors will arrange informal nighttime outings to famous cafés, operas, theaters, and nightclubs. If these are not part of the tour, you'll go "Dutch treat," but you won't regret paying for yourself. You are freed of trying to find an escort during the day, when you want to concentrate on ancient ruins.

❮ *You'll make new friends.* On my week-long tour of Israel, I loathed adjusting to twenty-five others. I hated getting up every morning at seven to catch the bus, and I resented being forced to see desert reclamation when I wanted to sit in a Tel Aviv café and watch the people. But within two weeks after returning home, I had had a date with the single man from the group, lunch with a girl my age, and received a dinner invitation from an older couple "to meet a charming Viennese."

❮ *Tours are economical.* Because they are arranged for a group, the operators are able to offer cut-rate prices. Also remember that the independent traveler during the summer season may not be able to find hotel accommodations in his price range.

And now the disadvantages:

❮ *The inflexibility.* You have to move along on schedule even though you might be particularly interested in the place you're visiting. Conversely, you'll have to stay with the group when the locale bores you to death; you've already paid for it. The group always wins. In Israel, we were riding through picturesque Jaffa on our bus. Every other minute, the driver stopped to oblige the shutterbugs' plea of "One more picture, please," but when I asked to get out for five minutes so that I could walk through the market section, everyone screamed, "We have no time."

⟨ *The boring meals.* To get a better room rate, tour conductors usually agree to the group's dining together at the hotel. That usually means second-rate food, with little choice of menu, instead of offbeat local cuisine. And you can get pretty tired of stringy duck with leftover orange sauce.

⟨ *The hidden expenses.* Tours usually do not include such personal expenses as laundry, gifts, theater tickets, or some tips. While an independent traveler is prepared to meet these costs and generally figures them in his total, a tour traveler is apt to be misled by what he assumes is an all-expense tour cost.

⟨ *The lack of freedom.* The tours operate on the principle of giving the buyers their money's worth, so they book every minute. The result is apt to be complete exhaustion and no chance to soak up local atmosphere. Even if the schedule permits "free time" from 8 P.M. on, you won't want to explore the town on foot if you've already been through six churches, two towers, and one waxworks in the course of a hectic day. Such a busy itinerary leaves little time to meet local people, and you can come home without having spoken to anyone except fellow Americans in your entourage, the concierge, the chambermaid, and shopkeepers who speak English.

If you want the freedom from care and loneliness that the package tour provides, try one. But be farsighted. Never sign up for one just because the price is right and you like most of the destinations. Instead, search for the tours that offer extras.

A busman's holiday can be fun. If you spend eight hours a day doing a certain kind ot work, you must like it. Logically, you should enjoy the people you'd meet and the places you'd go on a tour based on your professional interests. There are tours for architects that not only stress ancient edifices (which

anyone can visit for the price of passage and admission fee),
but feature meetings with architects such as Gio Ponti, visits
to unusual examples of contemporary design, such as England's Roehampton Estates. If fashion is your forte, you might
want a seventeen-day tour to *couture* capitals for "collection
viewing," with the added treat of meeting London's Digby
Morton or Rome's Fontana Sisters.

Even if you want to leave the office far behind, do not sign
up for some general tour where you'll take potluck with
people. Analyze your special interests, then enroll for a tour
that accents your favorite diversion. Is contract bridge your
off-hours passion? Maybe Charles Goren is leading an expedition to overseas bridge tournaments. Does your heart beat
faster to the strains of *Tosca, Otello,* and *Der Rosenkavalier?*
What could be more fun than to join forces with other opera
aficionados and hear Puccini, Verdi, and Strauss performed in
the fabled operatic halls of Milan, Vienna, and Berlin. Organ-
ized-interest tours have become such big business that there
is something for everyone. Horse lovers can travel round the
racetracks of South America without missing a bet. Garden
growers can coo over the *bonsai* and chrysanthemum shows in
Japan. There are tours for photographers, sports-car lovers, ski
bums, gourmets, golfers, theater buffs, jungle addicts, and
debutantes.

If your special interest is meeting single people, there are
even tours just for that purpose. Run by Gramercy Tours, 444
Madison Avenue, New York City, and called Bachelor Party
Tours, they are specifically for the lone traveler. Organized
some years ago by Richard Lowenstein, then a bachelor, who
found it was no fun climbing the Eiffel Tower alone, Bachelor Party Tours now take about six thousand people annually
to the far corners of the world. They are distinguished from
ordinary tours in three ways: they are confined to unmarried
people; they are divided into three age groups—twenty-one

to thirty-three, twenty-eight to forty-eight, forty-five to sixty-
five; they accent partying and night life.

What kind of people take them? A survey by Gramercy
shows that 41 per cent of the women were secretaries and
businesswomen; 18 per cent teachers; 19 per cent nurses. Of
the men, 30 per cent were in the legal, engineering, and
medical professions; 19 per cent were teachers; 18 per cent,
accountants; and 15 per cent, salesmen.

The company emphasizes that "it is not a lonely-hearts
club, not a marriage bureau, and not a tour of equal numbers
of men and women." A spokesman frankly admits that usually
there are more women than men "except in winter." But you
are with other singles within the same age group, and you
are sure of something to do every night. Don't count on finding
a husband though. So far, from all the thousands who have
taken the tours, the office knows of only fifty marriages—including Mr. Lowenstein's.

You can discover these special tours by investigating your
own professional organizations. If nothing turns up that way
that suits your purse or time schedule, ask the overseas airlines what they are offering in the way of special tours and
consult your travel agent. Also play Sherlock Holmes yourself. Read magazines like *Art World* and the *Saturday Re-
view* and look through the Sunday travel section of *The New
York Times*. The groups that sponsor offbeat expeditions need
the kind of members who read these publications, and they
frequently appeal through their columns. Some helpful tips:

❪ *Make a little list.* If you don't have any major interests,
list the places that appeal to you most, then go to a travel
agent for a tour that will touch at least some of them. You
tell the travel agent what you want. Don't let him tell you,
"I have a tour for $700 that will take you to Paris, Rome, Lon-
don, and Zurich," when you really want to ride up the Amazon
by riverboat.

❡ *Be realistic about price.* Read the itinerary very carefully, especially the conditions in small type at the end. Should you have to change your plans at the last minute, you want to get at least some of your money back. You might also be able to work out an arrangement for leaving the tour before the end and getting a proportional price cut.

❡ *Be careful that the tour you sign for is reliably organized.* On occasion, some ambitious person has decided suddenly to become a tour conductor. Sometimes the handful of zealous travelers who have counted on his trip are left stranded at the airport, sadder and wiser, because the neophyte conductor just couldn't get together enough people to fill the chartered plane. Be sure that your tour organizer is working through a big company and not merely trying to earn a free trip overseas by getting a group to travel under his guidance.

I have mixed feelings about package tours. In my heart, I think that if you are adventurous, ingenious, an expert in sign language, and really seeking the unfamiliar, a package tour is not for you—or me.

Yet the most glamorous, exciting, and unique trip of my traveling career was a prepackaged tour. It came about as the result of a tiny notice in the bulletin of the Seven Seas Journalists Association. The box read: "Journalists jaunt to South America. The SSJA will sponsor a twenty-eight-day trip to seven South American countries plus the Panama Canal Zone from August 3 to September 1. Cost of round-trip flight, excursions, side trip to Cuzco and Machu Picchu, first-class hotels, and some meals totals $800. This will be a working trip. Interviews can be arranged on any subject for members of the working press."

I had the money, but was a little timid about going. Apparently everyone scheduled for the trip was famous but me. I was awed by such august company.

I voiced this hesitation to Joe Morales, the public-relations director for the airline. "I don't work for a newspaper, I don't have a byline, and my only real qualification is membership in SSJA. If it would embarrass you in any way, I don't think I should go."

There was a long pause. I thought he was feeling his way toward admitting, "You're right." Later, I found out that he was holding his breath, for he needed at least fourteen people to make the trip possible. I was the fourteenth. Without me, there would be no expedition.

"Don't be silly," was all he said. So I went.

There is no difficulty getting to know your companions on a tour. In fact, you get to know them too well too soon. You can see other casual acquaintances for years and never realize any disposition toward temper tantrums, midnight telephone calls, reluctance to pay their own way, forgotten promises, and malicious gossip. But live with a group of thirteen others at the breakneck pace of ten stops in seven countries in twenty-eight days and you get to know their faults so completely that you sometimes wonder about their virtues.

Our group was really fourteen authors in search of a character or two. The cast:

NORMAN WELLES Dignified, white-haired, fifty-two, ex-Englishman, ex-editor, and current columnist. The "name" of the trip, he was expected to raise the tone of the group vis-à-vis South American celebrities.

ALLISON WELLES His wife. Dynamic, vital, the type able to cope with being cast away on a desert island. Her piercing British "my dears" and "how jollys" were sometimes disturbing.

ALAN KAHN The juvenile. Handsome, thirty-three, reporter for a Manhattan newspaper, traveling on a budget, he was more interested in saving money than in meeting girls.

EVELYN MARNER Divorced dilettante. The trip had been her idea, so she claimed credit for everything that worked out well. The things that were so-so she dismissed with an "I told you." She had her eye on . . .

CLARENCE YOUNG   Although paying alimony to two ex-wives, he was still a millionaire. Over sixty, he had little-boy qualities but little charm. His questions always revolved around currency and world banking. Only a wealthy man could drop gravy on his shirt so nonchalantly.

MRS. KNOWLES   She qualified for the trip by being the *mother* of a newspaperman. Seventy-two, quiet, always wearing clean white gloves, she looked like the president of the ladies' goodwill club back in Denver, her hometown. In fact, she was.

JOE MORALES   The tour leader. Handsome, gay, and amusing to the top of his wavy black hair. He had a wife and kiddies in the New Jersey suburbs—unfortunately.

THE AGING INGENUE   Me.

EXTRAS   Six dull businessmen-type newsmen, all happily married, all with their minds happily on their work.

One August day we all took off from New York to fly ten thousand miles across a continent with an area almost as great as that of Europe and the United States combined, a trip that was to take us from the Amazon across the Andes, up and down both Atlantic and Pacific coasts. Twenty-eight days later, we were back. In the intervening period, I had bargained with barefoot Indians in the markets of Ecuador, watched Argentines play *pato* (a mixture of polo and basketball), walked past armed sentries to interview the dictator-President of Venezuela. I had also learned facts about tours that travel agents, guidebooks, and even your best friends don't tell you.

❡ *Every woman traveling alone should room alone.* Because of the difficulty in booking hotel rooms in some countries, tour operators frequently try to pair off the loners. Don't let them do it to you. You may save $3 a night, but you'll lose comfort,

convenience, and the chance to read in bed. If you're old
enough to travel, you don't need a stranger for a roommate.
❲ *More men than women take "professional" tours.* The reverse
is true on the ordinary guided tour. The reason is simple: a
portion of the professional tour may be tax deductible. Business appointments can be sandwiched in between ruins and
receptions. We had four women to ten men on our Latin
trip—a favorable ratio in any language. You cannot expect
anything like this if your professional-interest tour concerns
fashions or gardens, but tours centered around archaeology,
architecture, photography, medicine, economics, and, amaz-
ingly enough, cooking draw the masculine gender.
❲ *Sign up for a tour organized by a travel agent nearby.* If
you live in New York, don't take a tour that originates in San
Francisco. It will only cut down your chances to meet people
whom you can see later. Find one that originates in or near
home base.
❲ *Leave the group when something better turns up locally.*
Meeting people of the country is much more important than
sight-seeing with your group. For example, the São Paulo
newspaper covered the arrival of our group, and as a result,
the editor of a woman's magazine invited me to lunch. I
skipped a coffee plantation and met Alda de Caraval, a Brazilian contemporary. We have corresponded ever since, not
just little Christmas notes, but long, tell-it-all missives; and
at yuletide, I send her my annual gift, last year's edition of the
Manhattan telephone directory. Don't worry if you've paid in
advance for a sight-seeing expedition. Keep the ticket. You
can get your money back later from the travel agent.
❲ *Expect the group to break down into the "ins" and the
"outs."* Cliques will form. The more-attractive souls will gravi-
tate to one another and the less-attractive souls will be excluded. On my South American expedition, mother-hen Evelyn
had warned me, "Don't expect the Welleses to bother with
you. They're very snobbish." Scared soul that I was when I

started the expedition, I dared not say more than good morning to the Welleses. From sheer social insecurity, I stuck with
the six newspapermen. Wasn't there safety in numbers? But
to my amazement, on the first evening in Rio de Janeiro,
Allison Welles telephoned me. "Jean, dear, will you join
Clarence and me for dinner tonight. We'd like to get away
from the group, and we'd like to get to know you." Just four
days away from the United States, the group was starting to
subdivide.

([*All tours will have boors in their bosom.* The boorishness
can take the form of pushiness, failure to pick up tabs, rudeness, practical jokes, selfishness, or complete lack of consideration. Life in the working democracy of tiny Montevideo
seemed all picnics and parks, sweetness and light, yet it was
there that I learned that life on a tour is not always beautiful.

The SSJA expedition was granted interviews with many
heads of state. The President of Uruguay had requested that
we submit our questions in writing, and I had innocuously
asked, "Does juvenile delinquency exist in Uruguay? If so,
what is being done about it?" Clarence garnered our queries
for deposit at the U.S. embassy on the day before the press
conference.

I promptly forgot all about mine and went off for a gay day
of touring the Museum of Fine Arts, dining on *carbonada* (a
Uruguayan stew of beef, rice, and fruit) at El Aguila, and
seeing the local ballet. It was one o'clock in the morning when
I wearily returned to the Victoria Plaza hotel with a the-
world-is-wonderful feeling. This was intensified when I got
my mail—three letters from home plus an official-looking document from the U.S. embassy in Montevideo.

I went up to my room, ordered a chicken sandwich, opened
the embassy letter, and nearly collapsed.

It read: "We regret to inform you that His Excellency the
President is extremely displeased with your question and has
asked that you be barred from the press conference tomorrow.

We are allowing you to remain in Uruguay, but ask that you refrain from doing anything further to embarrass the U.S. government. We are referring the matter to Lincoln White in Washington. Official action will be taken when you return home." The signature was illegible, but typewritten underneath was the identification, "First Secretary," and the seal was absolutely bona fide.

I couldn't believe it. My question had been harmless, but I could see that my professional—and private—life was finished. Who would ever want to be friends with a girl who had done anything so disgraceful? How would I ever get another job (because, obviously, I would be fired from the one I had)? Visions of a story in *Time* chased through my aching head. I started to count my savings; maybe I could move to some remote Mexican village and learn to weave baskets. . . .

It was two in the morning, but unable to bear my fears any more, I telephoned Clarence. "Clarence, something terrible has happened," I said abruptly. "Did they say anything at the embassy when you delivered the question?"

An angry voice shut me off. "I'm asleep," said this unsympathetic soul as he slammed down the phone.

Somehow I got through the night. At 7:30 in the morning I telephoned Joe Morales. "Joe, I'm afraid I've disgraced the whole group," I confessed.

He wasn't a bit perturbed. "Just stay calm, Jean," he counseled. "Clarence thinks the government translator confused 'juvenile delinquency' with 'sexual intercourse.' I think personally it's all a practical joke. Come down for the gaucho trip in an hour and we'll see what's what."

Down I came, my eyes showing the strain of the agonized night. Clarence wouldn't look at me. We separated into two cars to attend a gaucho barbecue and horse show. But I was too depressed to enjoy seeing the cowboys in *bombachas* (baggy pants), and the *maté* tasted like witch's brew.

Allison dragged me to a corner. "I found out everything,"

she confided. "Clarence stole the stationery from the embassy as a joke. He never dreamed you would take it seriously. Oh, Jean, he is so ashamed."

It was no joke to me.

"He wants to give you a diamond pin to make up for it," Allison added in her British English. Things were getting better. "But I told him that a gift like that wasn't a bit suitable for a girl like you."

"Why did you do that?" I asked dully.

"Two bottles of champagne would be much more proper, and we could all have a party."

At that point, Clarence thought it was safe to approach. Looking like a beaten beagle, he stared at me piteously from the safe distance of three feet.

"Can you ever forgive me?" he pleaded.

My mother instinct and sense of sportsmanship won out. "It was a terrible thing to do, but, yes, we can still be friends," I said magnanimously. I waited for him to renew the diamond pin offer—in vain.

"I'm going to send you some champagne," he promised.

"Make sure it's imported," said Allison.

The two bottles of Piper Heidsieck arrived, and I invited the group to a cocktail party. But the champagne was flat, and Clarence didn't show. He had gone to a cocktail party at the embassy.

❨ *Tours follow a personality pattern.* At first, you will be a collection of individuals, going your individual ways. Then you will enter the era of good feeling, when you will adore each other. This will turn to hate, reverse to toleration, and eventually come around to a final, "This has been wonderful despite everything."

No matter how nice a group of new friends seems at first, the mutual-admiration attitude cannot last. It was in Santiago, Chile, that our era of good feeling came to a violent end. The

Peking Opera Company was in town, and with his usual finesse, Clarence managed to get tickets through the local bank. He immediately invited Allison, Norman, and me to share his wealth. I was getting dressed for the gala when the telephone rang. It was Alan, and he was beside himself.

"Jean, I was supposed to get those tickets. I'm going to do a story on the Chinese troupe. You must let me go in your place."

I wasn't taking orders from Alan. "But Clarence invited me."

Alan countered, "He had no right to that ticket."

"Well, take it up with him." I slammed down the phone.

Two minutes later, Evelyn rang up. She and Alan had become great buddies. Each of them satisfied a need in the other. He was a male escort, and she paid her own way.

"You're a bad girl," she scolded. "You have to let Alan go."

She was trying to make me feel guilty. I suggested that we all meet in the lobby and straighten things out.

Ten minutes later, a real brawl was going on in the center of the fancy Carrera Hotel. Alan was yelling at Clarence. Clarence accused Evelyn of interference. Evelyn attacked me, complaining that I didn't care what I did as long as I had a date. Onlookers stared in astonishment at this group of badly behaved *norteamericanos*. Into the midst of the melee strode the usually stiff-upper-lip Welleses. No one would dare dispute their rights to tickets or anything else.

Magnanimously, I offered to give up my place to Alan. Anything to have peace.

Allison would have none of that. In her best *grande dame* manner, she commanded, "Oh, no, Jean, you've been invited, and it would be bad manners not to go. Norman and I will skip the performance. We've already been to Peking." Alan, Evelyn, Clarence, and I went to the theater in silence. Two enemy camps had been established.

❲ *Special tours enjoy special opportunities.* Before I went to South America, I knew nothing about that continent. I had certainly never heard of Cuzco and Machu Picchu. Yet these two wonders made up the touristic climax of the trip, because better, more informed minds than mine had organized the tour. In Cuzco, 11,207 feet high, former capital of the Inca empire, we joined visiting Italians, Germans, Japanese, and Australians in gaping at the relics of the long-dead civilization, while long-necked llamas watched us with disdain. From Cuzco, we traveled by single-track railroad to awe-inspiring Machu Picchu, a mountaintop sanctuary used by Incan rulers in times of distress. It was so well hidden that its existence had been forgotten for centuries until its rediscovery in 1911 by American archaeologist Hiram Bingham. The view from the mountain was suddenly blurred for me when Alan shoved me oh-so-slightly; he quickly apologized.

It was in Ecuador, where the churches gleam with Incan gold and the Indians are as picturesque as postcards, that the group received its most exciting invitation. We happened to arrive in Quito in time for the inauguration of Camilo Ponce as President, and in our rooms at the hotel were fancy invitations to the swearing-in ceremonies and the gala ball. We were too busy getting ready to pay much attention to the steep streets, white houses with red tiled roofs, and Indians drinking *chicha* ("corn drink"). The men were frantically bribing waiters to lend them their uniforms for the white-tie affair, and the women were haunting beauty parlors. I was the only female with enough foresight to have brought along a formal dress, so I was feeling uppity.

In the late afternoon, we entered the auditorium for the inauguration ceremonies. With great fuss and fanfare, the rites began, and we watched attentively.

Suddenly Allison poked me. "Where's Clarence?"

He had been in his seat just a few minutes before. We all began looking furtively around the great hall. As we glanced upward toward the flower-bedecked boxes for the VIP's, we

saw a tall, gaunt figure signaling frantically from the Arch-
bishop's box. There, among the purple-robed church dignitaries, was Clarence.

A few minutes later, Allison nudged me again. "Look at the
stage," she commanded.

On the platform were the fifty-one Senators of Ecuador,
standing severely at attention while the new President took the
oath of office. Dressed in white tie and tails "with decorations,"
they were regal enough for an eighteenth-century French
court. But their ranks had been swelled by a new member.
Clarence was there, too. Dressed in his finery borrowed from a
hotel waiter, he was waving cheerfully at our little group.
It was too much. Allison and I exited in a spasm of laughter;
we knew that Clarence would be dining out all the next year
on this story. The incident welded the group together again;
we began to speak to each other once more.

Everything was coming to an end—including my money.
In Ecuador, when I discovered that I had only a few dollars
left, I promptly invested in four of the long, lavishly decorated
candles that come in lovely candy-box colors. The pink, yellow, and green ones were too pretty for me; I bought black
ones to go with my white living-room walls. Later, I discovered that the black were for funerals, not for mantelpieces.
Meanwhile, I inveigled the males of the group into carrying
the candles by hand, so that they wouldn't be broken.

By the end of the trip, I felt far more secure. When Allison
looked at me on the flight home and quipped, "Dear, you've
been such a good foil," for once, I snapped back.

"Allison, dear," said I, "there's no foil like an old foil." For
once in my life I had delivered the perfect squelch.

Back at the airport, we separated. Clarence, Evelyn, and I
shared a cab into Manhattan, and I promptly celebrated my
return by sitting on my candles in the taxi, breaking them all.

"Good-bye, Evelyn," I called. "I hope I see you soon." To
my amazement, I meant it.

"Jean, I've lived with you for twenty-eight days. What will our relationship be like now?" worried Clarence.

A month after our return, the "ins" and the "outs" gathered at the SSJA for a report to members. In the meantime, Clarence had eliminated me from his social calendar in favor of women of his own income bracket. Joe Morales had cropped his wavy locks to the crew-cut length suitable for a hardworking publicity man. Alan appeared sweet and good-humored; I couldn't imagine him having a temper tantrum. Evelyn was busy organizing next year's expedition to the Far East, but she still hadn't forgiven me for not immediately giving up my Peking Opera ticket. Allison rated a hearty kiss; I won a curt nod.

One by one, Evelyn introduced each of us to the audience, each time with superlatives: "Norman Welles, the noted correspondent" . . . "Alan Kahn, the rising young writer" . . . "Clarence Young, the authority on international finance." When she came to me, she paused and said, "And this is Jean Baer. She interviewed teen-agers and went out with the men."

Coming from Evelyn, it was the supreme accolade.

CHAPTER 13

Buymanship

The customer is not always right—particularly when she is a female traveler abroad, avid for bargains, nervous about being "taken," and anxious about customs duties to pay coming home.

Taken away from the security of familiar stores and shopping situations, charge accounts and the time to "think now, buy later," she often ends up making two major mistakes:

She buys something she doesn't need or want.

She doesn't buy things she really wants, because she can't make up her mind.

Among the greatest delights of the woman traveler is to see everything that's to be seen, buy some of it, and get it back home safely. In the course of acquiring possessions abroad, I have come dangerously close to breaking my back, forfeiting my airline credit card, and suffering a nervous breakdown, but I have become a woman of property. My apartment bursts with interesting things, my closet is stacked with Paris originals—and everything cost me far less than it would have in this country.

To be a successful shopper in a foreign land, you must follow the rules of buymanship.

1. *Don't Buy Gimmicks.* In the pleasures of travel, your taste may suffer from the excitement of the moment. Stay away from pointless souvenirs. If you drop into a little antique shop, don't pick out some china monstrosity because it will set you back only $2 and will fit nicely into your handbag. Select something you can imagine in your home.

When I was in Russia, I felt I simply had to have a memento of my tour through the Soviet Union. Outside of caviar, there was little for the tourist to purchase. Finally I bought a balalaika, the handsome triangular Russian equivalent of the guitar, even though my ear for music is nil and I never got further on the piano than "Chopsticks." The balalaika is now taking up room in my hall closet along with similar mementos—the rococo cuckoo clock from Germany, the fancy tassels from Sicily, and battered straw hats from around the globe. Moral: do not buy badly designed, poorly constructed, or useless objects just because they are cheap.

2. *Buy Something You Can Really Use.* It's much more fun to search for something definite in a foreign antique store than to hunt in the "copper corner" of your local furniture emporium. Part of the fun of going it alone abroad is the opportunity to window-shop where you want, to poke around in unusual stores when you have the urge, and to treat yourself to something appealing without unsolicited advice.

I am a collector by nature, need, and just sheer love of owning things. The farther I get from home, the stronger becomes the urge to acquire. I used to just buy until my money ran out. The result was a set of twenty-four gold service plates for which I have absolutely no use in a two-room apartment where I am maid and hostess combined. Now, I'm smarter. I purchase objects for which I have a definite use, and I get them abroad, where I have the fun of looking and, concomitantly, spending less money than I would at home.

You can collect demitasses, buy a charm in each city for a superb gold bracelet, assemble one-of-a-kind dinner plates, add to your print collection (a signed Léger lithograph cost me $17 in a Left Bank art shop in Paris). I heartily recommend purchasing foreign kitchen equipment. On each trip, I pick up one ancient copper pot, the kind that sells for $15 or $20 in an American antique shop. Overseas, these run about $2 if you are lucky. Once home, I send the shabby pot out for retinning and refinishing—and for another $2, I have a beautiful piece of burnished-copper kitchenware.

Jewelry is often a good buy. Bargains still abound in little shops, if you have the time and energy to search. In West Berlin, you can buy antique garnet earrings on the Keithstrasse for about $10, a little stickpin for less than $4. In a shop next to Athens' Grand Bretagne Hotel are old Greek pins that look as if they once belonged to Electra. I bought two at $5 apiece.

3. *Act on Impulse.* If you see it, love it, and can afford it, buy it. You'll regret it if you don't. Riding on a bus in Elsinore, I spied a wooden blanket chest in a corner window. I got off the bus, walked into the store, asked the price. It was only $20, and this was the chest I had been seeking for years. I bought it. It cost $50 to ship to the States, but it was still half the price that I would have had to pay here.

4. *It's Only Money.* Naturally, if you are on an extremely strict budget, you aren't going to have an extra dollar to spare. But if you allot $100 for presents—either for yourself or others—adjust. If you want it badly enough, get it; worry about your budget later. Just rationalize that ten years from now you'll be $50 poorer—and how much can that really matter?

On my first European expedition, I was a strapped cub reporter, and every penny counted. My mother's favorite possession had been a dozen Lalique crystal plates. I decided that I was going to buy a complete set of glassware to go with them. At that time, the set of sherry, brandy, wine, water, and champagne glasses totaled $100 plus shipping charges. I scraped together the cash by doing without on the trip—

without lunch, without fancy excursions, without buying a single souvenir.

I remember the momentous day when I strolled into the Lalique shop on the Rue Royale in Paris.

"I'd like a set of everything, please," said I timidly to the clerk, who looked far more expensively dressed in his cutaway than I did in my neat gray wool jumper.

"What pattern please, madame?" he inquired.

"What do you have?" I was so ignorant, I thought that everything would be the same pattern as Mother's plates.

He showed the various styles to me. Name-dropping, he practiced French salesmanship. "This pattern is Rose; it belongs to the Baroness Rothschild. . . . We call this one Mystique. . . . General de Gaulle uses this. . . . This is the Royal Crystal. . . . Many of the ex-kings living at Estoril use this type."

I started to perspire. What if I made the wrong choice? I couldn't very well return it.

The salesman understood perplexed prospects. "This is the pattern used by the Duchess of Windsor."

That was it. Any woman who could make a king give up his throne had something. I'd take her brand of glassware.

Eventually, the glasses and I got back to Mount Vernon. We had two oak cabinets in the dining room, and in one of them the Lalique went on display. It represented so much to me in the way of both beauty and uneaten French lunches that I used it only on state occasions.

One day, as my father was reading in bed and my brother was listening to the radio in the sun parlor, I walked through the dining room. There was a terrible crash—and to my horror, I saw all the Lalique tumbling down inside the cabinet. Shelf after shelf of those precious glasses crashed down on top of one another.

I was silent. My insides contracted as I remembered all the *pâté* and the *mousse au chocolat* I had gone without.

Said my brother, "I'm sure glad I wasn't walking through the room."

Dad was more understanding. "I guess a shelf got loose. Must have been the cat." He saw that I was still numb from shock and added a piece of fatherly wisdom: "Honey, it's only money. You can get it again."

And I did. The very next summer I went back to Paris and bought my second set of the Duchess of Windsor's Lalique pattern. I've used it and loved it ever since. Even when a glass crashes to the floor in pieces, I don't mind. Good crystal breaks with such a superior sound.

5. *Start Shopping in the Local Department Store.* It can be GUM in Moscow, Nordiska Kompaniet in Stockholm, Galeries Lafayette, Aux Trois Quartiers, or Le Printemps in Paris, Harrods in London. If you don't know where to go, consult the concierge at your hotel. Find the store, then start your "just looking, thanks" approach in the basement and work your way up floor by floor. Note what the local women are buying and buy what they buy. If you see a crowd heading in one direction, follow it. You might just find a buy. I did this in Paris and discovered linen suits by a famous French ready-to-wear maker on sale for $20. Once you have cased the big store, you can make your way toward the markets, bazaars, and specialty shops. Often you will find that things cost less in the department store, just as they do at home. Alert department stores cater to the American buyer; many have English-speaking hostesses.

6. *The Technique of Haggling.* You can no more dicker over price in most European department stores or fine specialty shops than you can at Saks or Neiman-Marcus. Trying to barter down the prices in Nordic or Anglo-Saxon countries is a waste of time. When the sign announces "fixed price," or even if it doesn't in the British Isles, Benelux countries, Austria, Scandinavia, Switzerland, and Germany, it means just what it says. You have much more chance of haggling in

Balkan and Latin countries and in the Middle and Far East.

Haggling calls for a definite technique. If there is a conspicuous "fixed-price" sign, don't bother to try. If a clerk waits on you, save your bartering for another shop. However, if the owner himself looks you over, waits a few beats before naming the price, and eyes you thoughtfully, here's your chance.

You have three choices. You can play the waiting game: counter with an amazed, "That's out of the question," and start looking over other items in the shop. You can act coy and confess, "I don't have that much money." Or if you have no time for a "tennis exchange," make the man an offer. Start by offering half of the named price. This technique can boomerang. If the owner sees that you lack haggling experience and are also determined upon ownership, he will set his price so high that even at half price you are paying too much.

7. *Stop Worrying About Getting Gypped.* If you like an object, buy it. If you then learn that you have paid more than you should, stop fretting. The true value is what the article is worth to you.

A Turkish guide once escorted me through the great Covered Bazaar of Istanbul, a wonderful place for a woman to go crazy—gold and silver, rugs, antiques, shoes, and matches. The only things I didn't see on sale were fezzes. After a morning of sight-seeing that involved mosques, minarets, and muezzins chanting prayer calls, I was utterly dazzled by the display of jewels. I knew just what I wanted. The Turkish girls all seemed to wear gold bangles on their wrists. I was going to get a set of bangles.

"I will bargain for you," offered my guide, Fatima. "Remember, it's the weight that counts. Watch for the little mark on the inside that means the bracelets are twenty-four-karat gold."

Soon I was beginning to feel like a professional appraiser. I didn't talk, lest my American voice give me away, but at each stop, I borrowed the magnifying glass from the vendor and hunted for that hallmark.

Finally, I found six bracelets. They averaged $30 apiece.

"I will pay," offered Fatima. "You can give me dollars or traveler's checks back at the hotel."

It was a deal. Fatima forked out the Turkish liras; I placed the bracelets on my left wrist, where they jangled happily the way real gold does, and we left the bazaar.

When I described the expedition to my Turkish host at dinner, the gentleman regarded me ruefully. "Unfortunately, we have a black market here in Istanbul," he admitted. "Your guide probably made as much on that transaction as you paid. You might have done better on your own."

That was seven years ago. I have worn the bracelets every day since. The fact that Fatima made a profit on them or that I may have overpaid doesn't matter any more. What does matter is that I love them.

8. *Quit Fretting About Authenticity.* If you love something, get it. What's the difference whether or not that alabaster pot really belonged to Madame de Pompadour? You can always tell people that it did.

9. *Don't Be Too Sensible.* You *can* check out every purchase by comparing values in every other shop and flea market. You may find it cheaper somewhere else, but you may return to find it gone, too. You may think you're better off without it, but when you're back home, you may never forgive yourself for letting it go.

10. *Don't Worry About the Language Barrier.* You can accomplish a lot with a pencil and paper, pocket dictionary, smile, and your filled billfold.

11. *Take Your Checkbook with You.* I used to start all my trips on a strict budget. I would take a certain amount of money and carefully allot dollars for foolish spending. Then I would see something I had craved all my life and would not have any money to buy it. I learned from experience. Now

I take my checkbook. The balance really doesn't matter; it's
having the book that counts. In any major city, there is usually
a branch of an American bank that, if you look respectable,
smile nicely, and turn on all your charm, will cash a modest
check. It helps if you know someone who will vouch for you,
but this is not essential. Big stores will also cash checks for
merchandise. This may involve a cable home to a friend—
"Cover bank account $200 pronto"—but it's cheap at the price,
particularly when you remember that checks made out in
foreign countries usually take three weeks to clear. By that
time, you should be able to get home and clear things up
yourself. In a pinch, your bank will make a personal loan.

12. *Take Your Purchases with You.* It may mean extra expense, but it saves a lot of worry about loss and breakage.
You can't cart along a nineteenth-century Biedermeier cabinet, but you'll do much better packing two eighteenth-century coffee cups in assorted slips and girdles square in the
middle of your grip than you will sending them home by mail.
I trust myself more than I do any foreign post office. When I
purchased a Sèvres breakfast set at the Flea Market in Paris,
I wrapped it in pages of the Paris *Herald Tribune* and packed
it in between a red evening dress and my blue bathrobe. If
you find this procedure means too much overweight, pack a
small suitcase with dirty clothes and things you won't need
immediately upon arrival at home and ship that—not your
acquisitions. Exception: you can rely upon fine stores like
Den Permanente in Copenhagen or Harrods in London to
make proper shipping arrangements, but don't trust some
little clerk in a tiny store to do the same.

Devoting too much time to worry about overweight is penny
foolish. When you spend $1,000 on an overseas holiday, pay-
ing $30 more for the peace and comfort that comes from
having your purchases ride with you on the same plane is
worth it.

13. *Shop at Airports Only if They Are "Free Ports."* Other-

wise, everything costs more. Be forehanded and buy your gifts in town.

As a guide for similar shopping addicts, here are the places in which you'll find some of the outstanding flea markets, antique or junk shops, and auction houses:

LONDON

In the *Portobello Market* in the Notting Hill Gate district of London, the atmosphere is slightly hysterical; vendors sing-song their wares, which range from snuffboxes to torn Spanish shawls, in rich Cockney accents. Most stalls are open only on Saturdays. Go early.

The Bermondsey district in southeast London is still called the *Caledonian Market* by most people. It is open Fridays from 9 A.M. to 4 P.M. You'll find mostly junk, and certainly the market is not what it used to be.

Petticoat Lane offers more atmosphere than legitimate antiques. It is reminiscent of New York's Lower East Side in the old days. Stalls feature fabric lengths and old clothes, along with bric-a-brac, and very rarely a real bargain. However, it's a good Sunday-morning excursion.

The *Auction at Sotheby's* on Bond Street is as typically English as Ascot or crumpets and strawberry jam at teatime. On the day of a really big sale, the auction rooms are chic chaos; but on an ordinary morning, all is peace and tranquility. Elderly Englishmen, portly Germans, and a pink-cheeked Frenchman or two browse among the paperweights, jewelry, and silver. There is also a book-auction room, where the only sound is the occasional whisper of paper.

PARIS

The *Flea Market* is a "must" (Métro stop: Porte de Clignancourt). This sprawling Marché aux Puces is a major tourist attraction as well as heaven for serious antique hunters. Open Saturdays, Sundays, and Mondays. Parisians in the know go strolling in search of treasures on Sunday morning, but the time to find the best buys is on a cold winter Monday afternoon, when the vendors want to go home and get warm. Prices are high, but you'll find everything from old curtain rods and tiebacks to Louis XV crystal chandeliers. There are several sections. Try Vernaison or Paul-Bert for cheaper prices.

The *Swiss Village* (*Village Suisse*), Avenue de Suffren near the Champs de Mars (XV), in Paris is a more chic version of the Flea Market. The stalls, run by pseudocelebrities of the stage and literary world, stand on the original site of a Swiss village constructed for the International Exhibition of 1900. This market is closed on Tuesdays and Wednesdays. It is more expensive than the Flea Market, but there is less junk.

As for the *Hôtel Drouot* (6 Rue Rossini), the French themselves insist that you can get a real bargain at this government-regulated auction house, in everything from first editions of Voltaire to perfectly matched Louis XIV dining-room chairs. Clients, from housewives to film stars, inspect the merchandise from 10 to 11 A.M. Monday through Friday and all day Saturday. Sales take place from 2 to 6 P.M. Monday through Friday. It is closed Sundays and in August. If you can't manage French, go to the second-floor offices and ask for help. Remember, government tax ranges from 8 to 20 per cent, depending on your purchase.

ROME

The *Flea Market* in Rome, officially the Mercato di Porta Portese, is on the banks of the Tiber (a cab ride from the Via Veneto will cost about $1.25). About a hundred thousand tourists and locals turn up every Sunday for this market, which opens at sunrise and continues until one o'clock. The market covers acres, and the merchandise includes such items as war medals by the ton, live canaries, winepresses, altar candlesticks (which many visitors convert into lamps), and ancestral portraits (all the women look just like Lucrezia Borgia). Good buy: earrings for pierced ears. Skip the moldy, weather-beaten items, the old-clothes stalls and fake cameo booths manned by circus-type barkers. Wear old clothes (the crowd is worse than the mob in New York subways during rush hour), and do as the Romans do: never pay the first figure quoted or you'll be considered a *fesso* (Italian slang for "sucker").

MADRID

The *Rastro* used to be a bargain hunter's best bet. It still is interesting, especially Sunday mornings, and you *may* turn up valuable works of art and genuine antiques. It's safer to go with a Spanish friend as a guide; take his advice on how to bargain and what to buy.

PORTUGAL

For bric-a-brac bartering, go to *Feira da Ladra*, Campo Santa Clara, in Lisbon. It is open Tuesdays and Saturdays. Outside Lisbon, *Feira de S. Pedro*, Sintra, is open every second and fourth Sunday of the month. You'll find exciting pottery as well as squealing pigs.

ISTANBUL

The *Covered Market* is a gem for jewelry-seekers. If you've the wherewithal, the diamonds and sapphires are impressive. You can find everything here, including swords, coffee urns, and rugs.

ISRAEL

Shuk Hapishpishim (Hebrew for "flea market"), in the old quarter of Jaffa (adjoining Tel Aviv), features a jumble of old clothes mixed with Oriental copper and brass work and occasional European items. I particularly liked the brass kohl pots (kohl is an earlier version of mascara). Bargaining is expected. The centuries-old market in Nazareth is a typical Arab *suq*, selling exotic spices, Arab drums, and other goods from tiny shops on dark, cobbled lanes. Bedouins ride to Beersheba every Thursday morning at 7 A.M. to trade camels, but don't succumb to temptation and buy one. The late Mrs. Roosevelt did—and U.S. customs wouldn't let it in.

KABUL, AFGHANISTAN

Should you venture the camel-caravan route to this Moslem monarchy, you'll find an old bazaar in Kabul with bargains galore. Watch for hand-tied carpets, karakul skins and hats, old coins, guns, and postage stamps. Most merchants speak English and German—unless you can handle Pashto.

HONG KONG

Hong Kong is one big bargain basement, but it is on *Cat Street,* located in Victoria's West Point area, that you'll find a compact world of shouting hawkers, Oriental "disc jockeys" playing secondhand records on worn phonographs, cubbyhole shops shared by several merchants, and sidewalk sellers who display their wares on the street. You can take your choice of a battered cigarette lighter or a piece of hand-carved jade, and you are expected to bargain; but, remember, U.S. customs requires comprehensive "Certificates of Origin" that specify that the goods you purchased are not from Communist China or North Korea.

VIENNA

The *Dorotheum Auction* can be a treasure trove of everything from Hapsburg relics to petit point. It is open most of the year, and there are special commodities for sale on certain days of the week. It opens at 10 A.M., and you have all morning to look over merchandise. If you give a professional bidder your top figure, he'll work for you during the afternoon session for 2 per cent. Experts pin a starting fee on everything.

ATHENS has a local flea market on *Pandrossou Street,* a
nice walk from Constitution Square. You'll find charming old
brooches and bracelets, ancient icons that start at $10 and
zoom upward (these are a wonderful touch in a modern apartment). If the merchant likes you, he'll ask you to join him for
a cup of coffee.

Shopping Ideas from All Over the Map

NAIROBI, KENYA

Leopard sandals cost just $3. An elephant-hair bracelet
bound with gold (sounds terrible, looks good) will run you
$3 in town, but up to $6 at the airport. . . . Good investment
is a brown-felt safari hat for about $8. Get it at Ahmed's.
Don't pick the typical khaki cotton; get it in felt in the Aus-
tralian Army version and you can turn the side snaps up for
shooting.

PARIS

A shopper's heaven. Some offbeat suggestions: Buy a
special hairbrush at Alexandre, 120 Faubourg-St-Honoré.
For $7.50, you'll feel like a pampered darling. . . . Treat
yourself to a bra made to order at Berlé, 14 Rue Clément-
Marot. They keep your measurements, and you can reorder
from home. . . . Visit the Louvre Museum and head for the
chalcography department. In case you can't even fracture
French, go through the main entrance and head for the ladies'
room. Instead of transacting any business there, walk up two
flights and go into the room on your right. You'll find thousands of prints—mainly of old Paris, but also a limited number of lithographs by modern masters such as Cézanne,
Picasso, and Léger. Good buy: one or more of the prized
Turgot maps of eighteenth-century Paris, $3.50 apiece. . . .
At Dehillerin, 18 Rue Coquillière in Les Halles, pick out a
piece of copper kitchen equipment. I like the sugar scoops,

$6—lovely to use with summer strawberries. A tin *bouilloire,* which looks like a giant tea caddy, to cook rice in is about eighty cents . . . Go to any of the department stores and invest in some artificial flowers. You can buy six tiny black roses for about $2 each. Baste them on the puffed sleeves of a basic black dress and you'll have the look of a femme fatale for a minor investment. Full-blown roses cost about $3.50—one-fourth of their cost in American shops. . . . A dress from a Paris dressmaker in just as few days? Sounds impossible? It isn't. If you know a Frenchwoman, see whether you can pry her dressmaker's name from her. If not, try the concierge at the hotel. My treasure is Madame Denise Reboh, 17 Rue de Reims (XIII); telephone, KEL 89-69. You can probably get the latest Dior model (or Givenchy or Patou) made to order for you at department-store-at-home prices. A wool dress may run about $40 plus fabric; evening dress, from $50 up. Whatever it costs, it's worth it. Try to have two fittings. It might be a good idea to have a dummy made (cost, around $30), leave it with the dressmaker, and order clothes by mail as long as your measurements stay the same. . . . An alternative is to buy fabric. Max on the Champs-Elysées, right near the Rond-Point, has a choice selection of *haute couture* brocades, satins, flannels, and jerseys. . . . Pretty garden flowers adorn the new Porcelaine de Paris; I like the toilet-paper holders patterned in roses. Available at Raymond, 100 Faubourg-St-Honoré. . . . For buys in bric-a-brac, go to the Rue de Paradis; you'll find gold-plated butter dishes with knives for about $2.50 each; Limoges-Haviland is cheaper here than anywhere else. Very feminine white piqué gloves spattered with delicate red roses run $2.50 a pair in summer at Henri Roy, 271 Rue St-Honoré.

SPAIN

Cork wallpaper sells here for $5 a roll; costs $20 a roll in the U.S. My friend Wauhilla bought ten rolls, carried them home in a $2 valise, and papered her living room and hall. . . .

You can buy colorful strips of raffia for $1 each on the Costa Brava; put them on a strip of tape and attach them over a door. They come in every color of the rainbow. Vaguely reminiscent of the old bead hangings, but much more chic. Dogs can go in and out, but flies and mosquitoes can't break through. . . . You may want an authentic *torero* shirt, wonderful for wear with pants, skirts, suits; purchase it in white or black at Ripolles, the oldest shop in Madrid that sells the wardrobes of the bullring. . . . Loewe (in Madrid, Barcelona, and San Sebastian) is high in value and price for leather wallets, handbags, and lightweight luggage for air travel. . . . For a look of sheerest femininity, complete with pleats, tucks, and fluted lace, treat yourself to one of the handmade batiste nightgowns at Gurrachuga, 72 Calle Alcala in Madrid. . . . Majorcan synthetic pearls are cheap (from $1 to $10 for a three-strander) and lovely; but as a precaution, have them restrung when you get home. Mitzou, 27 Serrano, Madrid, is known as the "suede queen" of Spain. At her boutique you can buy everything from gloves to a high-fashion suit. Her suede is 100 per cent waterproof and can be cleaned with ordinary lighter fluid. Expensive.

BRAZIL

Antique brass saddle shoes run around $10 a pair. You can use them purely for décor or hang them on the wall as a planter. . . . The hand-shaped Brazilian good-luck charm comes in all woods, sizes, and prices. I like the polished-mahogany four-inch brass-trimmed one for about $5.

COSTA RICA

One of the most charming decorations at the Pan American Union Building in Washington, D.C., is the Costa Rican donkey cart that adorns the lobby. Smart shoppers who visit Costa Rica will make the effort of acquiring one of these specials, gaily painted in bright red and blue. Costs range from $10 to $120 for a one-ton cart, plus shipping. Can be used as garden planter or as indoor bar.

HOLLAND

A set of sterling-silver demitasse spoons at any top jewelry shop will run you about $10 and make your coffee taste better. Antique wooden cooky molds also cost $10 and make wonderful kitchen trim. The Dutch polish the molds with shoe polish to give finish; take this off and restore the original surface veneer when you get home. . . . If you've yearned for a tiled fireplace, buy a dozen Delft tiles and do it yourself.

GREECE

You can buy wonderful six- by nine-foot woolen rugs, woven in red-and-black wool, for about $10. Visit a saddler's shop and buy donkey bells. These are very elaborate, pure-sounding brass bells in the form of horseshoes decorated with blue-and-white glass beads. Use the bell on your door. . . . Worry beads are fun. They are colored beads for fingering, not for praying; from fifteen cents up. According to legend, they should help you make decisions. . . . On the island of Mykonos, you can have a skirt woven to order in colors of your choice for $9.

GERMANY

Best buy in Germany is the cutlery. At the J. A. Henckels shop in Frankfurt am Main and in branches throughout West Germany, you'll find poultry shears, beautiful steak knives, carving sets, scissors, and hundreds of other kitchen necessities. A lemon squeezer in stainless steel is something you can't get at home. . . . Söhnges in Munich and Berlin has wonderful sunglasses and spectacles—and you can get delivery in a few hours. . . . You can get beautiful dinner sets at 30 per cent off by visiting the factory of Staatliche Porzellan-

Manufaktur Berlin. . . . Loden-Frey, a department store at 7 Maffeistrasse, Munich, offers everything from Bavarian loden cloth to elegant clothes. And in every antique shop in every city of Germany, you'll find Meissen china. Pick up a piece, whether it is soup ladle, cooky jar, or dinner plate—you'll love it forever.

IRELAND

Handsome are the Sybil Connolly shawls, mammoth black-fringed shapes that do things for a simple red skirt and white blouse. They cost about $15 and come in medium and large lengths. . . . Get a skirt made in a handsome tweed for $9.40 at Irene Gilbert, Ltd., 222 South Frederick Street, Dublin. . . . Shannon Airport's free port shop is famous for bargains. You might like the Irish coffee glasses, $4 for six plus a glass cloth with the recipe for this warming drink. A fashion note is the natural-colored Aran cardigan sweater for about $15; you can also get it in the lumber-jacket style. Take note of the wool that is used in draperies and chair coverings at the airport. It is called Bainin and is a thirty-inch handwoven tweed. Comes in natural, red, and green and can be dyed any color.

FINLAND

If you've always yearned for a truly magic carpet, forget your budget and buy one of the lovely Ryijy rugs. Hand-woven, they retail in the States at an astronomical price, sell for about $150 in Helsinki. . . . If you're hunting for something for less than $10, invest in one of the lovely brass *kalevala* bracelets copied from old Finnish designs.

ITALY

Since time immemorial, Italians have been known as great shoemakers, but except for casual and playshoes, don't buy ready-made footwear—it won't fit your foot. Do get a pair of shoes made to order at Ferragamo, Rome and Florence. Other best bets on the Italian scene: A straw or raffia full-length coat will run just over $30. A gold-plated altar stick two feet tall will cost around $10. Don't turn it into a lamp; instead, put a fancy candle in it and let it spiral upward from your coffee table. My Italian favorite is the Gucci (8 Via Condotti, Rome) three-way bag. It costs $42.50 and will last for years. Basic version is black satin with reversible cover, suede on one side and calf on the other. If you prefer, you can have a colored cover. Gucci recently developed a larger, sportier version of this perennial success. . . . You can buy silks by the yard at Galtrucco, 18 Via del Tritone, Rome. . . . For medium priced ready-to-wear try these three Roman shops: Mademoiselle, 114 Largo Santa Susanna; Spring 126 Via Salaria, Viser, 154 Via del Corso.

AUSTRIA

What could be better than sleeping on fine sheets and pillowcases that make you feel like an Austrian empress? These lovely linens are available at Braun's, 1 Graben, and other top Viennese shops. I like the pillowcases that button, the quilt covers with diamond-shaped panes. . . . If your grandmother's brooch is good, but the setting is unfashionable, take it to Mr. Mixon, 10 Habsburgergasse, Vienna, for resetting. . . . You can buy handsome dark-gray cardigans at any of the women's shops on the Kärntnerstrasse. If you see a sweater you like, but object to the fancy silver buttons that delight the Austrians, ask the clerk for plain dark wooden ones. *Caution:* Do not buy lederhosen; they look fine on wiry mountaineers, not on ladies with overstuffed rear ends. . . . Loden cloth is a good buy; you can get a handsome coat made at home. . . . The crystal is outstanding at world-famous J. & L. Lobmeyr, 26 Kärntnerstrasse, Vienna. If you like offbeat handcrafts and house furnishings, visit Oesterreichischer Werkstatten, 15 Kärntnerstrasse, Vienna.

DENMARK

You can spend a fortune at Den Permanente in Copenhagen, but for a moderate-priced object, I recommend the teak plates at $1 apiece. Wonderful for Christmas gifts. . . . An amusing object is the corded lion for $6. . . . At Skagen, the artists' colony on the North Sea, you can buy original oils for about $15, and they're good.

PORTUGAL

If you have a use for it, you can buy an antique pistol for anywhere from $8 to $50. . . . At Madeira Superba, located in Lisbon at 75A Avenida Duque de Loulé and in the Ritz Hotel, you'll find elegant petit point and gros point handbags. They are all hand-made. Prices start at $35. . . . You can do your shopping the easy way in Lisbon at the Centro de Turismo, 60 Rua do Castilho. Under one roof you'll see picturesque items from all over Portugal—rugs, pottery, peasant-type wool skirts, fishermen's plaid shirts, and shawls from Nazaré that make wonderful evening wraps. . . . For silver, I recommend Mergulhão, 162 Rua de S. Paulo, Lisbon. Take your choice of everything from one-of-a-kind spoons and little salt dishes to major serving pieces. This company does work for Tiffany.

LONDON

At N. Peal & Co. in the Burlington Arcade, you'll find thousands of cashmeres, Shetlands, and tartans. It is best to acquire a sweater and then buy a length of matching fabric in the store's textile department and have a skirt made to your measure—or you can just purchase the fabric and get the skirt made at home. . . . Hunt & Winterbotham, 4 Old Bond Street, have had their own fabric mills in the west of England since 1532. Take your pick of mohairs, gabardines, camel's hair, cheviots, and many others. You can get custom tailoring done on the premises. . . . Liberty & Co., a deservedly famous tourist institution on Regent Street, is an excellent place to pick up gifts; it's just as much fun to see the old-world atmosphere of the store as it is to buy. Select from Liberty silk and cotton prints by the yard, tablecloths, scarves, napkins, and handkerchiefs. . . . Looking for children's toys? Hamley's, 200–202 Regent Street, is the perfect place. Your choice can include anything from miniature English racing cars and fabulous puppets to dolls and English games that are fun for both Lilliputians and adults. . . . At Davison Newman & Co. (established in 1650), 14 Creechurch Lane, you can purchase a pound of the very same brew that went to the Boston Tea Party. . . . For the ultimate in extravagance, have a pair of riding boots made to order at Peal & Co., 48 Wigmore Street. . . . You can go wild among the collector's pieces at the London Silver Vaults in Chancery Lane, but you can also discover inexpensive trifles such as Sheffield-plate cheese spoons for $5. . . . Visit Foyle's, the largest bookstore in the world, at 119–125 Charing Cross Road; it might be fun to pick up an original edition of Shaw. . . . Keep browsing among all the bookstalls on Charing Cross Road and acquire an old print or, better still, a book of English prints. You can frame them all when you get home and use them for unusual wall décor. . . . For those who love amber, Sac Frères, 45 New Bond Street, offers all varieties of amber earrings, rings, pins. . . . You and Queen Elizabeth can have something in common—makeup. Purchase a new lipstick, base, or rouge tint at Cyclax, 58 S. Molton Street, and you'll be buying the brand used by Her Majesty. . . . Travel-tired skins can benefit from a dose of old-fashioned cucumber soap or cucumber night cream. You'll find these cleansing aids, plus sweet-smelling lavender blossoms and pomander balls, at Savory & Moore, 143 New Bond Street, an old-time chemist's shop founded in 1792. . . . Flower perfumes from Floris (89 Jermyn Street and 2 Beauchamp Place) are a good from-you-to-you present.

Sample Red Rose, Lily of the Valley, Honeysuckle, or Steph-
anotis to see what flower suits your personality. Do ask to
see the letter written in 1863 to Mr. Juan Faminias Floris by
Florence Nightingale, thanking him for the "sweet-smelling
nosegay" that helped cheer her sickbed.

ADDIS ABABA

Do your shopping in two spots—the New Market and Her
Majesty's Handicrafts School. A good souvenir choice is an
ivory-handled flyswatter made of a real horse's tail; cost, from
twenty-five cents to $2. Good buys are the monkey-fur rugs. A
four- by five-inch circle of black-and-white fur will run about
$10, and the prices go up accordingly as size increases. They
are lightweight—but they do shed. Hand-painted wall panels
that tell the story of the Queen of Sheba's visit to Solomon can
be had for $15. I love the gold-fringed red-velvet ceremonial
parasols used by Ethiopian women. These come in shades that
range from rose to ruby, prices that run from $6 to $15. Fit
for a queen on a commoner's budget.

So far, I've been primarily discussing the purchase of decorative objects. Now let's talk about buying clothes abroad, and
let me make the point that every woman should go abroad as
nearly naked as possible, and once she gets there, she should
buy, buy, buy—as long as her dollars and her disposition hold
out. If you are paying a visit to Paris, Rome, London, Madrid,
or Hong Kong, make sure that you allot money for at least
one outfit. If each fall you purchase a cocktail dress and a
daytime number, buy these two costumes abroad, and don't
consider the cost part of your travel budget.

Believe it or not, you can have that Tiffany look at bargain-
basement prices. You can have a dress and jacket made out of
fine silk in Hong Kong for only $30; then be really chic—keep
the name and address of the tailor and airmail him costumes
to be copied and returned by mail. You can pick up a knitted
suit at Luisa Spagnoli in Rome, with alterations included,

for as little as $45. In Paris, you can find Balenciaga cast-off
models at Anna Lowe on the Avenue Matignon. There are
also stores in Paris that specialize in reduced-price clothes—
for example, Sèvres 33 at 33 Rue de Sèvres, which is entirely
devoted to sweaters. Don't be scared to wander into any store
and ask, "How much?" You may be surprised at the answer.
Even the *haute couture* houses have ready-to-wear *boutiques*
and have sales of their model clothes. After all, Dior, Givenchy,
and Cardin wouldn't be in business if they existed solely on
the patronage of Hollywood stars and wives of Greek ship-
owners.

My first on-the-spot contact with *haute couture* happened
in the United States, where I handled a public-relations job
for Jacques Esterel, the guitar-playing *couturier* who has cre-
ated many a beguiling number for Brigitte Bardot. As we
traveled the length of the Eastern seaboard, showing off
Jacques' newest concoctions to American misses with money,
I kept my eyes on a fetching apple-green satin dress with
matching sleeves in apple-green lace. This was paired with a
coat in the same spring-green.

I became happier and happier as the costume got dirtier.
"Do you want to sell it?" I asked Jacques just before he and
his newfound dollars left New York for Paris.

"Try it on," said he.

I did—and the dress was so tight that I could barely fit
into it.

"I'll make one for you in Paris when you come this fall,"
offered Jacques.

"I thought you might sell me this as a leftover model. The
actual costume will cost too much," I muttered, a little cha-
grined over the difference between the dress's waistline and
my own twenty-five-inch circumference.

"Five hundred dollars each," said the canny *couturier*.

I stared. "Brigitte makes a lot more money than I do."

"Come into the shop and say hello anyway. I'll take you

to lunch," offered Jacques, appreciative of my efforts with the American press.

In Paris, I felt a little hesitant about the lunch offer, but the memory of that beguiling costume kept gnawing at my brain and my pocketbook. One day, passing the swank corner of Avenue Matignon and the Faubourg-St-Honoré, I saw the sign "Jacques Esterel." In I went. Five minutes later, he and I were exchanging pleasantries.

"Do you still want the dress and coat?" he asked.

"Of course, but I still can't afford it."

"It's yours," said he, "for the cost of just the material."

Five fittings later and $150 poorer, I left for home, carrying proudly my first—and last—*haute couture* purchase: eighteen pounds' worth of lining, weights, ruffles, tulle, and satin. It still makes me feel expensive just to put it on.

HOW TO CROSS
THE U.S. CUSTOMS BARRIER

No matter where you venture outside the United States, you are bound to find at least one man waiting for you at the dock, airport, or border point when you return to this country —the customs inspector.

Contrary to popular belief, the American inspector does not have orders to be hard on returning Americans. He just has to do his job. That job is to see that you comply with a set of complicated regulations. The best way for you to save time, money, nerves, and a possible tangle with the law is to learn what these regulations are well ahead of time.

EXEMPTIONS. As a tourist, you are entitled to bring back a certain amount duty free if you have been out of the United States for at least forty-eight hours, if the merchandise is for personal and household use rather than for resale, and if you haven't claimed an exemption on another trip within the pre-

vious thirty-one days. The exemption is based on the wholesale value of the items unless they were made to order for
you. Your goods are generally valued by customs at a standard
discount of 40 per cent under the store's retail price, so a $100
exemption really works out to about $166 in retail purchases.
There are some exceptions to the standard 40 per cent
discount, but a substantial allowance in value is usual except
for items made to order for you.

DUTIES. When you bring in more than your exemption,
you have to pay duty on the surplus (again, on the discounted
value). Don't wait until you are face to face with the inspector
to learn the bad news. Find out beforehand what kinds of
articles are duty free and what kinds aren't. Remember that a
20 per cent duty on a $40 Luisa Spagnoli suit from Rome will
run the price to $48—still well under the $80 that a Spagnoli
outfit costs in the States.

Some goods are banned. Jade is one of the many items that
may not be imported without a special license or a certification
that they were not originally produced in Communist China
or North Korea. Tourists in Hong Kong are most likely to
encounter the problem of goods that come under the ban.
You can keep out of trouble by securing a copy of the booklet "What U.S. Citizens Must Know About Buying Chinese-
type Goods in Hong Kong" the minute you arrive at the airport. The booklet lists goods for which a "Certificate of Origin"
must be obtained and bona fide stores in which to buy.

There are three steps you can take to speed up the formal-
ities on your return. The first is to keep all your receipts in one
quickly accessible place, such as your wallet. This not only
makes things simpler for the inspector, but enables you to
make out your declaration without fuss or forgetting. The
second is to pack all your purchases together so that the
harassed inspector can get to them easily. The third is, when
you make out the customs declaration, write yourself a re-
minder note as to the exact nature of your purchases. I re-

cently returned from Greece and, in going over my slips, found out that I had purchased an *amphora*. It hasn't turned up yet, and I haven't the vaguest idea what or where it is.

Use your charm on the customs inspectors. They are judge, jury, appraiser, critic—and also men. A friend of mine had bought several dresses in Europe and wished to avoid paying heavy duty. At the same time, she wanted to be honest. "I bought them abroad—but I've been wearing them for six solid weeks," she declared, batting her eyes at the gentleman. The customs inspector smiled, put a white check on her luggage, and passed her through. Incidentally, you always have a choice of several inspectors. Don't be in a hurry. Pick your line carefully—select the man who looks as if he had a good breakfast.

CHAPTER 14

More Than Manners

The minute you go abroad, you become the foreigner.

To gain admittance and acceptance overseas, you will need two passports—the official document that proves your American citizenship and the good manners that you should also carry with you.

When you cross the Atlantic, Pacific, or even the southern border of the United States, you have done far more than exchange Main Street, U.S.A., for a stay on foreign soil. You have become the alien. Your behavior as the stranger in a strange land, your adaptability, and observance and practice of local customs will decide whether you are accepted as friend or enemy.

You have achieved a new importance. You are not just a tourist. You are now an ambassadress of the United States. The residents of foreign countries will evaluate your country by the impression you make.

You can never become acquainted ahead of time either with all the customs or with the psychology of the peoples you will meet on the trip. Whatever you do learn in advance will help. But you must go with an attitude of receptivity and respect and a willingness to understand the reason for the unfamiliar

252

mores and not scorn them as "peculiar" just because they are strange to you.

Most of the errors people make in foreign countries stem from ignorance, not arrogance.

For us, the "future" is the foreseeable future. But the Hindu or Buddhist in Asia, expecting to return to earth in a series of reincarnations, feels that it is perfectly realistic to think of the future in terms of thousands of years.

We judge others by their emotional response to us. But aristocratic Malays never laugh and seldom smile, because they feel it is not good taste to show their emotions.

In North America, a businessman who made more than one appointment for the same time would be considered a bad risk. In South America, it is customary for a businessman to make several appointments for the same hour; an uninformed North American who arrives on the dot for his four o'clock date may feel offended at having to wait for more than an hour. However, if he knows the custom, he may not like the wait, but he will comprehend the reason for delay.

We chuckle when a rich old man—or even a poor one— marries a pretty young thing. But in Nepal, it is no laughing matter; men are barred from taking a wife more than twenty years younger.

South American men are considered by women to be very sexy. Yet Latins frequently embrace other men as a greeting— a gesture that the tall, silent, more repressed *yanqui* would think of as effeminate.

A Middle Easterner's idea of law and order is far different from ours. Recently, an Iranian girl told me the sad story of a Mr. Said, whose wife had cheated on him. The husband's brother immediately went out and killed the seducer.

"What did the police do?" I asked.

She looked at me with pity for the innocent question. "Nothing," she shrugged. "It was a matter for the family—not for them."

The longer a visitor stays in a country, the more difficult the country can seem. A nod of the head does not always mean yes. A smile does not always connote approval. People may promise the visitor that they will do something by the next day—and a week later she is still waiting.

How can the American woman visitor avoid suffering from the condition anthropologist Edward T. Hall refers to as "culture shock"? According to Mr. Hall, culture shock is "simply a removal or distortion of many of the familiar cues one encounters at home and the substitution for them of cues which are strange."

The coward's solution is to escape—both from the country and into the comforting thought that "everything in America is best."

The wiser woman will not sit in judgment on the mores of other peoples, other lands. If she is smart and wants to get the most out of her overseas sojourn, she will follow these six basic rules for the guest abroad:

1. She will learn everything she possibly can about the traditions and social customs of the countries to which she is going.

2. She will show genuine interest in the way of life she finds when she gets there.

3. She will not gripe about any inconvenience she finds. (The British like their beer warm; we like ice in practically everything.)

4. She will not be the "American millionaire." Showing off her wealth will only make her unpopular.

5. She will not brag about how far ahead we are in the United States. Some countries do not attach the importance we do to mass production and scientific development.

6. She will practice as many of the local customs as possible and avoid making herself conspicuous by practicing the opposite.

These preachy words are fine in theory and I'm sure that

every American woman means to carry them out when she first goes abroad. But the art of overseasmanship is a tricky one, and often, with the best of intentions, the woman traveler makes mistakes simply because of lack of knowledge or lack of courtesy. The first is forgivable, the latter is not. Courtesy costs nothing, and as Menander said, "Manner, not gold, is woman's best adornment."

Here are a few pointers:

❡ *Keep Out of Arguments.* You will certainly rub a Briton the wrong way by telling him that we "came over and won the last one." A Greek may give you the cold shoulder if you announce "we supported you for years." Overseas is not the place to discuss politics or old wars. No matter what you think about De Gaulle, don't discuss him at the top of your lungs in a crowded French restaurant. Khrushchev may be an object of your scorn, but the place to talk about him is outside the Soviet Union. Whatever Hitler did, he finished doing it two decades ago, and there is no point in analyzing his methods and madness in the Germany of today.

❡ *Food for Thought.* If foreign friends ask you to be their guest for lunch or dinner at a restaurant, *eat.* Do not say, "I'll just take an omelet," or, "Your food is so rich that I just can't digest it." Your friend will properly interpret remarks like this as rudeness. No matter what the state of your digestion, make yourself eat something light first, then a main dish. If calories count for a lot with you, you can always order a plain grilled steak. But whatever your food choice, make your hosts feel that you enjoy their country's cuisine. Diet the next time you are by yourself.

Do not smoke between courses at a dinner party. (In England, it is considered very bad form to smoke before the Queen's toast!) Wait for the hostess or host to offer cigarettes or give the signal. The French particularly feel that tobacco ruins taste and are offended if you light a cigarette just before the soufflé.

Different countries have different eating customs. In Japan, try to use chopsticks. Any Japanese will be delighted to come to your aid. The technique is easily mastered. If you really get stuck, most inns will be able to produce a fork. If you cannot separate your meat into bite-size chunks, pick up a whole piece with your chopsticks and bite off a morsel. Drink from your soup bowl. And if you've always longed to make loud noises when eating soup, here's your chance! It's expected. Eat all your rice; food is not wasted in Asia. You can use toothpicks both during the meal and after—but shield your mouth with your hand.

You have probably looked forward to a real Swedish *smörgåsbord*—the Swedes pronounce it *smer-ghos-boord*—but have wondered just how to approach it, just as I was bewildered by the *rijstafel* in Holland. You will find a large table—sometimes a huge table, for the *smörgåsbord* may entail as many as fifty or even one hundred dishes—in the middle of the dining room, easily accessible to a parade of guests. The routine is this: the first time around, help yourself to fish—sardines of all sizes, salmon, shrimps, prawns, smoked eel, herring in half a dozen forms; on your second plate, you take the cold meats, salads, and, if you like, cheeses, such as the dark, sweetish *getost*—goat's milk cheese; the third round is reserved for the hot dishes—Swedish meatballs, tiny sausages, herring pudding au gratin. Never mix the fish and meat. For the Nordic trencherman, all this is just an appetizer, perhaps washed down with ice-cold *aquavit*, a caraway-seed-flavored spirit that is not sipped but gulped. American appetites are usually more than satisfied by *smörgåsbord* and dessert—possibly the delicious little Swedish pancakes.

In Switzerland, don't miss the fondue. This is a Helvetian version of Welsh rabbit—made with Emmentaler or Gruyère cheese, white wine instead of beer, butter, a dash of nutmeg, and a healthy spoonful of kirsch, the cherry spirit. When the blend has been melted in a chafing dish, you impale a piece of French bread on the end of the fork, dunk, twist, and eat. If you share this specialty with the opposite sex, you should be prepared for the special touch at the end of the meal: Swiss tradition dictates that the one who loses the bread off the fork owes the men (or the ladies) a kiss.

⟨[*Liquor License.* When you are a guest in a private home at cocktail time, do not ask for Scotch, bourbon, or American-type drinks unless your hostess offers them. Liquor can be very expensive abroad, and most homes are not equipped with whiskey. It is perfectly permissible to ask, "What do you suggest?" You are always safe in asking for sherry in Spain, port in Portugal, vermouth in France and Italy, and vodka in Russia.

As for the social etiquette of wines: broadly speaking, it's red with meat or game, white with fish, fowl, oysters, or hors d'oeuvres. You can drink champagne all through the meal and, if it isn't cold enough, send it back for more chilling. Never dilute a vintage wine with water, and never use a swizzle stick. Don't fill a wineglass up to its brim; leave room for the wine to breathe, so that you may enjoy its bouquet.

Good manners dictate that you become familiar with the *skål* (pronounced *skawl*) ceremony in Denmark. There are rigid rules for this ceremonial toast. Here's what you do. Wait until someone gives the signal, then raise your glass, look the recipient squarely in the eye, nod your head, loudly say, "*Skål,*" drink bottoms up, and never permit your eyes to waver from the eyes of the recipient. When you finish, hoist your glass again and bow. Then, and only then, should you lower your eyes.

Incidentally, you may find the word "bar" over a shop in Sweden. Usually this is a milk bar, where meals are sold self-service style.

⟨[*Language in action.* Make an effort to learn a few words of the language of the country—the natives will be flattered, and it doesn't matter how bad an accent you have. Your

vocabulary should include the terms for "Good morning,"
"Good-bye," "Delighted to meet you," "Please," "Thank you,"
"Excuse me," and "I'm so sorry, but I don't speak German"
(or whatever the language is). You also should be able to say,
"Here's to you," or some version of the local toast. Acquire
these terms and you'll find the natives more friendly. A smile,
an apologetic shrug, and expressive pantomime will get you
by in any spot.

On the other hand, do not assume that because you are in a
country whose people speak a language other than English,
no one about you will understand what you are saying in
your own language. Making personal remarks about the
people you see on the street, in buses or streetcars is rude,
regardless of a real or imagined language barrier. This can be
true even after you leave a particular country. I remember
flying out of Moscow to Copenhagen on an Aeroflot jet. Next
to me was a woman, bound also for the Danish capital, who
spoke excellent English. I assumed that she was a Dane and
told her in great detail about all my "difficulties" in the Soviet
Union and how I couldn't wait to get to Europe. "Interesting,
but Russia just isn't for me," I concluded, and I went on to
a discussion of current fashions.

As the jet swooped down on Copenhagen, I turned to my
neighbor and told her how much I had enjoyed talking with
her.

"Did you?" She raised her eyebrows. "That is strange. You
see, I am a Russian and a proud Russian."

Differences in meaning between British English and American English can cause a girl trouble. The words are the same,
but the usage—and the implications—can be as widely at vari-
ance as Tagalog and Urdu. English slang is particularly tricky.

I nearly died of embarrassment when my English host (supposedly a happily married man) said, "Take a nap this afternoon. I'll be coming along to your room to knock you up in
time for tea." He didn't mean what I thought he meant at all.

He was merely going to rap on my door to wake me. When a Londoner gets a good screw, he brings home a big paycheck. When he summons courage to meet adversity, he keeps his pecker up. When he gets the wind up, he is frightened.

"Bloody" meaning "very" is considered extremely vulgar in England. "Closet" usually means water closet, not the place to hang your hat and coat (which is a wardrobe).

Here is a short vocabulary that may be useful:

AMERICAN	BRITISH
Ticket office	Booking hall
Store	Shop
Rare (meat)	Underdone
Elevator	Lift
Candy	Sweet
French fried potatoes	Chips
Drugstore	Chemist's shop
Apartment house	Block of flats
Raincoat	Mackintosh
Bar	Public house or pub
Syrup	Treacle
Run (stocking)	Ladder
Run (for office)	Stand
Orchestra seat	Stall
Prep school	Public school
Grade (in school)	Form
Streetcar	Tram
Subway	Tube or Underground
Gasoline	Petrol
Sedan	Saloon
Hood (of an auto)	Bonnet
Baby carriage	Pram
Two weeks	Fortnight
Vegetable and fruit store	Greengrocery
Vaudeville theater	Music Hall
Oatmeal	Porridge
Roast (of meat)	Joint
Huckster	Coster or hawker
Check baggage	Register luggage
Swim	Bathe

If you head for Scotland, never refer to people or landscape as "Scotch." It's "Scot," "Scotswoman," or "Scottish," unless you are talking about drink or broth.

Even if your French does not extend beyond the *merci, très bien,* and *combien* stage, you will manage fine in France, but you should know that the word *douche* means shower in French. I learned this on the Riviera while swimming with a handsome lad from Marseilles. When once we emerged from the bright blue Mediterranean, he cheerfully suggested, "Wouldn't you like to take a douche?" I gulped, ignored the suggestion, and gave him the brush-off. Later in my hotel room, I consulted my Anglo-French dictionary and realized that he had had a very good idea. Other interesting Gallicisms: *baiser* as a noun means a kiss. Used as a verb, *baiser* has extremely vulgar connotations. Likewise, *exciter* refers to physical excitement.

⟨[*The Glad Hand.* Shaking hands is the expected gesture abroad far more than in the United States. You shake hands when you meet people and again when you leave the room. In Europe, one shakes hands with the saleswoman, hotel manager, and often the headwaiter. This routine reaches its height in Portugal, where the boss in the office shakes hands with his employees almost every morning.

When a woman meets a Continental gentleman, she should immediately take off her glove. Then he is free to kiss her hand. It is certainly not true, as one "authority" wrote, that a man will peel back the glove and plant a buss on the wrist. He won't. When in doubt as to whether her hand is going to be kissed or shaken, a woman can do no better than extend the hand limply and see what happens. If she's working for a firm handshake while he's maneuvering to get within kissing range, the result can turn into pure judo.

In the Far East, the greeting routine is different. In Japan it is a bow from the waist, or even several bows, depending on the status of the person greeted. Do not offer a handshake, but be prepared to accept one should your Japanese friend follow the Western custom.

Indians greet each other in still another manner—by pressthe hands together as in prayer and slightly bowing the head at the same time. The same custom is practiced in Thailand and other countries that have felt the influence of the Indian religions, either Hinduism or Buddhism.

❧ *Sitting and Standing.* In Europe, save in Scandinavia, a lady is always seated at the gentleman's right. She also walks on the gentleman's right. Exception: in a theater where this practice would put a woman in an aisle seat. In Scandinavian countries, the lady is placed at the heart side, on the gentleman's left. From time to time abroad, I have been terribly surprised to find myself walking practically on the curb, with my escort on the inside, but that's the European system.

In England (and elsewhere), people queue up at bus stops, cinemas, railroad and booking offices. Take your place at the end of the line, and do not tread on the heels of the person in front of you. There are long lines in Russia, too, but there Intourist seems to maneuver all Americans to the front ranks immediately.

Abroad, it is customary for young women to rise when an older woman enters the room—and always when being introduced. Incidentally, should you be invited to a cocktail party, don't expect that a hostess will introduce you to all the guests. You'll be expected to fend for yourself.

❧ *Calling Cards.* You will need plenty of visiting cards. Leave them at the U.S. Embassy if you are staying in a capital more than a week. Sign the register and give your address. Visiting cards are useful to exchange with newfound acquaintances, a practice more usual in Europe than in the United States. I found my business card particularly useful in Germany, where people are impressed by title and rank. Incidentally, write your address in the lower left-hand corner of the cards.

❡ *Reciprocation.* Outside the United States, women just do not pick up the check if there is a man along. However, it is good form for the single woman to give dinners or luncheons in restaurants, first warning the headwaiter not to present the bill at the table. In London, where pubs close at a certain hour, you can reciprocate by asking people back to your hotel for a brandy. For drinking purposes, a hotel is home to the guest.

It is one thing for you to return hospitality, another to embarrass people by thoughtlessly imposing on local custom. Arabs are particularly generous, and they regard a guest as a sacred trust. Even in the poorest home in Syria, the host will proffer coffee or tea in the cold months or a sort of lemonade-orangeade (*gazoz*) in the summer. If you admire an object in an Arab home too enthusiastically, you may be embarrassed by having your host present it to you.

❡ *Special Tipping.* In European theaters, the usher must be tipped or she'll call attention to your lapse (theater programs are not free, either). Guides everywhere receive tips. When members of the clergy or any religious order show you around a church or other religious establishment, it is best to give a contribution to the church. When staying the weekend in a private home, tipping is expected, just as it is in the United States. For instance, should you rate an invitation to a fancy British weekend in Suffolk, you would give a pound each to the butler and the maid. Always tip the cloakroom attendants. However, should you indulge in a Dior or Ricci, do not tip the saleswoman. She would be insulted.

❡ *General Tipping.* For some strange reason, women spend a lot of unnecessary nervous energy worrying about how much to tip. To avoid extremes, remember these basic tips on tipping:

1. The bulk of the hotel tip is usually included in the bill as part of the total. Most hotels automatically add a service charge to your bill (varying from 10 to 20 per cent, depending

on the country). Many restaurants do the same, so if in doubt, always ask, "Is service included?"

2. The only people you should tip during a hotel stay are the porter who brings your baggage to the room and the bellboy who brings a message to your room or who runs out to get you cigarettes. Otherwise, don't delve into your bag until you're ready to leave.

3. On departure, you will have to shell out. You should always give the concierge something—a minimum of $1 at a first-class establishment and $5 if you have been there a week and he has been helpful. Give the chambermaid about the equivalent of a quarter a day. If you have used the room waiter, take care of him in the same way. The man who has shined your shoes should get ten cents a pair.

4. Never give the concierge a lump sum to distribute. That's trusting human nature too much.

5. In restaurants, tip in addition to the percentage only if the service has been extraordinary. Local diners let the service charge do the job; however, you may want to leave the small change.

6. Watch taxi drivers. They frequently take out the tip before they give you your change, so you are really being taken for a ride. Read the meter and count your currency.

7. Whenever you don't know what to tip, give 15 per cent. Better err a little on the generous side, but not so much that you make yourself ridiculous. A fair tip will earn respect. A too-lavish one will add to the reputation Americans have achieved for trying to buy their way everywhere.

Here is a country-by-country guide:

AUSTRIA. Hotels and restaurants add a 10 to 15 per cent service charge to your bill, but tip an extra 10 per cent for special services. Tip 15 per cent in other cases; for luggage, about three schillings (a schilling equals about four cents) per bag. In restaurants, tip about 5 per cent in addition to the 10 per cent on your bill. You'll also be expected to leave a tip for the strolling musicians in a restaurant and will find a plate waiting to receive it. This should be five to ten schillings per guest.

DENMARK. All hotels and restaurants add a 15 per cent service charge to your bill. This is sufficient. Should it not be added, give 15 per cent. The only member of the hotel staff who will expect something extra is the porter and then only if he has rendered special service.

FRANCE. Hotels add a 10 per cent tax and a service charge of 15 per cent to the bill, but still you are expected to tip the bellboy, porter, chambermaid, waiter, and anyone else who does anything for you. If you don't, they'll ask. If the service charge has been added, you can get away with a small addition. If it hasn't, tip as you would elsewhere—15 per cent of the bill. Even with a service charge on the bill, you will still be expected to tip the wine waiter—one or two new francs.

For the woman alone, it is also a good idea to tip the telephone operator when you enter the hotel. You'll need her to help you find people, places, and things.

Taxi drivers expect a 12 per cent tip—more for a short ride.

At theaters, the ushers will expect one franc.

Porters at railroad stations get seventy-five centimes (fifteen cents) per bag from the French but expect double that from Americans with heavy luggage.

Guides on sight-seeing buses expect a tip of one and a half to two new francs.

GERMANY. There is usually 10 per cent added to restaurant bills and 15 per cent to hotel-room bills. Nothing in addition is expected.

GREAT BRITAIN. Here some hotels add a service charge of 10 to 15 per cent and others do not. Find out what the custom is when you register. If a service charge is added, extra tips will not be expected except for extra service: for dining-room waiters (if you eat there) 15 per cent of your bill for each meal, for porters, and for the maid if you make a prolonged stay. Incidentally, you don't tip the barmaid in a pub, but you may buy her a drink.

GREECE. A service charge is included in hotel (15 per cent) and restaurant bills (10 per cent). In addition, you usually tip an extra 10 per cent, because Greek waiters really need your drachmas. A guide for the day should get about fifty drachmas.

ITALY. Most hotels will charge an additional 18 to 20 per cent for service and tax. Restaurants add to your bill a service charge of 15 per cent (in Rome, more) plus tax. However, most waiters, particularly in name restaurants, expect another 5 per cent from you. In restaurants where there is music, you will be expected to pay an extra charge or they may pass the hat. Contribute a hundred lire (sixteen cents).

Railway, airport, and hotel baggage porters generally expect a hundred lire for each piece of baggage. It is advisable to tip hotel chambermaids, bellboys, and waiters a hundred lire each time you call for them; otherwise, give them a round sum when you leave, according to services they have rendered and the length of your stay. Do not forget the hotel porter. Give him approximately 10 per cent of his personal bill, which includes stationery, stamps, long-distance calls, cables, newspapers, and so on.

RUSSIA. It is not necessary to tip in most places, but a 10 per cent tip is expected in restaurants outside the Intourist beat. The checkroom attendant—and you are always expected to surrender your coat in a public building—should get a ruble.

SPAIN. Hotels add a service charge of 15 per cent, and no further tipping is expected unless you have received special services. Fifteen per cent is also added to meal checks, but here, and also in Portugal, you are expected to give the waiter the small change.

ARGENTINA. Tipping has been theoretically abolished by law in restaurants. A service charge is added to your hotel and restaurant bills. It is, however, customary to tip approximately 10 per cent in addition.

INDIA. At hotels that do not include a service charge, the usual tip is 10 per cent. Taxi drivers are not tipped.

JAPAN. Give fifty to a hundred yen to the boy who carries your bags. The 10 per cent that restaurants and hotels add to your bill is sufficient. No tipping to taxi drivers.

❡ *Thank You.* Never delay writing your bread-and-butter notes, whether for a simple luncheon or an evening on the town. Sending flowers with your note is even better. In India, the custom is to extend an immediate return invitation to your hostess. In Sweden, people thank the host and hostess at the end of the meal, before they adjourn to the living room.

❡ *Punctuality.* At all diplomatic and official parties in all countries, promptness is expected. The same thing is true in unofficial England. Arrive five minutes late and you find that the predinner drink has been served and that the party is ready to move to the dining room for overdone Brussels sprouts. In France, you can be ten to fifteen minutes late. In Italy, as a rule, be on time for all meals, but if you are asked for five o'clock tea, you'll find that showing up a half hour late will make you the first guest. In Spain, the entertaining hours are so late, it is practically impossible to be tardy. When dining out in Spain, you will find that although you are asked for 10 P.M., no one arrives before 10:30 or 11. The South American dinner hour is also late, generally around 9 P.M. You may be from a half-hour to an hour late unless your hostess has specified *hora inglesa* (English time).

❡ *Cutlery Counts.* Don't be disturbed if you end up without eating utensils and a new course appears. In many countries, after the main course it is customary to place your knife and fork in a holder at the right of your plate. You save the knife and fork for the cheese and salad course. Dessert fork and spoon are placed above the plate.

Americans who travel abroad for the first time often wonder why Europeans handle their knives, forks, and spoons in ways so contrary to American custom. The Continental way of dining involves the simultaneous use of knife and fork. The fork is held in the left hand, the knife in the right. At no time is the knife put down and the fork transferred to the right hand. The knife is used not only for cutting, but also to press foods onto the tines of the fork. Don't try to follow suit unless you know how; but if you do, you'll decide that this way is much faster and more efficient.

My friend Lucille spent two weeks in an upper-class Indian household in New Delhi where English table customs were the rule. When she was about to set forth on a month-long trip throughout India, visiting friends of New Delhi friends, her Indian hostess said, "Lucille, I must talk to you. You've been driving the servants crazy."

Lucille began feeling very inadequate. It had been a little difficult getting used to all those retainers.

"You must do something about your table manners on the trip. The servants never can tell when you have finished eating!"

Then the story came out. The servants would hide behind a curtained entrance to the dining room to watch for cues: knife and fork crossed on the plate with the tines of the fork down means you're just resting; knife and fork crossed with the fork on its side means you want second helpings; when the knife and fork are in the center of the plate facing the diner, you're finished.

Poor Lucille had been sticking to the American custom of placing the knife and fork diagonally from the near right-hand edge of the plate to the far left-hand edge, and the servants never knew what was what or when. Her hostess thought she'd better mend Lucille's manners before she caused any more difficulties on the remainder of her trip.

❆ *Cleanliness.* Do not be embarrassed by the occasional co-educational toilet you may run into. Just ignore everyone else. They will be doing the same to you.

In Finland, the sauna, the famous Finnish bath, is a must. Nearly every home has one, and almost every hotel. First you steam, then you are scrubbed inch by inch all over and beaten not too gently with birch branches, and then you plunge into cold water. It's a fine, invigorating way to get clean, but you'll need to get your hair done when you finish.

A Japanese bath is something special. The Japanese never use soap in the bathtub. First they sit on a wooden stool outside the tub or pool, take the water with the dipper provided, douse thoroughly, scrub down with soap, and rinse completely. Then they get in the bath to soak. This may be a problem, for the Japanese like their baths hot. If you can't beat the heat, add a small amount of cold water, but not too much. Better not to get in at all than to ruin it for the next person. Your *tenugui* (towel) does triple duty as washcloth, towel, and fig leaf.

❆ *Religious Etiquette.* When visiting churches abroad, women should wear a head covering, stockings, and dresses with sleeves. Buy one of the little black lace head scarves that are sold in American department stores for just this purpose. (Saks Fifth Avenue sells them for $1.) For an audience with the Pope, women must wear a dark, long-sleeved, high-necked dress or suit plus a hat and veil. If you are not a Catholic, you need not genuflect or kiss the Pope's ring. You must take your shoes off before entering a mosque; usually there will be slippers for you to put on.

Far more important is the attitude you have about other people's religions. Americans show their interest by asking questions; but direct questions do not charm Orientals, and sometimes unknowing people ask things with penetrating rudeness. For example, on one occasion, my friend Lenore and her Indian friend Sita, along with some other American tourists, were in a car going to the famous Ellora and Ajanta caves.

One of the American women addressed Sita, a rich, reserved, well-bred Indian matron. "Can you explain to me the difference between *dharma* (duty), *karma* (doctrine whereby a man's actions in this life determine his position in the next), and *artha* (worldly success)?" She said this to Sita, a woman who accepts her religion on faith and who if she came to America would never ask anyone his religious beliefs or whether he believed in the divinity of Christ.

To the American woman, Sita was just an Indian in a sari, so she continued her cross-examination.

Finally, Sita answered, "If I'm a good wife and mother and do the things I'm supposed to do, in the next birth I'll have a better life. If I'm sick now, it is because I had a bad previous life."

It cost Sita much to make the explanation, but the American woman then said, "Tell me, does anyone really believe this?"

People in India have believed in the doctrine of responsibility for successive reincarnations for four thousand years. Later, in the privacy of their hotel room, Sita was ready to throw her cup and saucer against the wall. "That's why we hate Americans," she said bitterly to Lenore.

Moral: if you want to ask theological questions, ask a theologian—if he brings up the subject.

❦ *"My Country 'Tis of Thee."* Abroad, people make much more of their national anthems than we make of ours. This is true particularly in Britain, where "God Save the Queen" is played at the beginning and end of all public performances and everyone is expected to stand at attention.

One year I served as chaperone to the girl who had made the best doll in a contest in the United States. We visited six European countries on a goodwill mission, handing out dolls to less fortunate youngsters. It was a mammoth publicity junket that had been preceded by a year-long buildup and a week of festivities in the United States. The sixteen-year-old girl from the Midwest—I'll call her Suzy—who won top honors in the nationwide competition, had become a celebrity. With her doll, a fashionably dressed babe with a mammoth wardrobe of coats, suits, and dresses, she had appeared on the "Ed Sullivan Show" before an audience of more than forty million viewers, made eight other TV and radio appearances, been interviewed by all the wire services, been welcomed to New York by Mrs. Eleanor Roosevelt, and been guest of honor at a reception at the United Nations. This was heady stuff for a teen-age girl from a small town, and she became quickly accustomed to all the glamour, attention, and service that go with being a celebrity.

We arrived in London at five o'clock (a few hours behind schedule because of weather). At the hotel, there was a note from the tourist office. "You are free this evening," it read. "Will call for you at nine tomorrow morning. Beefeaters waiting to give you special greeting at Tower of London."

Because I didn't want to leave Suzy without anything to do her first night in London, I ordered tickets for a musical. The only seats were in a box, so I took them, feeling very magnanimous, since I would have much preferred to see some sad drama with Gladys Cooper.

We bathed, dressed (I in dignified black befitting a chaperon and Suzy in her best crinoline-skirted red velvet), had a proper tea in our room, and taxied off to Her Majesty's Theater.

"English theaters are different from ours," I informed Suzy. "They call their orchestra seats 'stalls'."

Suzy couldn't have cared less. She didn't like this quiet arrival with no one at the hotel to meet us.

We drew up at the theater, and a cheerful usher led us to the box, royally decorated in red plush. I continued my briefing, "See, Suzy, theaters in England have bars. We don't allow that back home." (This law has been changed now.)

Suzy nodded. I could see that she would rather be strolling the streets of New York signing autographs than sitting unrecognized in a box at a London theater.

The lights began to dim, and I realized that I had forgotten to tell Suzy that every British performance begins with the orchestra playing "God Save the Queen."

Oh, well, I thought to myself, she doesn't care. She'll just think it's "My Country 'Tis of Thee."

The music began. The audience rose. My prize charge remained glued to her seat, but for the first time in London, she looked happy.

"Get up, Suzy," I said, nudging her.

She looked at me blankly.

"Get up," I repeated. "That's 'God Save the Queen.' You must show respect by standing."

The smile faded. The teen-age eyes filled with tears. "Oh," she said with definite hostility, "I thought it was our American song—and that they were playing it for me."

❰ *The Feminine Approach.* Foreigners often sum up American women with the damning sentence, "They're all on the make." All American women are no more on the make than are all Swedish, German, or French women. However, Americans do sometimes tend to be thoughtless and flaunt convention abroad by doing things that would be considered perfectly all right at home but are improper overseas.

The woman traveling alone must watch her behavior in the Latin countries or she will be considered not quite a lady —and will be treated accordingly. Entering a bar alone in Spain or Portugal will certainly be considered a bid for masculine attention. Commenting on a movie to the handsome Latin stranger in the aisle seat on your right will be considered a pickup maneuver, whereas in America such a remark would not be misunderstood. Wearing an ankle bracelet will certainly give the Latin man the wrong idea.

Any woman traveling abroad will have a better time if she

exposes the best side of her nature to other human beings in other lands.

George Washington wrote a book on manners that he called *Rules of Civility and Decent Behavior in Company and Conversation.* His first rule: Every action done in company ought to be done with some sign of respect for those who are present.

All over the world, courtesy and manners are based upon plain common sense and consideration for others. Govern yourself by common sense and the law of kindness and you can't go far wrong.

CHAPTER 15

The Follow-up

In Manhattan, an elderly widow stood in line at Columbia University to enroll for the elementary course in Russian. Simultaneously, in Milwaukee, traditional U.S. home of German cuisine, a thirty-year-old department-store buyer sent out invitations to a Saturday-night *smörgåsbord*. A Cleveland divorcée called the dean at Western Reserve. "Have you a foreign student who would like to come to Sunday dinner?" she asked. A recent college graduate left her wheat-farm home and drove to the Kansas City library, thirty miles away, for books on the cultural history of France.

Separated by thousands of miles, these women differed in age, appearance, income, and interest, but they shared one thing in common: a determination to make a recent trip abroad an influence in their daily lives. They realized, as you should, that the most important part of your trip comes *after* you return home. The intelligent traveler uses her expedition for her economic, cultural, and social future, not merely as a remembrance of things past.

In advance, you have had the fun of imagining the most fantastic adventures. On the actual odyssey, you have absorbed new ideas, impressions, and experiences. But it is the follow-up from home base that makes your trip of a lifetime

273

affect your lifetime. What happens on the journey isn't half as important as what you do with what you have learned.

How can you utilize your trip abroad at home?

SOCIAL SATISFACTION

Mind Your Manners. The first thing to do, even before you unpack that last pair of mismatched stockings, is write to everyone who entertained you, however simply, en route. It doesn't matter how busy you are; let your piled-up mail go a few hours longer. Take the time to be promptly courteous. Do not write a miserly, ordinary, "It was so nice meeting you. Thank you for that elevator ride up the Eiffel Tower." Tell your newfound acquaintance your impressions of Europe, how it feels to be home, what you'll be doing in the next few weeks. Personalize. If you don't have the woman-hours to accomplish this immediately, send a brief, warm note and follow it up with a letter. Don't let the brief encounter deteriorate into a mere Christmas-card exchange.

In 1953, an alert grandmother named May crossed the Atlantic on the Holland-America liner *Veendam*. Aboard, she met an Indian girl who had been studying in California on a scholarship. The sixty-year-old grandmother and the twenty-year-old student liked each other. For ten years they corresponded. Last year the Indian girl, who had become a wife and mother in the interim, wrote, "You always go to Europe. Why not come to visit us in Bombay?" So May did and spent ten wonderful Asiatic days—with five servants at her beck and call.

Look Up Friends of Friends. The woman in Oslo won't understand why you wouldn't know "my friend Susan Sorenson in New Rochelle, a Norwegian married to an American." Don't bother explaining that New Rochelle is thirty-five minutes from Broadway and that you haven't been there

since you fled the suburbs at age eighteen. Call up Susie, tell
her that you bring regards from Norway. Invite her for lunch
(not to Schrafft's, but some place with a little éclat) and pick
up the check. That minor investment may make a whole
group of new friends for you. It works the other way, too.
One night a nice masculine voice on the telephone announced
that he was a friend of Mimi Dabek of Paris. The voice
belonged to a man who lived two blocks away, but it took a
French Cupid, five thousand miles away, to bring us together.

Keep Up with the Americans You Met on the Trip. If you
met a group of pleasant compatriots on the boat coming home,
give a small cocktail party and exchange post mortems. New
friendships may result. Perhaps most of the people you met
live in New York and you live in Detroit. Don't let that stop
you. Write to them, and next time you're in New York, invite
them for cocktails—in advance. You'd be surprised at how
many New Yorkers have friends in Detroit.

Take Cooking Courses. The surest way for a woman to
succeed by really trying is to be a good hostess. Anyone can
invite guests for highballs, with a few tidbits thrown in as
appetite cutters, or for a meat-and-potato casserole out of the
Ladies' Home Companion. But it takes skill to cook really
well. See whether there is any foreign-cooking course in your
community. Last year I took James Beard's masterful six-part
series and learned about everything from fifteen kinds of
soufflés to how to chop onions with a French knife. In New
York there is a course in Chinese cooking at the China Institute, and there are several others (one is given by Dione
Lucas, another by Helen Worth) that will painlessly make
you a competent cook of mouth-watering dishes. If none is
available in your community, organize one.

Entertain. I have achieved a certain amount of note, if not
notoriety, as an authority on pisco, the Peruvian brandy that,
after proper treatment, becomes a delightfully cheerful nectar
known as a pisco sour. I drank one and one-half in Lima and

was so invigorated that I was ready to cross the Andes on foot. A year later the magazine for which I work decided to give a South American fiesta, and as an unusual feature, I suggested serving pisco sours. Everybody cheered.

At that time, pisco was unavailable in New York, so I made arrangements for two gallons to be flown in from Peru. Efficiently enough, the brandy arrived two days before the fiesta—but no farther than U.S. customs. It seems that to import two gallons, I needed a liquor license, a six-month job to acquire. So the party was held without the introduction of pisco sours to the New York press.

Half a year later, I was allowed to rescue the bottles from the customs house and, since no one else wanted them, I decided to give a pisco party. The invitations read like this: "If you're aching to go Incan and if drinking you've been thinking, there's a potion known as pisco that's been banned from here to 'Frisco. . . ." The party was so successful that I gave one every May until I got tired of strangers calling me up and saying, "I understand you're an authority on pisco. Can you tell me what to do with it?"

For your information, pisco is now available in better liquor stores. It costs $7.95 a bottle in New York and is worth every penny. Here's the recipe for six pisco sours:

6 jiggers pisco	1 jigger water
juice of lemon	1 well-beaten egg white
1 jigger honey (heavy syrup will do if your bees are on strike)	

Shake thoroughly with crushed ice. Add a dash of angostura bitters to each drink.

If you want to add flair to your Peruvian fiesta, serve *anticuchos* with the drink.

Bife anticuchos are bits of spicy steak-on-a-skewer. Cut two pounds of round steak into one-inch cubes. Sprinkle gen-

erously with meat tenderizer. Let stand forty minutes. Combine one cup tarragon vinegar, one-fourth teaspoon chili
powder, one-fourth teaspoon saffron, two minced cloves of
garlic, twelve peppercorns, one teaspoon salt, and one-half
cup water in a bowl. Add meat cubes, turning to coat. Mari-
nate, covered and refrigerated, four hours or overnight. String
meat on skewers, brush with olive or salad oil. Grill in broiler
until tender and browned, brushing occasionally with the
marinade. Makes four to five servings. In Peru, *cocineras* do
this dish with beef heart; you might try it that way, too.

Some other party ideas that impress at reunions of your
overseas acquaintances:

Caviar and Vodka Party. If you are just back from an
Intourist view of Russia, you are probably loaded down with
caviar. That's all the Soviets will let you take in exchange
for any leftover food coupons that you paid for in advance.
Canny travelers usually trade in the unused paper for fine
beluga caviar, the kind that comes in separate grains as big
as cranberries and sells for $32 a jar at the Vendôme in New
York. If you are lucky enough to have some left, invite people
(who will appreciate it) to a Romanoff-style tasting. Spoon
the ice-cold caviar into a glass bowl and sink the bowl into a
bed of cracked ice contained in a larger silver bowl set upon
a silver tray. Surround it with side dishes of hard-cooked
egg whites and yolks chopped separately, chopped onion, and
tomato wedges. Serve only vodka—in Martinis, with tonic,
or with iced bouillon (for bull shots). I served the latter
and was greatly embarrassed to overhear my maid-for-the-
day asking the guests. "Will you have vodka with your soup?"

Fettuccine Festival. Too many cocktail parties provide
nothing to munch except shattered potato chips and tired
deviled eggs. If you have invited veterans of the Via Veneto
—or even your regulars—why not surprise everybody by putting on an apron and whipping up a golden bowl of *fettuccine
alla Alfredo?* It's easy. Cook the noodles (two pounds) in

violently boiling salted water until they are just tender (*al dente*), drain, and toss with a pound of whipped butter and a pound of freshly grated Parmesan cheese. Toss at the table, of course, and with a golden fork and spoon if you want to do as the Romans do. A green salad and coffee will make a meal of your cocktail party and you'll have enough for twelve guests.

A *Coffee Party* can be made an international affair. If you don't already own a silver coffee service, borrow one. Put hot milk in one pitcher and you can serve French *café au lait*. Add a bowl of whipped cream and you can serve *Kaffee mit Schlag*—the Viennese way. Espresso-type coffee, combined with an equal quantity of steaming milk, sprinkled with cinnamon and a touch of grated orange peel, lets your guests enjoy *cappuccino*, an Italian favorite.

Irish coffee traveled from Shannon, Ireland, with San Francisco columnist Stan Delaplane and is now a favorite in the rest of the United States. To make one serving, place two teaspoons of sugar in a warmed wineglass, fill the glass about two-thirds full of strong hot coffee. Stir. Add a jigger of Irish whiskey and top with cold, softly whipped heavy cream. Don't stir.

Another elegant way of serving coffee is to add a dash of white crème de menthe, curaçao, kümmel, anisette, Cointreau, or some other liqueur to a demitasse of strong black coffee.

A *babka* (Polish coffee cake) makes a nice accessory for your international coffee party. You can buy a giant-sized one for $1.50 at Manhattan's New Warsaw Bakery, and I am sure that you will find one if there is a Polish bakery in your town.

A *French Dinner Party*. To really show off your cooking, you should give a dinner party for six in the grand French manner. I have one favorite menu that can be made completely ahead of time and never fails to impress.

First course is *rillettes*—the pork *pâté* of Touraine. It is difficult to find in the United States, but I learned how to make it in James Beard's class:

Rillettes or Rillons

1 pound lean pork, finely diced	¼ teaspoon cloves, ground
1¼ pound pork fat, finely diced	¼ teaspoon thyme
1 chopped onion	water to cover
2 teaspoons salt	
freshly ground pepper	
¼ teaspoon nutmeg	
1 bay leaf	

(The difference between the two is that the *rillettes* are ground or pounded, the *rillons* left in small diced pieces.) Mix ingredients, cover with water, and cook until the water has evaporated and the meat has browned. Remove bay leaf, drain off fat, and reserve. Return meat to heat and cook until crisp and brown. For *rillettes*, mash in a mortar or grind. *Rillons* are left as they are. Pack in pots, cover with reserved fat.

Second course is French chicken Calvados. You need:

5 lbs. chicken pieces (legs, breasts and thighs)	3 small tart red apples, peeled, cored and chopped
½ cup butter	1 tablespoon chopped parsley
⅔ cup (about) Calvados or apple brandy	⅛ teaspoon crumbled thyme
⅔ cup thinly sliced onion	salt
2 small inner stalks of celery (white part only), thinly sliced	pepper
	⅓ cup heavy cream

Sauté chickens in hot butter until golden but not brown. Pour one-quarter cup of the Calvados over the hot chicken pieces and immediately light the brandy. Let it burn out. Remove chicken pieces; keep warm. To the pan juices remaining in the skillet, add onion, celery and apples; cook slowly until soft and nearly cooked. Add parsley and thyme. Stir in another one-third cup of Calvados. Return chicken pieces to this sauce. Cover and cook over low heat for thirty to forty minutes or until chicken is tender. Taste sauce and season as desired with salt and pepper. Just before serving, remove from heat and stir in cream. (I do everything else the day before, heat the dish on the night of the party and add cream). Do not boil again and if you are of the reheat school and feel like indulging your guests, you might add a bit more Calvados. Serve with plain buttered rice or with boiled new potatoes. You'll have enough chicken to feed six.

A salad and cheese course should follow; and for dessert, give your guests fresh strawberries (the frozen ones are fine, too) with *crème fraîche d'Isigny*. You can make this by combining one cup heavy cream, thickened slightly but not whipped, with one-half cup sour cream.

Learn About Wine. One of the joys of travel is getting to know foreign wines in their own habitat and showing off your knowledge back home. Why not pursue the subject? Consult your liquor dealer. Start a cellar. Then your friends will know just what to give you at Christmas. Don't sip dinner wines exclusively. Experiment with *apéritifs.* For instance, mix white wine with a little cassis (black-currant syrup) and you can have a Kir, named after Father Kir, hero of the French Resistance and now mayor of Dijon. Or try La Seine (red) or Lillet before dinner. You may like one better than Scotch, and it is certainly less expensive.

CULTURAL SATISFACTION

Go to Language School. Discs are fine, but it's much more fun to go to a class and learn with others. It's useful to speak a foreign language before your trip abroad but even more practical after you have traveled. For then you'll know what language you really want to study. If you reside in a large city, there are usually Alliance Française groups. If you live in or near a university town, there are adult classes in German, French, Spanish, Italian, Portuguese, and sometimes in Swahili. Local high schools provide many adult language courses.

Join Special Foundations. America, the melting pot, is full of Italian-American Foundations, Friends of France, the Committee to Save Versailles, Friends of the Near East, and so on. Find out the nearest group that appeals to you and join. A friend of mine has found a whole new world in her hometown by joining the Asia Society.

Hobbies Make Your Trip Stay Alive. On my first trip to
Vienna, I went to the third "reopening" night at the world-
famous Staatsoper and heard *Der Rosenkavalier.* The performance had such an impact on me that the very minute I got off
the plane in New York, I rushed home, dropped off my luggage, and walked to the nearest record store to purchase the
Vienna Company's recording of the Strauss opera. Now whenever I'm sad, I play the first side, where the Marschallin
decides she's growing old; when I'm happy, I run the waltz
side.

You can collect *fado* records from Portugal, carnival records
from Rio, or street songs from Montmartre. Mount slides, or
put trip mementos into scrapbooks, but don't bore people by
showing countless photos of yourself in front of the Monte
Carlo Casino or the Parthenon.

Read. Now that your trip is over, you know what you'd like
to know. Ask your local librarian to map out a reading program. Have you wondered about the common denominator of
French genius, which produced the Napoleonic Code, champagne, the Suez Canal, Debussy, and crêpes Suzette? Hundreds of books have been written about the French character
and its manifestations. Fascinated by the German postwar
recovery? Learn the psychological and economic factors behind the "miracle." Have you decided that your next expedition will be the U.S.S.R.? Start to prepare now even though
the starting date seems years away.

ECONOMIC SATISFACTION

Deduct Your Trip from Your Income Tax. If you are a
decorator who purchased fabrics abroad, a publicist who attended a public-relations conference in Germany, a home
economist who toured schools overseas, you may be legiti-
mately entitled to deduct a portion of your trip. Consult an

accountant who knows the legal angles. It's certainly worth looking into.

Go Into Business. I nearly died last summer when I wandered into one of those chic little Manhattan *boutiques* and saw one of the Mexican work shirts, the kind I had bought for my twelve-year-old cousin for $1, priced at a whopping $24. In Mexico I had dallied with the thought of buying a dozen and trying to sell them at home, but the effort seemed too great. Many similar things described in "shop-wise" columns of fashion publications are the basic bricks that can be built into a business: Basque shirts, Peruvian ponchos, antique Brazilian horseshoes. My friend Madeleine has advanced one-third of the way toward a mink coat by selling Indian bangle bracelets. She brought two dozen home from India for gifts; their popularity gave her the idea of going into the bangle business in a small way. She buys the bracelets for twenty-five cents each at wholesale and sells them at a 200 per cent profit. Her "egg" money is becoming mink money.

Use Your Knowledge to Acquire a New Job. The fact that you have been abroad and liked what you saw may open the way to a new career. International firms (such as IBM) want personnel with international interests. Knowledge of a language and an understanding of foreigners and their problems can prove useful to import-export firms and other organizations with offices abroad.

A Two-Way Street. Up to the present, it has always been the American woman who roamed the globe and the European, Oriental, or South American who played host to her. Things have changed. The State Department's new policy of encouraging foreign travel to the United States has laid the foundations of a reverse tourist business. If you have been warmly welcomed abroad, extend your own welcome to friends and friends of friends. It isn't only the rich who come to the United States these days; busloads of workingmen and women tour our country every day.

Recently a Dr. and Mrs. Lob telephoned me at my office. "We are friends of Marcelle Henry of Paris," they said in fractured English, and I had a chance to return some of the hospitality that had been shown to me in France.

Assure your friends abroad that you will give them the same warm welcome that they gave you. Do not hold back just because you don't live in New York, Chicago, or San Francisco. Foreigners will find a visit to a Kansas wheat farm, a New England village, or a curio shop in the middle of the New Mexican desert just as interesting as an excursion into rural England, Austria, or India would be for you. Extend your invitations and maybe you'll receive a cable: "Have ticket. Am traveling."

Meanwhile, don't put off your international hospitality. One way of practicing it is to welcome children of foreign friends to your home. A prominent Chinese family entertained Jane for breakfast, lunch, and Christmas dinner in Hong Kong. She didn't know how to repay their warmth and friendship to a stranger. But at their request, she looked up their daughter, a student at Marymount, upon her return to New York. Then she asked herself, "If I were a parent, what would I want to know?" She wrote a long letter, detailing how the girl looked, the way in which she had changed her hairdo, where she had gone on dates with American boys. With the five-page accounting, she sent step-by-step photos, taken with a Brownie. This small act of thoughtfulness won her friends for life.

If you live near a college or university where there are foreign students, invite one or more for a Thanksgiving or Christmas dinner or just plain potluck. A friendly gesture to a lonely African freshman or a Peruvian pre-med student may bring you a world of satisfaction.

Another way of keeping your trip alive is by interesting yourself in an international organization such as UNICEF or the AAUN (American Association for the United Nations). My stepmother runs a series of panels at which the consuls general of various countries brief local townspeople on how they can work for international understanding.

YOUR TRAVEL FUTURE

The time to start planning your next trip is right now. You may decide to revisit more extensively the places you saw briefly on your first spell of globe-trotting, or you may venture off into foreign byways that you never knew existed until you started traveling.

You may want to go to summer school abroad and study a foreign language there. You can do this in six-week sessions at, say, the Sorbonne in Paris, the University of Santander in Spain, or the University of Grenoble. Or you may elect, as one friend did, to take a four-month leave of absence from your job, borrow the money from the bank, and live abroad. Is it worth it? Her comment: "The best thing I ever did—furthermore, my boss encouraged me."

Your first trip alone is the hardest to plan but the most rewarding. You are bound to come home a happier and wiser woman—wiser because you've discovered that it is more fun to see new things outside the U.S.A. than to be a fixture in your own living room; happier because you will have learned what Edward Gibbon meant when he wrote, "I was never less alone than when by myself."

It all adds up to one indisputable fact for women who adventure on their own: you can really go places when you go it alone.

Ten Days in Paris, Rome, and London

For the timid souls abroad for the first time who are confused by strange surroundings, strange languages, and strange money, I offer a plan for coping with the three major capitals of Europe on a short visit. These outlines are for women who know no one and who want to make the most of a few days' visit.

THREE DAYS IN PARIS

First Day. Rise early and put on your most comfortable walking shoes. If breakfast isn't included in the price of your hotel room, stop at a nearby café and ask for "*Café crème et croissants.*" Find your way by Métro or bus (the concierge will tell you how) to the Seine, the river that describes an S-shaped curve through Paris, reflecting so many historic monuments that you can get to know the city without leaving the water's edge. Walk from Notre Dame downstream to the Eiffel Tower, preferably on the Left Bank (La Rive Gauche). You'll see lovers with arms entwined, fishermen willing to

285

wait all day for a nibble, *bouquinistes* who sell everything from trash to an occasional bibliophilic treasure at their riverside bookstalls.

At the Eiffel Tower, the iron-lace Parisian landmark left over from the World's Fair of 1889, you can take the elevator up or climb the five hundred steps to the observation tower. You might eat lunch at the restaurant on one of the three platforms, but instead I suggest you descend, turn right, recross the Seine on the Pont de l'Alma, walk toward the Arc de Triomphe, and then stroll down the Champs-Elysées. When you come to a café called Fouquet's, sit down and order a Pernod or an *apéritif*. While the world revolves pleasantly around you, decide to indulge yourself in an extravagant midday meal; there can be no better introduction to Paris. You might try Taillevent, 15 Rue Lamennais; the luxurious Berkeley, 7 Avenue Matignon; or Lasserre, 17 Avenue Franklin D. Roosevelt, where the roof slides open every once in a while to eliminate cigarette smoke. All are expensive.

In the afternoon, walk off your lunch in two museums: the Louvre (see *La Jaconde*, French for the Mona Lisa, and the Venus de Milo) and the Musée du Jeu de Paume, which houses impressionist paintings. The two museums are separated by the beautiful Tuileries gardens. If you still have the energy, cross the Place de la Concorde to the Guignol in the Champs-Elysées gardens and enjoy watching French children enthusiastically cheering the marionette show.

Don't bother with dinner at night. Go back to your hotel, soak yourself in the tub with the new French bath salts you've just bought en route, rest, and go to a show. If your French is adequate, you might want to attend the Comédie Française, or the Théâtre de France. The acting is tops, and you can buy a bilingual program. If French is Greek to you, head for a popular music hall, such as Bobino or Paccra. The program will be a cross between a circus and Radio City Music Hall minus the movie, and you will be sitting in a French audience;

few Americans get this far from the familiar. Be sure to buy one of the "discs" that will be on sale in the lobby, and if your appetite is back to normal, try a half-pound *pâté* sandwich and a glass of Alsatian beer at a nearby *brasserie*.

SECOND DAY. Make this morning a shopping tour. You can lose your mind and your pocketbook in a stroll down luxury lane, the Faubourg-St-Honoré. Start at the Avenue Matignon and just keep going past the Rue Royale (where the street becomes Rue St-Honoré) until you hit the Rue Castiglione. You'll pass elegant Hermès, where gloves cost the earth but are one of the best buys in France; Pierre Marly, who not only fills prescriptions for spectacles but features a museum of glasses in the basement of his shop; Lanvin, and countless small *boutiques,* such as Rémy, Réty, Ramuz. Don't be afraid to walk in and price. During your promenade, you will pass several art galleries, such as Charpentier; again, walk in and inspect.

Leave the Rue St-Honoré and walk up the Rue de la Paix, stopping for coffee at the Café de la Paix in the Place de l'Opéra. Then head for Le Printemps or Galeries Lafayette, two famous department stores of Paris, both nearby. Both have English-speaking guides. You can lunch at the store *terrasse* or at nearby Au Coq Hardy, 16 Rue de Budapest.

In the afternoon, do Versailles but not *à l'américaine.* Instead of taking one of the guided tours, purchase a ticket to Versailles at the Gare St. Lazare and take the twenty-minute train ride. Or go underground into the Métro to the Porte de St. Cloud station and climb into the Versailles bus from there. You'll love the palace with its history and fabulous Hall of Mirrors, but also be sure to look at Le Hameau, the charming hamlet where Marie Antoinette played shepherdess, and Le Grand Trianon, where Louis XIV dallied with Madame de Maintenon.

That night, you may want to dine at Laborderie, 17 Rue Bergère and experiment with a taste of spicy Basque cooking.

After that, attend a performance of the Folies Bergère, a few blocks away. Don't let anyone tell you that this is too "touristy"; it's a legendary part of the Paris scene, and you will find just as many women in the audience as men.

THIRD DAY. Get ready to walk some more. This is the morning to explore Montmartre. From the high hill where the Church of the Sacré-Coeur stands, all Paris is spread out before you. Let your instinct guide you around the district of Montmartre with its squares, vineyards, bargains in mill-end fabrics at the Place St. Pierre. If you get off the bus at the Place Blanche, site of the historic Moulin Rouge, you can walk up the steep and meandering Rue Lepic, past the pushcart bazaar in the lower reaches, past the Moulin de la Galette, where Toulouse-Lautrec and his cronies used to drink and paint (then as now a working-class dance hall), to the Place du Tertre at the summit. On a warm spring day, it is pleasant to lunch here under the trees (La Mère Catherine has been popular for half a century). Or on your way down, look for Rue d'Orsel at the foot of the hill (south slope) and eat lunch at any of the restaurants there; prices will be posted outside the restaurant door. Another luncheon alternative is the Vert Galant (expensive) or Chez Paul (inexpensive) on the île de la Cité, for your *après déjeuner* destination will be the nearby Cathedral of Notre Dame and then the Ste-Chapelle with its exquisite stained-glass windows. The Ste-Chapelle is certainly the world's only thirteenth-century chapel in the courtyard of a police station. The Quai des Orfèvres, headquarters of "Inspector Maigret's" Police Judiciaire, is around the corner on the south side of the island, and the Conciergerie, where Queen Marie Antoinette spent her last days before losing her head to the guillotine, is nearby on the north side.

More walking now. Cross the river to the Right Bank and the Place des Vosges with its classically elegant façades. Walk through Victor Hugo's house at 6 Place des Vosges. You'll be amazed to see that Hugo excelled as an artist as well as author.

Stop at the Musée Carnavalet (closed Tuesdays) at 23 Rue de Sévigné, the Historical Museum of the City of Paris.

That night, leave the past for the present and explore the Left Bank. Sip a drink at either Aux Deux Magots or Café de Flore, where you'll see beatniks, existentialists, and scads of tourists. Then let your own appetite decide whether you want a delicatessen-type snack at L'Epicerie on Rue St-Benoît, a sandwich at the Montana, pancakes à la mode bretonne on Rue de l'Echaudé, or a real dinner at Les Charpentiers on Rue Mabillon. You could also go to the popular Brasserie Lipp for a dark beer or to Chez René. Don't miss venison in season or homemade tarts with crème fraîche topping at René's bistro.

For your last night, take the evening boat ride along the Seine. If it is winter and the Bateaux Mouches are not running, attend the opera—the singing won't equal the Met or La Scala, but the ballets are tops and the decor is magnificent nineteenth century. You might want to stop in and hear "le jazz hot" at any of the spots on the Rue de la Huchette. Or simply do in Paris as Parisians do: sip a last cup of coffee with a liqueur or brandy at a café before retiring.

ALTERNATIVES:

❪ In summer, swim in the Seine. The rebuilt Piscine Deligny is on the Left Bank near the École des Beaux-Arts, and the Royale is across the river at the Quai des Tuileries. Other athletic types might rent a bicycle. You can ride the Métro to the Neuilly end of the Vincennes-Neuilly line and look for a place that says "bicyclettes à louer." Stop at a charcuterie and buy some pâté de campagne, get yourself a small loaf of French bread at the boulangerie and a bottle of wine at the wineshop, put them into the basket of your bike, and start pedaling. In Holland, women of seventy-five still ride bikes.

❪ Eat your lunch in a tree at a place called Robinson. Take the Métro to the Denfert-Rochereau station and connect with a suburban line called Ligne de Sceaux, and that will take you to Robinson, named for the Swiss Family Robinson. A

number of restaurants there have tables set up on platforms
in the branches of old chestnut trees. You haul up your food
and drinks in baskets.

(*Attend a fashion show.* Go to any of the following: Balenciaga, Balmain, Cardin, Chanel, Dior, Givenchy, Grès, Griffe,
Heim, Laroche, Ricci, St. Laurent. Showings of important collections are usually held at three in the afternoon. Ask your
concierge to make a reservation for you, because you cannot
just walk in off the street. You'll sit on a gilt chair and be
given a cardboard program on which to pencil your favorite
numbers in case you want to buy, but very few women can
afford it. *Haute couture* prices for a simple suit start at $500.

(*Spend an afternoon browsing among books, bibelots, and
prints on the Left Bank.* Rue Jacob and Rue de l'Université
are your best treasure-hunting bets. Simone Barbier's book-
shop at 14 Rue de l'Université contains rare books on Paris,
and Mme. Barbier also conducts walk-lectures three times a
week. Lectures cost three new francs and are in French, but
the proprietress can also speak English. At 31 Rue Bonaparte,
you'll find the Librairie Bonaparte, entirely devoted to books
on the theater. There are thousands of old frames at G. Bac,
37 Rue Bonaparte, and everything from *marmottes* (wooden
blockheads useful as hatstands) to paperweights at Comeglio,
22 Rue Jacob. Paul Proute et Ses Fils, 74 Rue de Seine, has
prints that cost anywhere from a dime to $1,000.

(*Get your hair done.* Alexandre, 120 Faubourg-St-Honoré,
and Carita, 11 Faubourg-St-Honoré, are tops. Allow three
hours for shampoo, cut, styling, and set.

THREE DAYS IN ROME

FIRST DAY. Take your time about getting dressed, because
the pace is leisurely in this twenty-five-hundred-year-old city
on the banks of the Tiber. Breakfast at Rosati's on the Via
Veneto. (Many tourists head for Caffè Doney, but Rosati is

the haunt of Italian politicians, socialites, and writers such as Alberto Moravia.) Notice the statue of Julius Caesar at the bar—apparently drinking cocktails! Drink a *cappuccino* and eat *maritozzi*, the Italian morning cakes similar to *croissants*.

Then stroll down the Via Veneto to the Church of the Cappuccini. Take a look in the basement, where monks have adorned rooms with human bones, including lamps made with sacroiliacs. This is a very elegant Roman church; men kiss women's hands after Mass.

Keep going straight down the Via Veneto, Rome's Main Street, to Piazza Barberini. You'll find Gino Paoli's world-famous Italian knitwear at Leslie Boutique, 7 Via Veneto, just above Thomas Cook's. A knit suit will run you from $30 to $50. Roman ladies, who haven't the figures necessary for knits, don't buy them often, but on Americans, they are stunning.

Now you're ready for the Piazza di Spagna, one of the treats of your Roman holiday. Scan the map you've acquired from the concierge, turn right, glance at the chic shops on the Via Sistina (the Fabiani *boutique*, the Fratteggioni playshoes), and head straight for the obelisk at the top of the Spanish Steps. Lean on the balustrade and stare. On your right, looking down, is the house where Giorgio di Chirico paints; on the left, the house where the English poet Keats died; at the left, on the Via Gregoriana, the house where the Italian poet D'Annunzio lived. If you're young, you'll want to sit on the steps and muse. Someone may offer to buy you flowers; if no one does, treat yourself to a bouquet for thirty cents.

You should now be ready for a Roman meal. Walk over to Cesaretto, a tiny Tuscan place, on the Via della Croce. Take any free seat. You can join others, or if you sit alone, the waiter will shortly escort others to your table. The food is excellent, the Chianti genuine. A specialty is mozzarella cheese toasted on the fire, or you might try the *abbacchio* (baby kid).

By now, it should be about three o'clock. Your feet hurt and your head aches from impressions. So taxi back to the hotel for a real Roman siesta. An elegant woman in Rome is never seen out of doors before six!

At that hour, you may emerge, stroll for a bit, perhaps sit and read the lively *Rome Daily American* at the Café de Paris, across the street from the Hotel Excelsior. At dinnertime, head for nearby George's, 7 Via Marche. George's is owned by British gastronome Vernon Jarrett, and the cuisine is international. It will be perfectly all right for you to have a cocktail at the bar, where patrons play a drinking game called "The Bishop's Hat." At dinner, try the *scampi* (shrimp) or the gypsy-style chicken cooked in clay. This place is fairly expensive for Rome; dinner with cocktails and wine will cost about $8.

Now if you've the spirit and curiosity (you don't really need nerve), you can wander into Bricktop's alone. This is definitely a nightclub, but it is the one spot in Rome where you might feel comfortable without an escort—and you don't have to be without one for long. Bricktop is a Sophie Tucker-type entertainer who sat out the Nazi occupation of Paris. *Life* reporters frequent her place on the Via Veneto. If you're lucky, Bricktop will appear at midnight and sing her repertoire.

SECOND DAY. Rise early, breakfast in your room, and take one of the sight-seeing bus tours of Rome. Be sure to take the one that includes Vatican City and the Sistine Chapel with its frescoes by Botticelli and Michelangelo. Should you possess a large mirror, take it along and play the reflection game with Michelangelo.

The bus will bring you back to your hotel around 1 P.M. Spruce up, and then either take yourself for a chic lunch at Capriccio, haunt of the film and sports stars, at 38 Via Liguria, or go for *panini* (sandwiches) at the Strega Bar on the Via Veneto, after sitting for a while over an Americano cocktail (sweet vermouth, Campari bitters, dash of soda, and lemon peel).

After lunch, walk to the Marlborough Gallery on the Via

Gregoriana for a look at the best moderns. Then head for the Via Condotti and a shopping spree. Stop at Gucci and view the famous leather handbags and luggage. Look at shoes at Ferragamo; you can get a pair made to order in about eight days. Walk to nearby Myricae, 133 Via del Babuino, and browse through the second-floor models; I had a winter coat made in my choice of fabrics for $80. There are nice, inexpensive coral beads at the shop in front of the Spanish Steps. Keep going till your feet give out, and then stop for coffee at the Caffè Greco.

Back to your hotel to rest. Take a taxi to Trastevere and dine at Da Meo Patacca, 30 Piazza dei Mercanti (phone: 586198). You'll find the typical "picturesque" atmosphere of old Rome, complete with decorative gimmicks, Roman country cooking, and communal songfests at midnight.

THIRD DAY. You might take the morning tour to Tivoli and Hadrian's Villa. Have lunch there if there is a lunch stop; otherwise, eat at Giovanni's, 19 Via Marche.

In the afternoon, take a sight-seeing expedition to the Circus Maximus, the various Forums, the Coliseum, the Appian Way. Or if you are tired of ruins, go down to the railroad station and take the Roman subway to the Esposizione (next to last stop). See the new architecture of Rome on display. Walk over to the Museum of Roman Antiquities for a glimpse of ancient Rome. Or stop at the Museum of Folklore to hear recordings of dialect lullabies. Take a bus back to town, and to celebrate your last day in Rome, you might go for an Italian makeup at Luislele at 28 Via Due Macelli. If you have an introduction, try a drink at the Stampa Estera (Foreign Press Club) on the Via della Mercede.

That night, go to the opera. The Roman season is from late fall to early spring, but in summer there is outdoor opera at the Baths of Caracalla. If opera bores you, try a Rome-by-night tour, head for Alfredo's and the *fettuccine* routine, or go back to Trastevere and eat in any of the charming restaurants there. In summer, attend the Sound and Light spectacle at the Roman Forum.

ALTERNATIVES:

⟮ *If you pick up a man, suggest a drink at the new Hilton Hotel.* The bar there has the best view in town. Maybe afterward, he'll wine and dine you at the Palazzi alla Camillucia, 355 Via della Camillucia, now a restaurant and formerly the villa of Clara Petacci, Mussolini's mistress, or the Hostaria dell'Orso (Dante's former home).

⟮ *The Flea Market is open Sundays until 1* P.M. On Tuesday mornings after 10, you can get into the Flower Market in the caves under the Royal Palace. There's a bar where you can sip a midmorning *cappuccino* as you pick posies.

⟮ *Get a quick pick-me-up beauty treatment.* At Payot, on the Via Veneto, you can get a manicure, massage, or facial (no hairdos).

⟮ *Have your hair done.* Best hairdresser in town is Attilio at the Hotel Excelsior.

⟮ *Walk through the Borghese Gardens and visit the Borghese Art Gallery.*

⟮ *Try for an audience with the Pope.* Come to Rome armed with a letter from your parish priest or minister and present it to the North American College, 30 Via dell' Umiltà, or to the Vatican. This takes at least a week to arrange unless you have pull.

⟮ *Check on your stocks.* Merrill Lynch, Pierce, Fenner & Smith now has a Rome office, 76 Via Bissolati, where you can watch the ticker to see how your stocks are doing—and perhaps meet a stockbroker also on a Roman holiday.

FOUR DAYS IN LONDON

FIRST DAY. Rise early, ring for tea (the genuine British brew) and marmalade, and study your street map of London (if you are forehanded, before leaving home you will have ordered the Foldex Miniplan of London from Harriet Ship-man, Box 98, Belleville 9, New Jersey, for just eighty-five cents). Then start walking. Your hotel (maybe the Goring, the Meurice, or—for those with wherewithal—the soul-satisfying Connaught) will probably be fairly near Grosvenor Square, so stroll there and take a look at the American Embassy. You might enter and ask for a ticket to watch a debate in the House of Commons (you can order tickets before you leave home by writing to the American Embassy, Grosvenor Square, London, W.1).

At 10:30 A.M., jump into a taxi and drive to Buckingham Palace to view the Changing of the Guard. Watch from Queen Victoria's statue opposite the palace, as the crowds are so great that unless you are seven feet tall, you will see nothing by pressing against the railings of the palace yard. At 11:15 A.M., the old guard from St. James's Palace will march in with a drum-and-fife corps, and a few minutes later a troop of cavalry in full-dress uniform will ride by.

Don't bother waiting until the guard marches out again. Instead, stroll through Green Park to Piccadilly and thence to the Burlington Arcade, where you will find small shops featuring everything from candy to cashmeres. At the end of the arcade, turn left and then left again into Old Bond Street, said to be the richest street in all Europe. At Lewis New-combe, 41 Old Bond Street, visitors are allowed free use of a projection room to examine slides or films. Antique lovers will find everything to a connoisseur's taste at Frank Partridge (No. 144). Art addicts might want to drop into Fores (No. 123) for a look at sporting pictures and prints or go to see the old masters at Walker's (No. 118). At the end of Old Bond Street, you'll find yourself just across the street from Fortnum & Mason, London's most unusual department store. Be sure to visit the food department, where you'll find Hy-blaean honey from Mount Olympus, haggis from Scotland, all presented by a clerk dressed in cutaway coat and striped pants. Food isn't the only thing; Fortnum & Mason features floor after floor of wearables, including costumes by Dior. An inexpensive way to hobnob with the British aristocracy is to eat a quick salad lunch at Fortnum's Fountain on the ground floor.

In the afternoon, go to the Tower of London. In summer, take the twenty-minute boat ride from Westminster Pier that passes Somerset House, where birth, marriage, and death records are kept. Or ride the Underground, the British subway. At the historic Tower, wait on the first drawbridge, where a Beefeater will form a group for a conducted tour. You'll want to see the collection of armor, including the Fat Boy's suit worn by colossal Henry VIII, and it's worth waiting in line to get a look at the eye-popping crown jewels; they are exhibited in impregnable security in a room where Henry VI was murdered.

Your next move depends on the state of your appetite and feet. Either take tea at one of the reliable Lyon's Corner Houses or head straight for your hotel, order a theater ticket for the evening, and rest for a while. The Stratford Shakespearean Company plays at the Aldwych Theater, but there will be many musicals and dramas to choose from, and tickets cost much less than in New York. Most shows (not all) start at 7:30 P.M., and Londoners usually have a bite first and dine afterward. Try a drink and a steak at the Cock & Lion, a smart pub at 62 Wigmore Street. Another good pub is the Antelope at 22 Eaton Terrace.

SECOND DAY. Start the day with glamour. Treat yourself to a shampoo and set at Vidal Sassoon at 171 New Bond Street. Actress Margaret Leighton is a frequent customer. It's expensive; a shampoo and set will cost about $10. There's a second Sassoon salon at Grosvenor House, Park Lane.

This can be your morning for serious shopping. Start out at Wedgwood's showrooms at 34 Wigmore Street. Here everything Wedgwood makes is on display. Next, walk to W. Bill,

12 South Moulton Street, and you'll find a wonderful range of cashmere sweaters. Don't miss Marks & Spencer's (on the corner of Oxford and Baker Streets); this is a reputable chain store with its own make of clothes; you can purchase a Shetland sweater for just $7. Some British girls hesitate to buy dresses here for fear they'll meet themselves coming and going, but it's unlikely that you'll meet your best friend wearing the same little off-the-rack number at home. Right next to Marks & Spencer's, you'll find the Wallis Shop, a small, smart, and inexpensive store that features Paris copies—for example, a Chanel-type suit, complete with brass buttons, runs only $45.

You can meander along and lunch at Derry and Tom's Restaurant on the Roof on Kensington High Street, or head for Harrods Department Store in Knightsbridge, where you can buy anything from a white mouse to a grand piano, and lunch at the Contented Sole at 19 Exhibition Road or the Tun of Port, 31B Holland Street, which has a bawdy *Tom Jones* kind of décor. Incidentally, the young in heart and figure should make note of three special dress shops: Bazaar (Mary Quant) in Knightsbridge, the Twenty-one Shop at Woolland's, and the Tuffin-Foale Boutique at Harrods.

Make the afternoon a museum tour. Head for the Victoria and Albert Museum (South Kensington), where the "musts" are a collection of English furniture through the ages, the Raphael cartoons for the tapestries that hang in the Vatican Museum, and the newly opened Costume Court. Luckily, all three musts are grouped together, for the museum is said to have seven miles of passages. You may also want to visit the Wallace Collection, outstanding furniture, porcelains, paintings collected by the Earl of Manchester in what was once his private home, and the Courtland Institute Galleries at Woburn Square, with its exciting impressionist and postimpressionist paintings.

Stop for a proper British tea at the Hotel Connaught, 1 Carlos Place, and then go back to your hotel for a bath and change of clothes. Tonight you might visit the Royal Opera House at Covent Garden. If you have acquired a beau, perhaps he will squire you to the Savoy Grill, or the Mirabelle, or a private club. A good pub near Covent Garden is the Essex Serpent, frequented by opera and ballet performers.

THIRD DAY (SATURDAY). This is market day. Go bargain hunting at Portobello Market (open from 9 A.M. to noon). Collectors of antique jewelry and old china should try Kensington's Church Street; those on the alert for real bargains can try Camden Passage in Camden Town (open daily, but twice as many stores are open on Saturday).

Next stop: Marble Arch. Cross the road to Speakers' Corner in Hyde Park, where soapbox orators sound off, short of treason, about anything. While you're in Hyde Park, watch the British people at play—horseback riding in Rotten Row; swimming, boating, and sailing on Serpentine Lake; a crowd watching a painting exhibition on Hyde Park Corner.

For a change of pace, take the bus to St. Paul's Cathedral, the largest and most famous church in the city. It took those who followed Sir Christopher Wren's plans thirty-five years to build it. Then walk along Fleet Street, the journalism center of London, and lunch at the Old Cheshire Cheese (No. 145), an old haunt of Dr. Samuel Johnson. If you want to see the attic where the eccentric doctor worked on his dictionary, the Johnson house at 17 Gough Square, just off Fleet Street, is open daily.

Next, go to Parliament Square. At the far end of the Parliament Buildings, you will find a guide making up a party to conduct through the House of Lords and House of Commons. Or if you have a ticket of admission, go right in.

If you aren't completely exhausted, take a short taxi ride to the Tate Gallery on Millbank to see examples of the British school of painting. When you have had your fill of Turner, Blake, Stevens, and Pre-Raphaelites, go downstairs to have a look at the collection of international moderns. You can get a good cup of tea at the restaurant in the Rex Whistler Memorial Room; and, incidentally, this is an excellent pickup spot. Tonight you might attend the theater again. Or if you are in the mood for a leisurely dinner, go to the zany Elizabethan Room of the Gore Hotel (189 Queen's Gate) and eat the kind of meal Good Queen Bess had—everything from swan to suckling pig to syllabub. You'll wash down your peacock *pâté*, salmagundi, or lobster pie with mead or mulled claret. You'll eat with a bifurcated "dagger" (a two-pronged fork, which Elizabeth introduced into England from Italy) on wooden plates. There are rushes on the floor, costumed serving wenches, candlelight, a long refectory table, and music by minstrels. Watch that mead; it's deceptive. Other dining spots: the Salisbury, a pub on St. Martin's Lane; or the chic Ivy, 1–5 West Street. Both get a theatrical clientele.

FOURTH DAY (SUNDAY). Breakfast in bed (on kippers); read the Sunday papers; they are independent of the weekday editions. Go to Westminster Abbey, the great church where the British kings and queens have been crowned since 1066 and where many of them are buried. The graves of Chaucer, Browning, and Tennyson are grouped together in Poets' Corner.

Stop for a pick-me-up at the Grenadier, 18 Wilton Row, S.W.1, patronized by the young smart set that you read about in *Tatler* or *Queen*. Eat lunch at Cunningham's, 51 Curzon Street, Mayfair, W.1, but don't linger, for you should take a tour this afternoon to Windsor Castle, the Queen's favorite weekend residence. The tour includes Runnymede, where the Magna Carta was signed by King John in 1215, and Hampton Court, a palace with a thousand rooms, all haunted by the ghosts of Anne Boleyn and Catherine Howard. Get the hotel porter to book the tour for you.

For your last night in London, dine at a little restaurant called Le Petit Montmartre, 15 Marylebone Lane, Wigmore Street, or at Kettner's, 28–31 Romilly Street, and go on to a symphony concert at Royal Festival Hall, Albert Hall, or Wigmore Hall.

ALTERNATIVES:

❨ *For early birds.* The Billingsgate Market on Lower Thames Street, E.C.3, in existence since the seventeenth century, opens daily at 5:30 A.M. The leather caps of the porters are modeled on those of the archers who fought under Henry V at Agincourt. This fish market is open daily except Sundays. Covent Garden is London's best market for fruit, flowers, and vegetables. Best times for visiting are between 6 and 9 A.M. on any day but a Sunday. Smithfield is London's main meat market. Best days are Mondays and Thursdays, and you can get a rare ("underdone," to the waiter) steak at any of the nearby pubs. ❨ *Go to a sporting event.* The cricket matches at Lord's are usually held Thursdays through Tuesdays from May to September.

The Royal Ascot is held in early June and is one of the most important social events of the London horse-racing season. The royal party rides in a carriage from Windsor Castle along the course to the stands before the first race at 2:30 P.M. You can apply for tickets at Ashton and Mitchell, 2 Old Bond Street, or the Racecourse, Ascot, Berkshire. Admission to the Royal Enclosure is by invitation only.

The All-England Lawn Tennis Championships are held at Wimbledon, on the southern edge of London, at the end of June and early July. For tickets, apply to the U.S. Lawn Tennis Association, 120 Broadway, New York, New York, or to Alfred Hays, Ltd., 74 Cornhill, London, E.C.3.

The Royal Regatta takes place on the River Thames at Henley in early July and can be viewed from an enclosure on the towpath near the finish. Admission can be obtained from the Secretary, Henley Royal Regatta, Henley-on-Thames, Oxon, or at the entrance to the enclosure on the days of the regatta.

❡ *Go to the opera festival.* Glyndebourne Opera Festival tickets are offered first to members of the association, then sold to the public. Formal dress is *de rigueur.* Write to the Glyndebourne Festival Box Office, Lewes, Sussex. Send no money; you will be billed if your order can be filled.

❡ *Watch a program at Broadcasting House, headquarters of the BBC.* There are no regular tours, but the BBC occasionally arranges private visits.

❡ *Try the Day of Beauty at the Dorchester Hotel.* About $4.50 pays for the works (massage, makeup, and Turkish bath).

❡ *Meet people.* Meeting people in Britain is easy—and not only because of the language. A number of American associations, such as the American Legion, the Daughters of the American Revolution, and the Harvard Club, have branches in London. Other useful organizations: Academy House, 24 Kensington Park Gardens, W.11, provides hostel accommodation for overseas students; Newman International Center, 31 Portman Square, W.1, a meeting place for Catholics of all nationalities; English Speaking Union, Dartmouth House, 37 Charles Street, W.1, a meeting place for member visitors from the U.S. and Commonwealth nations; American Women's Club, 14 Queen's Gate, S.W.1, founded in 1889 for American women in London. In addition, several personal-service agencies undertake to arrange for Americans to meet British families in their homes. Two of these are the Visitor's Advice Bureau, 53A Lowndes Square, S.W.1, and the Tourist Hospitality Service, Kent House, Market Place, Great Titchfield Street, London, W.1.

London abounds in private membership clubs that will provide transient memberships if you have the proper sort of entrée. For example, Le Petit Club Français, run by Miss Olwen Vaughan, a Welsh lady who used to be head of the London Film Society, is usually open to visiting Americans in the arts. Try to get the name of one of these special clubs from a friend at home, and write a letter requesting temporary membership and stating your qualifications, *before* you leave home.

❡ *Investigate the family tree.* For Americans seeking to trace their family roots in Britain, the Society of Genealogists, 37 Harrington Gardens, London, S.W.7, has records that may prove helpful. These can be inspected for a fee of $1.50 for a half day or $2.50 for a full day.